Let's Talk About Six

Let's Talk About Six

A Life in the Season of a Liverpool Fan

Chris Perkins

Published by Chris Perkins

© Copyright Chris Perkins 2019

LET'S TALK ABOUT SIX

ISBN 978-1-916-15990-7

Contents

About the Author

Chris Perkins has been a season ticket holder at Anfield since the double-winning season in 1985/86. For the past 25 years he has been watching the game from Block 105 in the Kop. Chris has worked in Sales and Marketing all his career and this is his first foray into writing, fulfilling a lifelong ambition to write and publish a book. He lives in Warrington with his wife, two children and a dog.

Twitter @chrisperks1709

Acknowledgements

There are a number of people and organisations I would like to thank in the process of writing this book. The nature of the book means there isn't a need for too much research, but I have relied on a number of sources for background.

First of all, I would like to thank LFCHistory.com for the wealth of historical data on their website. It is a fascinating site that you can quite easily get lost in. Secondly, I would like to recognise The Anfield Wrap and their team of writers and podcasters. I have been a listener and subscriber from the early days and have always loved their insight and passion around the game, part of which has inspired me to write this book. I have been careful to write before listening to their podcasts so my thoughts are not influenced, but is good to get a sense check on what I see on the field. Finally, I would like to thank the Twittersphere in general, for providing me titbits of information and stats that have found their way into the book.

In putting the book together, I have had great help from a number of people. Tim, for pushing me to take this from a project through to the finished item, and for being the first to read it through, along with his son, Ben. I'd then like to thank my gang of freelancers, PositiveBoby for putting together the website, Ken for editing the manuscript, Frank for formatting it, and Prudence for designing the cover. Its amazing the talent you can find out there on the web

On a more personal level, I would like to thank the people who I go to the game with. I had thought that they would feature more in the book, but to be honest their level of banter left a great deal to be desired—on the rare occasion I actually went out!! I don't tell them often enough, but they are the funniest people I know—Bobsey, Whaley, Noel, Alex, Anthony, Rob, Ian, Sam and of course Helen.

The photo on the cover is courtesy of one of my best friends, Rob Burgess. Rob was unimpressed with his seat at the final, so he went for a wander and managed to blag a seat right behind the Liverpool dugout. It's the ultimate fans view of a magical moment!

I'd like to thank my sister Katy and my Auntie Pat who are my link with the past and are as passionate about the football as I am.

Finally, I would like to thank my beautiful family, Ange, Dylan and Rosie, for always being there and being my everyday source of inspiration x

To my mum, who always wanted to write a book,

and my Grandad

who introduced me to a whole new world.

And to my family,

Ange, Dylan and Rosie

who make all this worthwhile.

INTRODUCTION

Wednesday 4th July 2018

Today is where I start. I was on Instagram this morning, which is full of the players back at preseason training. The caption was 'The 18/19 season starts here.' It was attributed to Klopp, but I don't think for one moment he said it. That's the Liverpool marketing team using him as the figurehead, which he is so I guess that's fair enough. If Klopp says it, we all get behind it—I think that's a thing now.

Last September, I was driving to work, listening to a podcast as usual. It's John Gibbons, Mike Nevin and Si Hughes talking about their books, laughing about being a published author. Good on them, their books are really good too. I thought to myself, *I'm going to write a book.* It was as I was driving past Debenhams in Warrington. There's no blue plaque there now, but who knows what will happen. It's on record now.

For the next hour, while driving to work in Stoke (I hate driving to Stoke), I thought about and constructed the bones of my book. What do I know about? Not a lot considering my age. I know about Liverpool, it's been a constant in an otherwise inconstant life.

It's always been there from one of the first photos of me when Liverpool won the FA Cup final and I'm pictured with my Grandad at 18 months old with a Liverpool top hat on in their living room ... all the way through to my Instagram feed, which has all manner of Liverpool related streams. It's always there.

Today, as it goes, England are playing Columbia in the last 16 of the World Cup. I don't follow England, I'm from Liverpool. That's what I tell all the guys in the factory in Stoke. They all know I like football, so they want to talk to me about it (or rather they know I will talk back if it's football). I tell them I'm not really that bothered.

To be fair, as the tournament goes on, I am getting a little caught up in the positive sentiment around Southgate and the team, but ultimately, I couldn't give a damn. I want to know how Liverpool are doing; are they going to be ready for the first game? Are the players fit? How many games will be remaining when they win the league this year (because they will)?

Over the course of the hour driving to Stoke, I constructed this book. It's two books actually. The first is a diary of the season, my own views on the progress of the season, not every day, just when I have something to say. My aim is to try to catch the ups and downs, the feelings of euphoria and how we're going to win the league, coupled with the feelings of despair—and how we are going to come back from it and win the league.

I'll cover the games and my thoughts about what happened and the aftermath. The laughs, the jokes, the banter, the negotiation to get out early for more pre-match pints, the shit I take when I have to drive. Also, the ongoing soap opera of the Premier League and my reactions to how the media cover it all ... increasingly, I'm not a big fan of the media.

The second book is an autobiography, I guess. My life and how Liverpool has played a part in it. The defining life moments where Liverpool have been involved ... the 1986 FA Cup Final in terms of the greatest days, Hillsborough for the worst and the ongoing thoughts that have affected me since.

No one really knows about me, no one really cares. This is not an autobiography because I don't think people would be interested in me, I'm not famous – I'm not even particularly likeable – but to be able to talk about things that have happened and how I feel about them. A lot has happened – I'm 45 now – and I think about a lot of things but very rarely talk about them.

I don't know if that's a strong enough basis for a book. I've never thought of writing one before, I've read a lot though ... or quite a lot. I've never been to a creative writing class or researched how to write a book – that might be a better start I guess – but I have thought on occasion when reading a great format for a book.

David Peace, for example, I love David Peace. His Shankly book was amazing the way it was structured, so clever. Part 1 was so structured and rigid and repetitive. Page after page of text repeating itself, mesmerising to the point you built up a rhythm reading it. An incredible guy summarised into the monotony of season after season. You almost felt sorry for a man with an obsessive and boring life.

But then the second part of the book is so unstructured you see and feel the man disintegrate in front of you. From the rigidity of the first part, the second part is almost impossible to read. Imagine the man's life after he retired. A brilliant book, but not my favourite Peace book.

That would be *GB84*, an account of the miners' strike of 1984/85 (which will certainly feature later in this book). *GB84* is two books. The first is a story of the behind-the-scenes machinations of the miners' strike, a fictional thriller based around the secret services and the state-sponsored destruction of an entire industry and effectively a class of people. The second is the diary of a striking miner and the desperation of his struggle and the sacrifice those men and their families and communities made.

It's a great book and the idea of two stories as a format for a book has stuck with me. I don't think for one minute I am clever enough to bring the stories together, don't be expecting anything like that. But I would like to think one book serves as a backdrop for the other—how experiences of the past colour my view of the present.

The book isn't going to be in-depth analysis of football tactics. There are a load of podcasts and websites out there now that do some incredible analysis. Some of it is bullshit of course, but there are others who provide amazing insight into what is going on both on the pitch and in the minds of the players and managers. Sometimes I think I'm watching a different game ... or that my 34 years of being a season ticket holder count for nothing in terms of understanding what's going on in front of me!

I'm also not going to write about transfers. The whole thing leaves me cold. The over-inflated prices and media gossip over a bunch of players that we don't really know anything about. A highlights reel on YouTube and a student obsession with Football Manager and people think they're a scout. I leave all that to Klopp and his team, trust them to find the right players and support them when they play in red!

When I came up with the idea last year, mid-September time, I felt I was too late. The season starts the minute the last one finishes. No point starting six games in. Everything is already decided by then. So the question was when. Kiev was a month ago (I didn't go to Kiev, I was on holiday—that is another story), but I was away and it all seemed a bit raw. Now we are in the middle of the World Cup. I was going to wait until that finished, when the focus returned to Melwood and the soap opera of the Premier League.

But Klopp has spoken—the season starts here. So, this is where I start. At the end of May, I may just look at these two pages of text and laugh and think, *Well, there's another thing you didn't follow through on, you loser,* or I may have my book—or two books...

Tuesday 4th June 2019

Well, it's exactly 11 months on and I present to you ... a book. I can't tell you how proud of myself I am. For me, just writing this has been an achievement. No one knows about it, no one has seen it. (I have hinted at it with friends in a couple of pissed moments but have quickly covered my tracks!)

I thought this was going to be unique, but I see Si Hughes, one of the guys who inspired me to write this in the first place, has pre-published his review of the season on Amazon this morning, while I've been that focussed on writing it (and working and family life) I haven't even thought about how to start printing yet. I'd better pull my socks up!

It's not quite two books as I first intended—I'm going to say it's a book with a series of interludes. The main thrust of the book is the season; I could say the ups and downs, but it has been a season of many ups and very few downs—what a season it has been. I have to say probably the best season of football I have ever seen.

The football has been amazing from start to finish. And while you may think that would make it easier, I can assure you it doesn't. It means you only have half the emotions to deal with, half the number of words to use. There is a danger that the consistent success of the team makes the book quite boring because there's nowhere else to go. I hope not. Some might say it's a nice problem to have.

I am going to say the book was written 'on the hoof'. The vast majority of it has been written on my phone, frantically typing away with my thumbs when I have a spare moment and a thought comes into my head. I've tried to be as immediate as I can, writing before I have read anything or listened to podcasts so as not to distort my view. A good proportion of it has been written while sitting on the toilet, but please don't let that put you off!

I'm also not particularly well planned in my writing style. In an effort to get something out of my head, I just write and let it flow and see where I finish up. I've tried not to go back and edit this as it's how I want the book to read. So at times, please bear with it. I certainly haven't gone back and edited later in the season. This is about what I was thinking and feeling at the time and sometimes difficult to think about that nearly a year on. The chat about Karius last July is actually a little disorientating, now we have the best keeper in world.

The second book isn't a book at all. In putting this together, I realised that an autobiography of someone you've never heard of is a little bit self-indulgent, to say the least. I also identified a period in my life that told a little story about me and why I am so attached to the football. It is about why I love the football, but it is the attachment to it that is pertinent, the two are very different things.

It's a series of short interludes, which breaks up the story of the season, something a little different to break up the football and possibly make you appreciate it more—a bit like an international break. The interludes tell the story of how I came to be a Liverpool fan as a child and a teenager and how lucky I was to be supporting Liverpool during such a successful period. They try to put the football in the context of other things that were going on in my life at the time. As I said, in the first part of the intro, no one really wants to read about me, so I've kept it short.

I've enjoyed doing this most of the time; although at certain times there has been a pressure to write something down, which can be difficult in the context of work and family, particularly when no one knows I am writing it. But I have found time. My social media browsing time is right down, which is no bad thing.

I've also realised that I am not a writer and, as such, much of this has been a challenge when trying to find the right words to express myself. I have become an Audiobook fan recently and I am increasingly jealous of the writing talents of authors who can create so much using just words. This is not a piece of literature, it's just the thoughts of a man who is passionate about Liverpool Football Club and decided he is going to share that passion with anyone who might care.

I hope you enjoy it.

JULY

Friday 6th July 2018

Another warm night. I'm sitting out in the garden because the house is like a sauna. Ten p.m. now and a light breeze is cooling everywhere down.

Brazil got knocked out of the World Cup by Belgium tonight. Good game, Belgium looked really strong in the first half, incredible strike from De Bruyne who is a hell of a player. Fellaini played the whole game, put in the middle to disrupt the Brazilians and it worked. He's an ugly brute, but he's effective. Came on to score against Japan the other night and tonight was essentially there to ruin the game in one direction, while De Bruyne and Hazard and Lukaku were devastating at times.

Brazil had chances to equalise at the end but couldn't cut through in any meaningful way. Bobby Firmino came on at two nil down to try to resurrect things. He did make an impact but doesn't have the same influential role in the team.

I don't think anyone really understands him outside Liverpool. It was Bobby who made us tick last season. Salah got all the recognition, but it was Bobby pulling the strings. So underrated from people who don't see him every week or people who only watch and understand the game on a TV. He's not a TV player; he spends most of the time avoiding the TV camera, creating space elsewhere. If I was cleverer, I'd say something about antimatter and black holes. But I'm not, so I won't, I'll leave that to you (the reader).

This season, Bobby didn't even get in the top 100 list that they do in the *Guardian*. I shouldn't be the surprised. The *Guardian* football writers are like a bunch of bedwetting stattos. I used to listen to their podcast but had to stop in the end. No insight, just a group of posh blokes who all sound very pleased with themselves. They release that list day by day, and they had all the way down to 11 with no sign of Bobby. I was really pleased for him that he had got that recognition, that he had made it into the all-important top 10. But no, he wasn't in the list at all. Otamendi was. I'll leave it there.

Klopp talking today about the keeper, Karius. How the mistakes of Kiev are '100%' down to

the concussion. For me, that means he's staying and probably staying as first choice.

It's a difficult one, isn't it. I love stories of redemption. As I walked home from the pub after the final (I didn't go the final, but not bitter about it, no, not at all), I thought about Karius and I wasn't angry with him, I felt really sorry for the lad. He made two absolutely horrendous errors, but he didn't do it on purpose and now he was going to be the absolute villain. He was going to be the villain in his own mind, and in the mind of a large chunk, an overwhelmingly large chunk, of the supporter base. I wondered how you come back from that when every mistake any keeper makes in the next five years will bring a reference to Karius. 'Oh no, he's dropped a Karius,' 'Oh dear, he's Lorissed that one.'

It's a sliding doors moment... I thought about his redemption, how this time in four years, when he's the German No.1 winning the World Cup, in some godforsaken desert somewhere, he would be interviewed and talk about that moment in Kiev as the turning point. The catalyst to great things.

I also thought about tripping over him on a beach in Asia, having dropped out of civilisation, with a bong and a huge beard, broken by that night. It's a very delicate situation because he could go in either direction.

Since the turn of the year when Van Dijk arrived, I think he (Karius) has been awesome. The assurance that Virgil brings has rubbed off on everyone around him – Lovren, Robertson, Trent and the keeper – and they look like an assured unit. I was really positive about the whole thing.

I think the keeper, whichever keeper, needs to have the confidence that they are the man. I don't think you can rotate them, I don't think they can play with any confidence knowing that one sniff of a mistake and they are out. That breeds mistakes. It's been a bad situation for both of them. I think when Virgil came in, he was heavily involved in the decision to go with Karius and, Kiev apart, Karius was the long-term plan. He's had a couple of years to bed in; he's made mistakes, lots of mistakes, but to be fair he has then got his head down and come back from those mistakes.

At the time, I would have preferred Mignolet, I thought he was playing well and deserved to be playing, but I thought he was the best of two shit options and they both had to go. With Karius I could see the light, but with such an almighty howler in the biggest game in world football, it's going to be hard to forgive and impossible to forget.

I think with both of the keepers (Mignolet too but not sure it's relevant because he'll be out on his arse within the month) they have lost all the credit in the bank. They're branded with the mark of the shit error-prone keeper, and they're never going to get rid of that reputation.

Karius could be a world beater all season, head and shoulders the best keeper in Europe. But then he makes a mistake in a live TV game and we lose some points and the whole thing comes flooding back. The media jump on the easy but lazy narrative of him being error prone, the fans straight away jump on the lad and a season of good work is flushed away.

It happened to Mignolet, it happened to Moreno, and it happened to Brendan Rodgers in the end. There wasn't enough goodwill in the bank and no matter how much positive work they do they are one mistake away from being the villain ... the liability.

So, the pressure is on to get rid of him, or at least relegate him to back up. But what are the options? I'm listening to people divided into two camps—Alisson from Rome and Big Bob Oblak from Madrid. And I don't think most people have the first clue what either of them would bring.

A year ago, no one (outside football scouting circles who do this for a living) had heard of Alisson, he has one good season and now he's the main man. I'm not having it. I saw him play twice this season and the first time he conceded five! He played tonight; conceded two and Brazil are out. I'm not saying it's down to him, but he was nowhere near that shot from De Bruyne.

And as for Big Bob, well, I wouldn't know him if he walked into the back garden now and did a shit on the grass. But I do know that if I played in that Atletico Madrid side, behind that defence, my chances of keeping a clean sheet would be considerably higher. They both seem like very expensive options. I wonder what De Gea's market value is, or Neuer. If you're going to really break the bank, then do it with style. That said, neither of them have covered themselves in glory at this world cup.

Monday 9th July 2018

Monday, back in work. The country is going into minor meltdown around the World Cup. England beat Sweden over the weekend and in no time 'It's Coming Home' can be heard everywhere and has made it to number 1 in the charts.

Croatia awaits on Wednesday. I'm not a big England fan,

but I have to admit it is getting quite exciting. I remember the semi-final in 1990, loads of people crowding around the small TV in the local pub and everyone was really up for it. But since then, I've never been that bothered, the focus has always been on Liverpool and international football in general is a distraction.

I hate the international breaks, always seem to come at just the wrong time, just as we are getting some momentum, and then you worry that the players will get injured. It's not just England either, the players play for teams around the world. Watching it now, I don't think the quality of the football is anywhere near as high as club football; none of these national teams would get close to any of the top European club sides.

The thing I really don't like about it is the media coverage and the general England supporter bellendery that surrounds the national game. Already we have seen dickheads ripping up an IKEA because we beat Sweden and God help any holidaying Croatians if their amazing midfield of Modric and Rakitic actually click on Wednesday night.

But despite all this, there is a general excitement that I am getting caught up with. Southgate is this pleasant, unassuming (if a bit bland) guy who is clearly working hard to create a good team spirit, getting the public and the media onside. It's a young squad – not a particularly good one as it goes – who are performing well, and the public are behind them. God knows the public need something to get behind. Boris Johnson has just resigned and the whole political system seems to be burning down around Brexit. The football is relief from that if nothing else.

I'm not really a big fan of Liverpool players playing for England either. I can well remember losing John Barnes for best part of a season after playing for England. And Jamie Redknapp too, but that didn't have the same sense of loss, obviously.

In this World Cup, I think Henderson has been quietly brilliant, keeping the game ticking and moving, and has been England's best player through the tournament (with mentions for Pickford in goal and Trippier).

But I'm not here to talk about England. Amongst all the hype, Liverpool kicked off their pre-season with a 7-0 thrashing of Chester. First game of the season and the players only back in preseason training for a few days, two different teams ... one in each half, so we can't really read too much into the game, but at least the season has started. Seems like ages since the end of last season and this game means we are a few short weeks away from Anfield and winning the league!

Both Fabinho and Keita played a small part in the game, but the interesting one for me is Sturridge who scored twice and set another one up. What are we going to do with him? My guess is we will still sell him, but something in the back of my mind wants him to be this redeemed player. When he is on form and fit, he is a class player, an absolute world beater. Thinking of that season when he played alongside Suarez, we had an absolute gem of a player.

It's so sad that he's never been able to repeat that form, every time he begins to show it, his body seems to let him down, to the point where I don't think anyone has any confidence left in the lad.

But what an option he could be for us ... not a first team starter but a backup to the front three who could provide a more creative option than Origi and Solanke. I think deep down everyone wants him to prove how good he is. It would be criminal to let him go and him have the season of his life ... but maybe worse to have him sitting injured on our payroll for another twelve months.

Next match is Tranmere on Tuesday, moved forward because of the England semi.

Tuesday 10th July 2018

For fuck sake. Karius. Lad, what are you doing?

After my reasoned argument a few days ago, showing tolerance to a keeper under pressure, he messes up in a friendly at Tranmere and lets a goal in. We go from a comfortable three nil lead to finishing up 3-2.

And straight away it starts. The pressure starts. From the fans, from the media. Second game back and he spills the ball and the concussion shouts of Kiev are out of the window. And even the most reasoned fan is thinking, *No, this can't go on.*

I have been that reasoned fan for the past few weeks, showing understanding and empathy, but more than my desire to be a caring person is my desire to win the league. And I think the pressure that surrounds the keeper question is going to put winning the league in jeopardy.

I don't think the pressure is on Karius. I think he's beyond pressure, he's walking round in a bubble; everyone thinks he's shit, everyone is expecting mistakes, and he is merely fulfilling those expectations.

The pressure now is on Klopp. What's he going to do? He's played the concussion card, there's only so often he can say it's just a mistake. The pressure is on the manager to act, and if he doesn't act, then the next mistake that comes, whether it's the first game of the season or the thirtieth, will bring a world of criticism down on him.

Mention it quietly, but up till now Jordan Pickford has been bloody brilliant. Whether he's the right fit I don't know, but imagine the fume if we pinched him. Ha, ha. Bitter bastards!

Wednesday 11th July 2018

Well, it looks like it's not coming home after all. England knocked out by Croatia in extra time. They scored an early goal but missed too many chances in the first half. In the second half Croatia just stepped it up a gear and England barely had another chance. They were lacking in midfield, Dela Alli and Lingard were anonymous, and Henderson was left to pick it up. Faced with Modric and Rakitic, they were absolutely flooded.

It's a shame for them as they built up quite a following and level of excitement across the country. Gareth Southgate has been a breath of fresh air in his own unassuming way and the country has been drawn to him. Ultimately, I think there is a lack of quality in the squad overall and they have really ridden their luck in how the draw turned out to get this far. I guess the media recriminations will start today … we should run a sweep on the first person to mention Jack Fucking Wilshere.

With them out, we can now return to the deeply divided Brexit-ridden nation we were before a ball was kicked.

Friday 13th July 2018

Next signing of the summer. Shaqiri. My first thought is there's no U after the Q, which is wrong. That's my first thought before I begin to think about what sort of player he might be ... which isn't a good sign.

To be honest, at £13m for an established international, it's a bit of a no-brainer. With unproven players touted round at £50m plus, getting him at the release clause price is a bargain. I have heard all sorts of rumours about his shit attitude and the fact that he went to Stoke doesn't bode well. The word mercenary comes to mind. But what do we really know about what goes on behind the scenes and why footballers pick clubs?

I work in Stoke and they rate him very highly (they have quite low bar). I can only think he's in as a squad player and if he proves himself above then it's a bonus. If he reaches a stage where he is keeping any one of the front three out of the team, then we'll all be happy. I'm sure Klopp will see through the character of the guy, and if the character doesn't pass muster, he won't see the light of day. In that context, £13m is a steal.

Sunday 15th July 2018

Pissed.

World Cup final. France win it again. A good game, they beat Croatia 4-2. I thought they were a little lucky. Debatable free kick, which goes in as an OG, followed by a very questionable penalty and they are 2-1 up at half time when Croatia had been dominant. Two good goals in the second half from Pogba and Mbappe put it out of reach. Lovren came out yesterday saying he was one of the best defenders in the world. Looking a bit exposed now.

Liverpool had their next pre-season game yesterday. A goalless draw at Bury. I don't really know too much about it other than it was a stinking hot day and it couldn't have been a lot of fun, but it's all part of the pre-season routine.

At the same time Everton won 22-0 (yes, twenty-two) as part of their pre-season, so their whole planning process is going swimmingly. The final goal is hilarious, the Everton striker is one on one with the keeper, and the keeper literally walks off leaving an open goal. Twitter is alight with Evertonians thinking this is their season, comparing a 22-0 win to Liverpool's goalless draw. Gobshites, every one of them. They are currently 200/1 to win the Premier League. Draw your own conclusion from that, 22-0 or not.

Speaking of odds, I have had a look at the odds for the Premier League tonight and have to say I am a little miffed. There was an obscene number of combinations of bets on today's game and precisely none of them came in. But I did predict France to win the World Cup at the start and I did predict a France-Croatia final once the last 16 draw was in place, so it hasn't been a complete disaster.

The plan was to put the winnings from the World Cup onto Liverpool to win the league next year. This is not a rush of blood to the head, I do it every year, but this year is definitely the year (hence me writing a book about it). It's absolutely nailed on and I'm going to make a killing on it ... so imagine my disappointment to find we are only 5/1 to win the league. I was stunned. That sort of suggests that others think we are going to win it too. I was expecting double figures at least. I feel cheated.

As a person who is hopeless at betting (I wouldn't go so far as to call myself a hopeless gambler, I'm too anal for that), my first reaction was to see what I can get a better price on... What are the odds of us winning the league and Champions League Double (70/1 by the way)? 5/1 isn't worth having; imagine how much I'm going to have to put down to get a decent return. Bastards.

These people know though. That's why they have all of our money. The CEO of Bet365 got paid £190m last year (just one year). So many think it is our year. Even taking those rose-tinted specs off, it looks like we might have a chance...

COME ON, YOU MIGHTY REDMEN

Thursday 19th July 2018

It looks like Liverpool have signed the new keeper Alisson Becker. You never quite know when people have actually signed and confirmed, with all the hype and chat, but it was just on the BBC news, which I generally take as gospel.

I'm pleased to be honest, pleased that it's all sorted and we can all look ahead to the new season. The Karius thing was already getting toxic and was going to create division. The one thing about the Klopp reign so far is that he has united the club and eradicated the divisions and it looks like sense has prevailed. Karius may well be a great keeper of the future, either at

Liverpool or elsewhere, but now there is a new focal point for the team that we can unite behind, in the same way we have done with Van Dijk. We just need to eradicate these lazy media narratives about the defence now.

Liverpool won 2-0 at Blackburn tonight. Goals by Markovic (who I guess had a price tag sellotaped to his shirt) and Sturridge. Listening to the Anfield Wrap podcast, sounds like Keita is boss, he's the one I'm really looking forward to seeing, the type of player that Klopp was clearly happy to wait a whole year for ... he must be amazing. And by the sound of it, Sturridge is playing well too.

I don't think there's a Liverpool fan out there who doesn't want Sturridge to do well. I think they all know his level and are secretly desperate for him to find it again. I'd love to see how he could add an extra dimension to the front line, how he could change things in the dynamic between Salah, Mané and Firmino. My guess is he has lost that pace that he used to have but would love to see that touch and awareness, his ability to be in the right space or spot a tight pass or just turn play on its head.

As I write this, I feel like I am describing Bobby Firmino. Maybe that's not so far off the mark. I hear so many people ask how they are going to find a backup to Bobby, how he's such a difficult player to replace or replicate ... could it be Sturridge?

It was interesting in one of his Instagram posts last week; the comment was something like '45 minutes in a new role.' It would be great to turn him into the person who can unlock a difficult game, even if he can't do 90 minutes. There's a perception that he's lazy and unprofessional, but I don't think that's the case for a minute. It must be desperately disappointing to have that much talent but be constantly affected by injury.

Overall, I find it hard to get excited about pre-season. Three weeks to the start of the season. That's when I get excited. Can't wait for the first game of the season. Can't wait.

Sunday 22nd July 2018

Well, there's a bonus! Sunday night and I'm watching the news. Virgin Media have fallen out with UKTV over some of their channels and customers are kicking off about it. I have a quick flick through to see what is on the channel in question and what do I find? Liverpool in their pre-season game against Borussia Dortmund... Live... GET IN!

I knew it was on; I've been following it during the first half on my phone. Van Dijk scored in the first half. I've said previously I'm not too bothered about pre-season, but finding a sneaky half is a real bonus. Wife is out, kids in bed, beer in hand. COME ON.

Keita playing, first time I've seen him play for the reds (or the purples as it goes tonight). Sturridge too, and from what I've heard and read the two are linking up really well. You're reading the first chapter here and thinking, *He knows nothing about what's going on ... doesn't even know when they are on the telly!*

***

UPDATE. Lost 3-1 but don't quite know how. We were all over them for the majority of the first half. Sturridge looked quick and on form, team moving around him; Keita great, can't wait to see him. But then we conceded three goals. All about Pulisic. We have been linked with him through the summer, and he really made an impact on the game. Skipping across the edge of the area to win a penalty and then converting it. Great finish from the edge of the box for the second two minutes from time, and then came in on the right to shoot (which Karius messed up, obviously) leading to the rebound, which they scored from in injury time.

Look, we know it's a pre-season game. I thought they

played well at times in the second half, not taking our chances. Ojo plays and has a chance to impress but fluffs it. I thought Gomez was OK in the centre of defence too. One game closer to the big kick-off.

Just watched an incredible documentary on Bill Shankly on BBC2. Interesting, informative of an era before mine, and so emotional. I think above all it was the connection he had with the people. It's difficult to understand that connection in our modern society. It was a simple time, an honest time and the people loved him.

Nowadays, there is an untold amount of comment and reaction, so much content … the world lives on it 24 hours a day, 7 days a week. Trotted out, spun around, it becomes so vacant and vapid. I think real people tune it out. The media thrive on it, and gobshites who live their lives through social media get so wound up about it.

They don't understand. Football is about the people and the game. Not the inane chat that swims around it. There is so much talk it just loses its value.

Its 50 years since Shankly was in charge and in those days, we didn't have or need this content; we had the people and we had the match—every week. People talked about the match in work or in school in the lead up then reviewed and discussed the match afterwards. Face-to-face. People talking to people. None of the constant replay of sound bites, arguments on chatrooms and over analysis by idiots.

There isn't that much footage of Shankly. There's the famous footage, bastion of invincibility and all that, but beyond those famous sound bites there isn't too much. But tonight I have heard stuff I haven't heard before, new insights into football and life. And the scarcity of these insights makes them so much more valuable. He understood people, he understood life. That's why they loved him.

Tuesday 24th July 2018

Now, I have to start this by stressing I am no accountant but have seen something this morning that has put our transfer business into perspective...

Last week, we bought the new keeper Allisson for £67m, which is a world record transfer for a goal keeper. We then offset that fee by selling Danny Ward to Leicester for £12m, which brings the net spend to £55m. I fully expect us to unload Mignolet over the next couple of weeks and will probably get around £20m, which will bring net spend down to £35m.

And then last night Everton spent FIFTY MILLION POUNDS on someone called Richarlison from Watford?!?!? I've had to look him up. He scored five goals in 12 games at the start of last season and then hasn't scored since November. Apparently, Marco Silva, the new Everton manager, thinks he was really good. Fifty million!!!

If that is the market value right now, take it away from the Allisson net spend, and I feel like we are £15m in credit!!

He's an ugly bugger too, looks like a blue nose from the start.

Saturday 28th July 2018

The summer rumbles on. Can't wait for the season to start.

Social media is full of the LFC tour in the states. Sturridge looking good, Milner got the best social media game. Keep seeing pictures of Lazar Markovic. What's going on there? He's just hanging around ... it's cruel. Don't know whether to feel sorry for the lad, not getting a chance, or pissed off with him, seeing out his contract and not wanting to take a pay cut to go elsewhere. Klopp seems happy to put him in the shop window, but either no one wants him or he's happy to sit it out. He's never going to see a competitive game.

He had a good run for a while there, looked like a good option, quick on the ball with a great touch. He came on in a European game and looked the business and then was sent off for a petulant swing of the arm and from that point he just disappeared.

Liverpool playing Manchester United tonight. It's a friendly so all a bit of nonsense but that doesn't stop Mourinho and his mind games. What an odious man. As much as I have been brought up to hate United, this guy really is the pits. While I have a grudging respect for Ferguson, this guy deserves none of that respect. I have friends who are United fans and they are loath to get behind him and hate the style of football he is playing.

You can see it all coming apart at the seams. The mind games are going to ramp up over the next few months and it wouldn't surprise me if he's gone by the end of October. They just won't put up with it and it will reach breaking before too long at all. The book about his time at Real Madrid is a real eye opener. It became all about the media story and points scoring rather than the football, telling the team not to win because it would play into his hands with the media and Spanish football establishment. Scum.

You would like to think that United aren't going to get caught up in that and would just show him the door. After his brain haemorrhage earlier in the year, Ferguson has recovered and it would be great to think he still has the power to influence. He can't be happy with what is going on at the club.

The best thing about this is I don't think Klopp really gives a damn for the hype. He just wants to play football and win things, not get sucked into the media game. Every time I see him, I just love him more!

Sunday 29th July 2018

Liverpool beat United 4-1. Pre-season friendly or not, we battered them. A good all-round performance topped by a bicycle kick goal from Shaquiri to make it 4-1. He only joined the squad on Tuesday. He also got an assist for Sturridge in the game.

Mourinho already moaning. That the Liverpool first team were playing the United kids, even though our average age was 25 compared to their 26. That he hasn't been able to buy the players he requested. That one of his players has had the temerity to attend the birth of his child.

It's the Mourinho third season thing. The meltdown is going to be glorious.

Interlude 1 – Born to Be a Red

On the 16th September 1972, Liverpool played away to Arsenal at Highbury. It was a goalless draw. Bertie Mee and Bill Shankly were the respective managers. It was a different age.

It would have been a big game at the time. Arsenal had won the league and FA Cup Double – the ultimate achievement in English football at the time – just over a year earlier, beating Liverpool in the Wembley final. The two teams had finished third and fifth in the previous league season, and going into this ninth game of the season, they were on the same points in 3rd and 4th, just a point off the top. All to play for.

The game was a repeat of a thrilling title-deciding last game of the previous season, which had also ended goalless, although John Toshack had a goal disallowed to prevent Liverpool winning the league. The post-match reports start with Toshack talking about what an unlucky ground Highbury is for him after he had drawn another blank.

The excellent match report is a world away from the modern narrative-based report we are used to. After the opening Toshack story, the reporter Chris James of the Echo talks with clarity about the game itself and has high praise for a pressing midfield three of Hughes, Callaghan and Cormack breaking down the Arsenal attacks with their 'harassing, intelligent interceptions and solid passing.' Clemence is singled out as having an excellent game, making a number of crucial saves.

The game is famous as the game where Jimmy Hill came

out of the stands to replace the linesman who had gone down injured. Jimmy Hill was a well-known footballer and commentator and for many was the ex-pro who had become the face of football on TV at the time—the '70s equivalent of Gary Lineker but with a bigger chin and a bit more bite. I had heard of this story before, but I didn't realise until now that it was this game.

It was the day before I was born.

The Liverpool team on the day was relatively young with an average age of just 25. It was the team that had been born from Shankly's purge of 1970 when he realised his great team of the mid-1960s had grown old before his eyes and he had to make significant changes, which he did over the next 18 months.

This was the beginning of his second great team and the one that Paisley inherited in 1974. The team on the day was Clemence, Lawler, Lindsay, Smith, Lloyd, Hughes, Keegan, Cormack, Heighway, Toshack, Callaghan with a young Phil Thompson as the only substitute.

This team would go on to win the league that season as well as the UEFA Cup. It would form the backbone of the side for the remainder of the mid '70s and six of them would be in the squad for the European Cup Final in Rome in 1977—seven if you include Ray Kennedy who played for Arsenal that day. It was the start of an 18-year run of unprecedented success in English football.

The subsequent Liverpool managers never made the same mistake that Shankly had made in 1970—from that point the team evolved year on year, phasing in young players in place of old in an almost seamless transition over twenty years until their last league title win under Kenny Dalglish in 1990.

In that 18 years, Liverpool won 11 League titles, 3 FA Cups, 4 League cups, 4 European Cups and 2 UEFA Cups—24 major trophies in all. No other team in England at least has managed that level of sustained success over such a period. From 1972 through to 1990 was a great time to be a Liverpool supporter. I was born at just the right time. It took me through my childhood and my teens until I was 18.

***

There is a funny thing with history. There are some parts you remember as clear as a bell—these start at the point you are conscious of it all. Prior to that point of consciousness, it doesn't matter when something happened – it could be last week, or it could be 50 years ago – if you aren't aware of it you have to go back into the history books, it might as well be a world away.

When I look at that 18-year period, my point of clear consciousness is about halfway through—I'm going to put a stake in the ground at the European Cup Final in Paris in 1981. I watched that at my Nan and Grandad's and can remember Alan Kennedy scoring. I can remember his celebration more than the goal—the way he ran away pumping his arms in the air.

For the two or three years before that I am aware of Liverpool, could name the team, watched for the results. This is obviously before the internet, and the information at hand is limited.

Prior to that point, it's just history. Of the players who played that day in 1972, Lawler, Lindsay, Cormack might as well be Elisha Scott and Billy Liddell—they are just names from history. Even though we might be able to picture them in colour rather than black and white there is little conception of them as people and players, even though it was only a few short years before.

Larry Lloyd was different; I remember him as part of the 'We Hate Nottingham Forest' side of the late '70s and early '80s—that he ever played for Liverpool was a world away. In writing this, I have had to draw that distinction between the conscious and the 'pre-conscious'.

I think the starkest example is the European Cup wins. I know all about 1984; I was 12 and sat there watching Grobbelaar's spaghetti legs in Rome having been to most of the home legs in the run to the final. That was only seven years after their first win in Rome, which I was too young to comprehend, and as a result they might as well be a thousand years apart.

I think back seven years now and it takes us back to 2011 and Roy Hodgson—well, actually I don't want to think about that horrendous time, but it seems to have passed in an instant and I can remember every step in between.

So to be born into a Liverpool supporting family in the early '70s was really very fortunate. It wasn't the whole family who followed; in fact, from quite a large extended family there were just three or four of them – all on my mum's side of the family – but they had a big impact in steering me into following the team in my early years and my first season ticket, which is still my most prized possession 34 years on.

AUGUST

Wednesday 1st August 2018

It's August, which means the season is just around the corner. Just 10 days or so. We kick off against West Ham next Sunday lunchtime.

Coverage of the reds has quietened down since the United game at the weekend. They are at a training camp in France, so other than what comes out on social media there isn't a lot to see. Other than the pictures of Alisson in action ... he's absolutely massive!

Over here, the start of the season is in everyone's mind. Media beginning to ramp it up, social media going for it too. I've already seen threads on Twitter talking about the line-up for the first game (my guess is Alisson, Clyne, Gomez, VVD, Robertson, Milner, Fabinho, Keita, Sturridge, Salah, Mané). Players still coming back from their holidays after the World Cup, so I can see them being phased in over the first couple of months.

There is an opening set of four matches before the international break, and I think he already has his squad ready for those games. The likes of Henderson, Lovren and Firmino who are only coming back now, I think they'll get phased in after that break.

That gives some of the new starters a chance to establish themselves in the team and create some competition in the squad, which is a good thing.

I think that is something where Liverpool have fallen behind some of the rivals, the difference between the team and the squad. In their heyday of the '70s and '80s, it was all about the first 11 (or 12 really with a single sub). That was always the focus. Were you in the team or not?

As time has moved on and there have been more and more subs on the bench (I heard someone say it's 11 in the Champions this year FFS), I think other teams have moved more towards the squad game and Liverpool more than any other still have their eye on the first team, the starters. I don't think that is necessarily the club itself, the team and the manager. It's more about the view of the fan and the media especially.

While Ferguson was rotating players for years and the likes of Giggs (in his pomp) and Scholes and Beckham would be rotated between starters and the bench, supplemented by the likes of Quinton Fortune (where did I drag that name from?), the media would be quite forgiving and talk about a squad game. But when Liverpool dared to rotate the likes of Gerrard, it was always sensationalised as DROPPED, or that we were playing a second-string side.

On the other hand, it's a while since Liverpool have had a depth in their squad. In 13/14, we basically played with 13 players plus a load of kids (and Aspas obviously), and last season in the run up to the final, I think half the Kop had cramp in their toes worried about another injury ... it was literally the last men standing. Thinking back, it's probably peak Houllier since we had a proper depth of squad and what happened then? We won three trophies and qualified for the Champions League.

It looks now like we are at a point where we have that depth again. Since Klopp arrived he has been targeted in his buys and hasn't let that many go. Rather than wholesale change, he has slowly evolved the squad to a point where we have our best chance in years of really challenging. Aside from the team I mentioned above for the first game, there is a strong squad of international quality players... Trent, Lovren, Wijnaldum, Henderson, Ox, Lallana, Firmino, Shaqiri, before we look at the competent fillers like Matip, Klavan, Moreno, Grujic, Origi, Solanke, Ings (some of whom will move on before the week is out), and then there are the kids... Curtis Jones, Camacho, Ojo etc.

I think some people prefer the whole transfer side of things to the actual football and are never satisfied with the squad, always wanting more. Thankfully, Klopp doesn't seem to be like that. He has clearly selected the platers that he wants to build the squad and nothing else will do. The pursuit and acquisition of VVD and Keita, waiting a year for the right player to arrive, shows this is a long-term strategic plan rather than a 'buy six and hope three work' approach of others (like Brendan Rodgers and his committee).

The other really positive thing that I like about Klopp is his reinvention of players, both those who are playing well but had managed to adapt and improve their game (Firmino) and those who have fallen out of favour but he has shown faith and reintegrated them (Moreno, who was great until his injury last season, and Karius who was spot on from Christmas until the second half in Kiev).

I'd much rather have a manager who is developing players and creating a culture of trust within the club than one who is buying and selling for marginal gain ... and to an extent I would include Benitez in that, as much as I love him.

(Can I just take this moment to nail my colours firmly to the Benitez mast? Just want to get it out there early on, before the season has started. If you didn't support Benitez, you were a shithouse and if you want to put the book down now, that's fine by me. Hopefully you've already paid for it. As I write this now, surrounded as we are by this Brexit nonsense, I wonder if there is a relationship between those who supported Benitez and those who voted Remain ... life's good people. All the rest are *Daily Mail* reading, racist, xenophobic idiots who voted Leave to 'take back control' from Europe and called Rafa a Spanish waiter ... life's shithouses. For a while there, it hadn't occurred to me that any Liverpool fans would have voted Leave, but apparently they did. I know, disappointing, isn't it!)

Where was I? Oh yes, how much I love everything about Jurgen Klopp and the positive impact he is having on the club. The talk before the World Cup was buying Fekir, but he didn't pass the medical and that should be that. Some cling on to the hope that we may buy him, but not having him there opens opportunities for others like Curtis Jones. Hopefully he will be given a chance to show what he can do, like Trent has been for the past couple of years.

That's the type of club I want to support, one where local lads come through and prove themselves with the best in world, far more satisfying than continually taking a chance on the next big thing. And with silly money being paid for players in the current market (Richarlison ... £50m ... blueshite ... FFS), the lottery is becoming very expensive.

That said, and to contradict two pages of writing, Martial looks like he's on his way out at United. How much would he be?

Thursday 2nd August 2018

Charlie Adam. Discuss...

He's just been on TV as the match summariser for the Rangers game in the Europa League spouting his drivel again. He seems to be everywhere in the media at the moment. I can only assume he is injured. I'd be really pissed off if one of our players was doing media work during pre-season.

He's already been warned by Stoke this week about talking too much in the media. Talking about the bad apples in the

Stoke squad, talking about the previous manager, Lambert, and how he expected the rest of the squad to be water carriers for Shaqiri. The club are fed up with him, the fans are fed up with him, and here he is up in Glasgow on TV again.

Earlier this week, he was on Radio 5 talking about Shaqiri and, although being very gifted, he doesn't track back or do any defensive work for the team. Pots and kettles. There is a key difference of course; Shaqiri may not be tracking back because he's lazy. Adam doesn't track back because he's lugging that fat arse around after him, he probably wants to track back, just isn't bloody quick enough. What a cheek. (Fat arse cheek).

The funny thing is his comments have been everywhere accompanied by a clip of him tripping over the ball while trying to take a corner. What a disgrace. How he ever ended up at Liverpool I will never know... They were very dark times.

Sunday 5th August 2018

The wait for the start of the season is driving me mad now. Liverpool beat Napoli 5-0 yesterday in a friendly in Dublin. They look so sharp going forward and assured at the back. First game for Alisson who keeps a clean sheet. Goals from Milner, Gini, Salah, Sturridge and Moreno ... with an incredible 60-yard assist from Sturridge. Even the new kit is boss.

I have said this every year since 1991, but I think we've got a bloody good chance here. The squad that has come together, the clear passion and enjoyment of the squad playing together; they look like they're having fun and there's a genuine level of excitement building amongst the fan base.

We have to remember, of course, that City amassed 100 points last season, which is almost unheard of. It doesn't matter how good you are playing, if one of your rivals can get that many points then it's going to be very difficult. I think we need to aim for 60 points off the first 25 games, that's 2.4 per game, and then we must be in with a shout. That's when we find out how good we are.

I'm big on points per game (ppg). It's always in my head. 2.5 ppg is 95 points and wins you the league (except last year). Two ppg is 76 and pretty much gets you in the top four. As I'm out walking the dog I'm generally calculating ppg, how many we have, how many we have to get if we want to be up there... It's constant mental gymnastics. Another place it seems to happen is when I'm in the shower!!

I'm a big fan of the alternative Premier League on RAWK, which is done by Prof. Always a great way to follow the league, playing to par. As much as I like to follow it, I think it's a little dated now and doesn't work with a league with a very dominant top six.

As I remember it, it's three points for every home win and then three points for any away win against the bottom seven and a point against the top 13. That just doesn't work anymore. I think there is so little between the teams outside the top six that we should be expecting to beat each of those teams home and away. I also think it's a little harsh that if you win a game that you expect to win, you just stay on par... Where's the fun in that?

So, last year, I created my own alternative league on a similar basis but with different points expectations. Basically, we need to look to beat each of the bottom 14. In the alternative league, each one of these games is worth 2.5 points. Beat one of the bottom teams and you are half a point ahead. In all, the games against the bottom 14 are worth 70 points (28 x 2.5) and the games against the rest if the top six are worth 20 points (10 x 2). Against the top six we should look to score four points across the two games, that's a win and a draw. All in all, that gets you to 90 points, which should be enough to win—or be very close.

In my own little sad way, I have all of this set up on a

spreadsheet, along with league tables of the top six against the rest of the top six and against the bottom 14. Last year, City won both leagues by a long way; overall their PPG was about 2.7. No one came close; no one has ever come close since the Premier League began. This season Liverpool need to do better against the rest of top six but more importantly need to be more consistent against the rest at the bottom.

Wednesday 8th August 2018

Last friendly of the pre-season last night. Beat Torino 3-1. It's been great preparation but so pleased we can now move on to the real thing—West Ham on Sunday.

Another good team performance last night, topped off with Gini's goal, which was a fantastic team effort—that's two goals in two games for Gini. Hoping he has a good season. With the new arrivals into the team, you wonder how that affects the rest of the players in the squad, who is the first name on the team sheet, who is going to spend more time on the bench.

The automatic thought that comes into my head is Gini would be one spending more time on the bench, but I'm hoping that isn't the case. He has been a funny one to gauge since he arrived. He was very much unheralded, no one really knew too much about him and he was a surprise when he arrived, but he went straight into the team and has been consistently in there when he is fit.

He's the player who does all the work that you don't always see. You think he's had a quiet game or question his contribution only to find he's clocking up the miles, creating space, making links. He's the player you miss when he's not playing, and things don't quite click—the Ronnie Whelan of the Klopp era (one for the dads there).

The game that jumps out for me where he was outstanding was the Manchester City game last season – when we beat them in the league – he was everywhere. Christ knows how he managed to keep up that pace and movement for the whole game.

Not scoring goals, not being flashy, just being consistent and there for the team. If you weren't in the ground for that game, you wouldn't know how good he was. In the final minutes of the game, as City came back from 4-1 to 4-3 and very nearly equalised, I remember watching Gini and thinking, *Please don't fuck up, I don't know how you are still running around the pitch here, but don't be the one who messes up and be remembered for that when you have been outstanding for ninety-odd minutes.*

I think there is an opportunity for him this season. I saw a thing that said Klopp made 5.5 changes per game in the league last season, that's half a team for each game. When you think the front three and the keeper are fairly unchanged, then it stands to reason that the rotation comes largely from the midfield. Gini is going to get his game, as are Milner and Lallana. I can also see Shaqiri and Sturridge being pulled into the midfield rotation, if not as starters then definitely as substitutes.

Thinking back to the start of the 16/17 season, Klopp played a style and formation that was so exciting. Closest thing I could call it is 2-1-7. Two centre backs, Henderson at the base of midfield and then the other five attacking players plus the two full backs (Milner being one of them) just doing whatever they wanted. They were everywhere; it was difficult to see a formation, just seven players swarming all over the opposition defence with Henderson seemingly in control of every movement. I can see that happening again this season.

Thursday 9th August 2018

So it looks like we were the unluckiest team in the Premier League last season – and that is official – so say the independent experts. They have analysed every game, looked at every decision that was made that affected the game – goals and penalties that were given that shouldn't have been, those that weren't given that should have been, incorrect offside etc. – and decided that Liverpool were ROBBED of 12 points—yes, ROBBED! The bastards.

Add those 12 points onto our total and take away the three points that City were GIFTED from bad decisions and guess what—no, we still didn't win the league!!! City were that good we couldn't even catch them with a fifteen-point swing. But it does put us closer, much closer.

The law of averages says that we won't be hampered by bad refereeing to the same extent this season and if you add those potential points to a more consistent approach, an outstanding transfer season giving us the strongest squad we have had in years, excellent preparation through pre-season and what seems like the universal vociferous support of the team by the fans, then this is the year.

No prizes for guessing who the luckiest team was—United of course with six points.

Friday 10th August 2018

Season starts this weekend, tonight to be exact, United playing Leicester on the TV.

It's always really exciting, walking up the steps to see the pitch for the first time in the season. I can remember doing it with my Grandad in the main stand in the early '80s, and 30-odd years later the effect is still the same. The pitch looks so green and lush and the stands that surround it create this enclave. I always think it's amazing there is space for 50,000 people, all coming for the same thing—to shout on the reds.

Seeing the same faces who sit all around—you recognise them like they haven't aged, but they are all 25 years older than when we all sat there for the first time. They look the same but are a full generation further on, like me I suppose.

Transfer window finished yesterday, so hopefully we can concentrate on the football now. It always annoys me the first few weeks of the season when people are still talking about transfers instead of getting behind the players that are already there. None of that this weekend—we have our players, and this is our year.

There was a fair amount of business yesterday, Everton bought nearly a full team of players you'd never heard of—they need that to support the striker you'd never heard of either. Wolves and Fulham have both spent a lot too and the talk is they are strong enough to finish in the top half of the table. I think for the past few seasons you could pick any three out of ten to go down at the bottom and my guess is that will be the same this year, with those two teams included.

No more purchases for Klopp, which I'm happy with—squad is picked and settled. I think Shaqiri could be the buy of the season (wonder how quick that opinion will change!) and I really hope this is the season where Sturridge can fulfil his potential.

He's a different player to that of 13/14, certainly not as quick, but he's a class player, a player that can create things and change games, and if he can do that as a bit part player and be happy with that role then he is invaluable. I think everyone has fallen in love with the idea of him being boss again!

Danny Ings was the only player to move on. It's the best thing for him. It's been so sad for him the past couple of years. When he joined just before Klopp arrived, he showed some real passion and was the sort of player you like to have around the team, someone who gives his all. And then he has two horrendous injuries and, in that time, Klopp has moved the club onto a new plane—to a level where Ings just couldn't compete.

Everyone was happy to see him back, both fans and players, and really cheered him on, but you could see he wasn't going to fit in at the level Liverpool have raised themselves to. So he moved on to Southampton, back to his hometown club, where I am sure he will do well and be a real local hero. Good for you, Danny, best of luck.

Sunday 12th August 2018

First game of the season. Liverpool 4 West Ham 0.

Great to be back at Anfield. An assured display by Liverpool, completely in control, never under threat. West Ham offered very little and Liverpool never really had to get out of a low gear to put four past them.

Salah gets a tap in after great work from Keita out to Robertson, Mané gets a couple – the first on the stroke of half time that just about kills the game, and then the second was probably offside – and then Sturridge taps in with his first touch of the game having been on the field for about 10 seconds. I would be made up for Sturridge if it wasn't for the Salah first goal and 3-0 double that I was just about to win. Thanks Daniel.

Through the team, they played well. First time I've seen the new keeper and he's massive, not just tall but built like a brick shithouse too. Didn't have to do very much today, but just looked assured. He's really good with the ball at his feet and the calmness flowed through him and VVD. Gomez had a couple of dodgy moments with Arnoutovic but they didn't offer enough threat for him to have a bad game.

Trent and Robertson were threatening moving forward and are essentially attacking midfielders rather than full backs... Robertson got an assist for the first and then set up the second with a great ball.

I thought the best two players on the pitch were Wijnaldum and Milner. They seemed to swap positions at the base of midfield and then take turns to push forward. Milner just seems to get better and better. Every season you think he's going to play fewer games, but he'll be playing every week if he continues this form. Keita was quieter than I thought he would be, but you could see the quality and the potential for the rest of the season. He was almost playing himself into the season, getting the measure of everyone and then every so often getting the ball to his feet and running with it. That's where he's going to be good, running at players with the ball, and with players around him running into space, that's going to be a massive weapon.

And what can you say about the front three? Salah was a constant threat despite the attentions of his man marker. Bobby and Mané had a couple of duff touches, early season rustiness we can put it down to, but still managed a couple of goals and an assist. They were all off by the end, replaced by Shaqiri, who had some magic little touches, looking forward to seeing more of him through the season.

So a good start to the season. Top after the first game on goal difference. It's nonsense really, they never even used to show the table until the third game, but if they're going to show it now, we might as well be top. According to the BBC, I'm a 'traditionalist'.

One thing to note about the game today was how bad the referee was throughout. That can sometimes get lost in the wake of a 4-0, but it has to be said he was abysmal. He always is, the Manc bastard. He didn't stop us from winning today, but in a tighter game he could have done. He probably thinks his performance will go under the radar and he lives to referee another weekend, which is bad considering what a train wreck of a display it was.

I had to drive today, which is probably why I can remember so much of the game. I was hoping for a boozy start to the season, but the rest of the lads decided that they'd rather be on holiday. I can't complain too much as I'm missing the next home game on holiday. When I let them know that a couple of weeks ago, the reply I got on WhatsApp was 'It begins.' I don't think I'm going to live down missing Kiev, especially after the odyssey that the rest of them went on to get there.

Bit of an easy target for missing a game. Only after that both Bobsey and Whaley announce that they're on hols ... and I end up driving. Lightweights.

Tuesday 14th August 2018

General consensus about the weekend is Milner had a great game and so did Keita. I agree on Milner, I think he's going to be the go-to guy for the first part of the season. Solid, full of energy and running, not afraid to throw a tackle in, tactically astute and contributing key passes and assists. Every year, you think he's going to be phased out with the introduction of new players, and every year he shows that experience is priceless and age means nothing.

A season at left back, redefining what that role can be from a midfield perspective, a season starting on the bench until it came to the crunch and ended up being the driving force to the Champions League Final.

We beat Man City in a great game in 13/14; Milner came on at half time for City in that game and was possibly the most influential player on a visiting team that I can remember seeing. He does the same for us now ... never flashy but running his bollocks off, popping up everywhere and dictating the game through sheer force of will but somehow doing that in an understated way. The trick is to manage him through the season so he is fit and on top form when we need him.

I stick by what I said about Keita. Despite the rave reviews, I think he was holding himself back and getting the feel of the game and the pace of the league. I was more excited about what he is going to do than what he did on Sunday; he's going to be amazing when he's got the measure of the players around him and the players playing against him. Worth waiting for.

Amongst the few comments I have made so far, the ones about Richarlison (Everton's new £50m striker in case you had forgotten reading this at the end of the season) may be a bit misguided. Scored two at the weekend. It was a good job Mané got two as well. Can do without all that crowing from the blue shite.

Saturday 18th August 2018

Saturday evening and Liverpool don't play until Monday night. I hate Monday night kick-offs. I hate the wait. Watching all the other teams play, the mental gymnastics of what we have to do, where we'll be if we win, lose or draw.

The only thing I hate more than Monday night games is Monday night games at Anfield. What a waste of a weekend they are. At least when they're away from home, it's an additional game I get to see. I hope you're not reading this book under an assumption that I am a home and away supporter. Unfortunately not. No refunds though. It's difficult enough with two young kids to get a pass for the home games sometimes, never mind the aways!

Monday night is Crystal Palace, which means Roy fucking Hodgson. Christ, I hate that man. There's so much added needle in wanting to beat that bastard. He makes me angry just thinking about him. I think I'm angrier about it since he came back to the Premier League. Following the debacle at Liverpool, he was the most infuriating, insufferable prick of a man, loved and adored by the bed-wetting media, inferring that his outright failure at Liverpool was more to do with the club than the man.

He was bang average, no ambition, no tactical nous, no people skills. He was absolutely awful. And that may be OK for Blackburn or Fulham or any other shithouse team whose measure of success is avoiding relegation, but it wasn't alright for Liverpool. And then he gets the England job and it was horrendous.

Standing pitch side in his England blazer, working his way through the qualifiers, beating second-rate teams, being talked up as an intellectual ... a thinker (on the basis that he could read a book). The Liverpool job was an aberration. He was rewriting himself as world-leading football authority, a renowned coach. Not a journeyman who had played 4-4-2 football for average teams in minor leagues.

Until the Iceland game. England get beat by Iceland and Hodgson falls to the ground with a bang. He resigns minutes after the game, so he doesn't have to face the press. Then he gets hauled up in front of them the next day, and he sits there not understanding why he has to sit there and answer his questions because he's already resigned. Nothing to do with the millions he had been paid by the FA. All to do with having to face the music for an atrocious campaign. The country saw him for the fraud he was, the fraud that we had known he was for years. And off he slinks into the darkness never to be heard of again.

At that point I was quite happy with the whole Hodgson situation. But now he's back, playing his one win in three, two banks of four football. He kept Crystal Palace up last season, so they think he's great. He'll probably keep them up again and will get the freedom of the city or some such bauble. And the media seem to have forgotten his England shambles, he's the darling again. Bang average he is and a nasty piece of work to boot. I hope we batter them. Rant over.

(Everton won today, Richarlison scored again. He's going to make a show of me!)

Monday 20th August 2018

Monday Night Football. Palace 0 Liverpool 2.

That's a good away win for Liverpool tonight. There will be a few teams who go there this season and come away with nothing.

Another solid performance. I think they call it winning ugly. Midfield three of Gini, Milner and Keita all played well. I don't know where Milner gets the energy from. Henderson came on after an hour and played well too. There was a lot of talk about him starting tonight, but that would have been harsh on Wijnaldum after last week and he had another strong game tonight.

The front three struggled to get into a rhythm against an organised back four but continue to put in the effort and make it hard for the opponents the whole game. I think the big plus from the game was the keeper and defence. Alisson looks assured in goal, in control. And then he pulls out a couple of absolutely belting saves. A clean sheet was a great positive from the game. Benteke couldn't hit a barn door, but there are other players such as Zaha who are a real threat, but nothing was getting past him.

Of course, to get to the keeper you have to get through the centre of defence and that just isn't happening. VVD is imperious. What a player. Just seen a great tweet from Martin Fitzgerald, he could watch a BBC crime series featuring VVD solving crimes with his headers. And he's right, they are a thing of beauty, controlled and timed to perfection. Gomez had a good game too and you can see the makings of potential partnership there.

First goal was a penalty. Nailed on for me. Sakho had about half a dozen goes at Salah and eventually he came down. Never in question. Unless you are Roy Hodgson of course.

Second came in injury time from a Palace corner, cleared to the edge of the box and then run the length of the field by a combination of Salah and Mané, who finished really strongly one on one with the keeper, which also happened to secure my two-goal bet, so a nice finish all round. Mané also keeping in touch with the free-scoring Richarlison.

The most satisfying part of the night was Hodgson's post-match interview. You could feel the anger coming through the radio speakers. It was perfect. We were lucky to come away with a win, it was never a penalty. Ha ha... Piss off Woy.

The build-up to the game today was very much secondary to the post mortem of the United defeat against Brighton yesterday. The meltdown continues, helped by Pogba coming out in an interview saying he wasn't really up for the game. It's all going wrong and it's wonderful! I give Mourinho till Halloween.

Wednesday 22nd August 2018

Couple of nights on from the Palace game. Still excited and would be looking forward to Saturday but am away on holiday tomorrow morning so have had to pass my ticket on. Holidays are great, but at the moment I'm gutted I'm missing the next game. Sure I'll be able to find a boozer and watch it there, but it's not the same. And then it's nearly a month until the next home game. That one is written in stone!

Much of the talk following the game on Monday is about the penalty. What nonsense. It was a nailed-on penalty and how it can even become a conversation is beyond me. Sakho had three swipes at Salah and was either too slow to keep up with Mo's footwork or too bloody clumsy to control his own feet in that situation.

I think it must be a media thing. They need a topic of conversation, a debate, a controversy. It's lazy journalism really. They should be talking about the tactical battle, the defensive control, in what was a tight game. Not a lot of goals to talk about so they seem bereft of ideas for how to analyse the game. Stick a microphone under the nose of Roy Hodgson two minutes after the final whistle and of course he's going to say it wasn't a penalty (as previously pointed out, the man is an imbecile), but that just adds fuel to the media fire.

At some point soon, Liverpool will get the credit they are

beginning to deserve.

Saturday 25th August 2018

Top of the league! Third game of the season, so the league table is officially out and we're sitting proudly at the top after beating Brighton 1-0.

Another case of winning ugly. Brighton played well right to the end, defended really well and disrupted our attack, while at the same time pushing forward and if it wasn't for Alisson making an incredible save in the last ten minutes, we would have come away with the draw.

I am away on holiday at the moment but never far from following the scores of each game. City drew at Wolves so dropped a couple of points. Even three games in, the general feeling is it's a two-horse race between Liverpool and City, so the idea of them dropping points is an opportunity. Even as I'm walking around Alcudia Old Town, I feel myself thinking about those points and is this an opportunity for us to go ahead of them... It's only the third game if the season, for God's sake.

Liverpool starts well enough and has enough chances to make it look as if this is going to be a straightforward win. Salah scores in the first half and I'm thinking my accumulator is looking safe... I need two goals in the game. Liverpool looking in control in midfield, safe at the back, although the front three aren't quite firing, disrupted by the Brighton defence.

Second half and although we have most of the game, Brighton have their chances too. Keita and Mané playing on the left are quieter; Salah seems to be playing everywhere, dropping deeper, both sides of the pitch. It's as if Brighton have worked them out a little and they have a couple of good counter attacks, should score early in the second half.

Gomez has another good game at the back alongside VVD (who is always good it seems). Alisson has a couple of moments at the back. The type of moments that if it was Karius or Mignolet, the crowd would have kittens, but because it's Alisson, people wonder at his skill with the ball at his feet. He tries to take on a player, gets it wrong and has to finish with a sliding tackle to get the ball away.

And then there's the 'dink'. I've a feeling the dink will be the GIF of the season, replayed alongside Keita's turn at the Crystal Palace game, the type of thing you watch on repeat a hundred times. Alisson receives the ball at the edge of the area with a Brighton player running in, he just 'dinks' it over his head. It's just brilliant. So cocky, yet so controlled.

All of a sudden, we have the best keeper in the world, he's never going to concede a goal and he's barely even made a save of note yet. That is until the last few minutes when he saves one low to his left from about six yards, wrong footed; he's going the opposite direction but manages to get his hands to it and push it away around the post. A nailed-on goal. Plucked away. Now he is winning us points. He is the best keeper in the world. Three points, top of the league!

Special mention here for the mighty Everton, who throw away a two-goal league at Bournemouth. Richarlison is becoming a theme here, although today it's not about scoring, it's him getting sent off and missing the next three games. Magic.

Sunday 26th August 2018

The dink is mesmerising on a loop. The dink is wonderful.

Monday 27th August 2018

Away on holiday. Today spent in a God-awful water park in Majorca (the kids thought it was great, so I guess that's all that matters). Two things in my head. The first is why have so many blokes got the name and date of birth of their kids tattooed on them? What the hell is that all about?

The second is the mental gymnastics going on around our points haul so far (9 out of 9) and how many points per game we need from now to the end of season to win the league. It's not even the end of August and the sums are happening. There's no hope for me. In the 13/14 season, the sums weren't happening until February. I've got six months of it and they won't go out of my head. In case you're interested its 2.31 ppg per game to get to 90 from here.

As I type, a little beep on my phone tells me Harry Kane has scored against United in the Monday night game. There's something special about United conceding a goal, isn't there? Although its only three games in, if they get beat tonight, they are at the threshold of crisis. More mental outbursts from Mourinho; more media coverage (beep, its two nil) talking about the third season syndrome. I'd said Halloween; he might not make the end of August!

Talking of United, I came across Michael Owen's piece from the coverage of the Liverpool game at the weekend. What a shithouse. How he'd always wanted to come back to Liverpool. Nonsense. I don't think I've ever seen a footballer who was more in it for himself. All about him. Angling to leave Liverpool because they couldn't fulfil his ambitions. And then he went for £8m. Given his standing in the game at the time, it should have been £30m, but I guess he did OK for himself.

At the weekend, he was saying that it was always the intention to come back to Liverpool after a couple of years at Real Madrid. How he was expecting to come back, but Newcastle put in a higher bid and it was out if his hands. Apparently, he even contacted Liverpool to see if they'd up the bid. Rafa probably told him to get stuffed.

As you might have gathered, Michael Owen is not my favourite player. That he is now an ambassador for LFC really annoys me. REALLY ANNOYS ME. And to have him and the clapping seal, Macmanaman, commentating on our games... Well, I'm just going to leave it there or I won't be able to sleep!

Beep, beep. It finished 0-3 at Old Trafford, according to the BBC website, Jose Mourinho 'cuts a glum figure.' Hee, hee!

Thursday 30th August 2018

Sitting in hotel trying to get the Champions League Draw. The WIFI is shit, so have jumped the phone onto 4G, it's now 17 minutes in and nothing happened yet. Had to sit and listen to David Fucking Beckham wittering on, when all anyone is really interested in is who we are playing.

We are in Pot 3, which it a bit more tricky, but really hoping we get a top team. Disappointed last year not to get one of the big ones. Would be great to get Bayern Munich or PSG his year. We play the Pot 1 team in early November... What a great trip that would be. Come on, stop bloody talking and start picking some balls.

Finally, they get going. Whoever worked the draw out must be really clever. The whole thing is like a test for MENSA. United come out the pot and there are only two options for them, they get Juventus. At last, the bastards get a tricky draw.

At last ... pot 3. Come on, you red men. We can get Atletico Madrid, PSG or Moscow. I think Paris would be the preferred option. We'll take on anyone! Kaka pulling the balls out, he's very well trained. I think the other one is Forlan, who looks very European and sophisticated, not at all like the oik who played for United.

Last one out the pot and we get PSG and Napoli. It's already the group of death and they have still got one team to pick. Bloody hell, they're going to be massive games. Imagine how good Anfield will be for those games. Doesn't bear thinking about. How am I going to contain myself!?

Red Star Belgrade. The final team in the group. They are a

massive name as well. Probably not as big as they used to be, but what a history. I can't wait already.

Of the others United got Juve and Valencia and Spurs got Barcelona and Inter Milan. There are going to be some great games. City managed to get the easy draw (of course) with Shakhtar, Lyon and Hoffenheim.

Interlude 2 – My Family

My mum and dad were both from Liverpool, baby-boomers born in the two years after the end of the war. As I grew up it was clear from an early age that they were very different families and backgrounds

My dad was born the year after the war brought up around Smithdown Road in Liverpool in a small terraced house. I don't really know too much about his childhood. I think the phrase for our relationship is estranged and it's been that way since the mid-80s so I never really had a conversation about him growing up.

It's another world in the same way that my son's knowledge of me growing up is next to zero. There is probably a point when you have enough interest in your parent's previous life that you actually sit down and have a conversation with them about it, but I never reached that point with my dad, so I have a very sketchy idea of him growing up.

He went to Liverpool Collegiate for a couple of years and then got a scholarship to HMS Worcester, which was some kind of posh naval academy. It was boarding school and I guess they drummed a lot of the Liverpool out of him. You wouldn't know where he was from now—the way he dresses, the way he talks is a million miles from what you would expect of a Smithdown Road baby boomer. I think he is ashamed of it actually. A couple of times, when he has been caught out on something he has said or the way he has said it, he has distanced himself very quickly.

From HMS Worcester, he joined Shell as an apprentice in the early 1960s and went off to sea on the big oil tankers, progressing his way through the officer ranks of the merchant navy. He was certainly well travelled, and Shell took him around the world many times throughout the '60s.

At some point his parents moved to a semi-detached house in Childwall and were the height of lower-middle class respectability. That was where we used to visit Grandma and Grandpa as kids, although post-divorce it was funny to hear my mum's absolute assassination of them as the 'jumped up snobs from smithdown.'

My mum's family were from Prescot. My mum was the youngest of three girls and was a lot younger than the other two. My Auntie Pat and June had been born before the war, but with my Grandad stationed away for the majority of the war, it wasn't until he got back that my mum came along. Her sisters were ten and seven by the time she was born. At the time they would marry young, so her elder sisters were married and having kids before my mum was even in secondary school.

They were more of a traditional working-class family. My Grandad had 'done his time' as a bricklayer before the war. When he came back from the war, he got a job as a maintenance man at a chemical factory in Speke and used to cycle there every day—he was there for 25 years until he retired in 1974. At some point, the family moved to Huyton, to the St Johns Estate just off Tarbock Road, and that is where my mum grew up.

My Grandad was a man's man, people (the women of the family) thought he was miserable, but he wasn't. He was just quiet. My Nan was this bubbly effervescent little lady, who would light up the room and was always warm and welcoming. My Grandad was too, in his own way, but he was quiet and quite dour sometimes.

He didn't suffer fools gladly, would never talk just for the sake of it. If he didn't have anything to say to you, then he wouldn't say anything. I'm like that now—people sometimes think I'm arrogant or aloof (I'm not, I'm just shy ultimately), but there was no arrogance or aloofness about my Grandad. He was just very well respected as being a quiet man.

When people visited, Nan would entertain them in the back room next to the kitchen, while Grandad would sit in the front room on his own, listening to his records or more often watching sport on TV. He would watch anything with a ball in it my Nan used to say. And as quiet as he was he always had an opinion on the football—it usually started with 'Jee-sus.' Grandad didn't smoke, didn't drink, didn't gamble—he had come from a well-known family of illegal bookies and pawnbrokers in Liverpool; he was a good, respectable, hard-working family man. In fact, he never gambled until I got him into it in the early '90s just before he died!!

My mum was bright and passed the 11+ to go to Prescot Grammar School. She wanted to go on to art school but my Nan and Grandad wouldn't let her—they thought art school was for beatniks, so she left school and got a job as a Comptometer operator in Lewis's. She had a more traditional time growing up in the Liverpool in the '60s.

She was there at the start of the Beatles and would tell us all about her nights at the Cavern just around the point they were becoming famous. As kids we used to think that was all a load of shit, until one day, just after she died, there was a new Beatles exhibition in Liverpool. There was a picture on the front of the Echo of the early Cavern with Paul singing and there she is, right at the front, probably only about 16 or 17.

At some point in the mid-'60s my mum and dad met, married in 1968 and then headed off to sea as a married couple. My dad was working, and my mum would go along and live on the ship. This was a massive departure for someone of her back-

ground, spending time across South East Asia, visiting faraway places such as Singapore, Bangkok, and Vietnam—they were there carrying supplies during the war.

I have been fortunate enough to travel in my life and I think the desire to do that comes from my mum and her experiences abroad. When we would visit Nan and Grandad's, the place used to be full of souvenirs from Asia and while I just took that as normal at the time, it was probably quite exotic.

In the early 1970s she returned back to England and they had me in September 1972. She was 25 by this point, which was late to be having a baby in those days. Her sisters were a lot older and had had children younger so there was a considerable gap between me and my cousins. My Grandad had always been working when my cousins were growing up, but around the time I was born he had a couple of heart attacks and was forced to retire.

My parents bought a house in the growing 'New Town' of Warrington, which was quickly filling up with baby boomers from Liverpool—a bit like Bob in 'Whatever Happened to the Likely Lads'. When I was born, they left the hospital with me a few days later and moved straight into their new house for the very first time; I always find that a bit mad, that they had never even slept there until they arrived with a new baby.

My dad still worked away at sea a lot and would be gone for as long as three months at a time, so my mum would spend a lot of time with my Nan and Grandad. It was only about 10 miles from our house to theirs. My mum would drive when she visited, but they didn't drive and would get the H2 bus, which dropped them off half a mile away where my mum would be waiting at the bus stop.

I think a combination of these two factors – my grandad retiring and my mum needing help being on her own – led to me having such a close relationship with my Grandad. I was the first of his grandchildren that he was able to spend the time *with, I was like his little hobby and I came to realise that I had a much closer relationship with him than many of my cousins.*

It was my Grandad who was the Liverpool supporter. There is a picture of me with him on the day Liverpool won the FA Cup in 1974. He has got me held up on his shoulder with a red-and-white top hat on—not even a toddler at this point, just a fat baby really, but I always think that is the point it all started.

SEPTEMBER

Saturday 1ˢᵗ September 2018

Half time and Liverpool are 2-0 up against Leicester. I'm sitting in a bar in Alcudia having just watched Liverpool control 45 minutes of football.

The word is control. From back to front. Started the game on the front foot. Salah should have scored in minutes but put wide. Mané scores after ten minutes after Robertson walks through tackles on the left. He had every right to go down after the second challenge but admirably stayed on his feet to put Mané through.

They then allowed Leicester to have some possession and move forward but always with an air of control. On the odd occasion the midfield let one slip through, Gomez and VVD are in control at the back. At one point, Alisson even has to make a save. They look so good in absorbing pressure across the team. There is a twenty-minute period where they don't even look like they want to go forward. It's as if Klopp has set them a challenge to see how well they can absorb pressure. Like a training ground exercise.

Then, at 40 minutes, they decide to push forward again. And guess what... Firmino pops up and scores a header from a corner right on half time. It's all about control. It's brutal really.

Almost an unchanged team. Henderson in for Keita, which just brings that solidity that's required for this type of game.

Leicester aren't a bad side and we clearly needed a solid and experienced midfield in Henderson, Milner and Gini. All three have been dominant. Immaculate.

It's not particularly exciting. It's impressive through. It's all about control. With the Champions League draw now made and a visit from Chelsea in the League Cup there are going to be plenty of opportunities for the rest of the squad. Clyne, Matip, Lovren, Moreno, Lallana, Fabinho, Shaqiri, Sturridge have barely kicked a ball between them. What squad depth. Liverpool have a tendency to focus on the first eleven and haven't graduated to a squad game in the same way other teams look at it. We now have the ability to do that.

They're out for the second half. At this point it's worth pointing out how much rhubarb Richard Keys has banged on. Just saying like. The fat hairy fuck.

***

Full time. A win. A hanging on win but a win nonetheless. Am I allowed to say game of two halves?

From the control of the first half, we have had the madness of the second. Almost from the kick-off Leicester were on the front foot and Liverpool had lost all that assured play. At the back it was VVD who seemed to lose his composure ... fouls leading to a booking. Good job Gomez seemed to have kept his head. He was outstanding.

At one point I thought it was all a cunning plan. To invite them on and pretend we weren't concentrating only to catch them on the break. But no, we really weren't concentrating!

Their goal. I could cry. Terrible back pass from VVD back to the keeper, which he salvages on the touch line on the right-hand side of his box under pressure from the attacking player.

It's a clearance. Of course, it's a clearance. Our keeper is so good it will be a clearance to the feet of Salah on the half way, which will lead to the third goal. I have to say I wasn't expecting the drag back. For a split second I thought that Alisson was the greatest ball-playing keeper the world had ever seen. A drag back under pressure ... on the touch line. He's amazing ... wait, what?

He lost possession of the ball, which two passes later was in the back of the net. The noise of a million balloons being popped was deafening. Lad, what have you done? Straight away, last week's incredible dink becomes a fluke. Mignolet and Karius wouldn't have dared to have done that... Whatever happened to Row Z?

After that it really was a scrapping, digging in display. No control at all. Some good defensive work particularly from Gomez, but no control. I don't think a clear chance for us either. Alisson looked solid for the rest of the game. No doubt there will be a flea in his ear tonight!

Monday 3rd September 2018

So much coverage of the keeper mistake. So much debate. But I don't really care because it didn't cost us anything and four games into the season we are sitting at the top of the league with 12 points. It may be early to say, but it's in our hands!

Lots of coverage and talk about the game. General feeling is we played poorly throughout. I think that can sometimes be dictated by the final result. At half time I thought we were well in control.

A lot more relaxed about the keeper mistake too. At the end of the day we won the game, so all it has cost us is our clean sheet record and a bit of the keeper's pride; much better for him to make that mistake when we are 2-0 up than to lose a game at a crucial time. He has had his warning... You can't dribble out of every situation, sometimes safety has to come first.

The interview post-match with Klopp was funny. He was

overly relaxed about it, like it was being forced, a smile that bordered on manic as he over accentuated the extent of his relaxation. So relaxed my guess is he walked back into the dressing room and picked Alisson up by the throat. I don't think it will happen again, that's for sure.

Good news of the day (apart from being top of the league) is the contract extension for Jordan Henderson. I think he's a great player and for all the focus on the front three, when he is playing, he is the heart beat of the team and central influence that dictates the pace and shape of the game.

He's had it fairly tough I think. Obviously spotted young and brought in as a player with huge potential, the first year he is played out of position but keeps his head down and contributes. In the 13/14 season, he was absolutely pivotal to that team. While all the focus for not winning goes to the Gerrard slip, for me the point it all turned was the Henderson sending off at the end of the City game. At that point we lost him for those final crucial games and the energy and the legs he brought to that team. If he hadn't have been missing, we'd have beaten Chelsea (or at least not lost to them), I'm convinced of it.

Since Gerrard retired, he has unfairly been cast as Gerrard-lite. It's difficult, near impossible to replace such an influential and globally iconic player and I think he has been cast as the poor replacement, rather than on his own merits. It's a shame for him, but for many he will never get rid of that tag, which is why he gets such abuse from so many quarters. They can't see beyond that Gerrard replacement thing.

I think anyone who has objectively watched him over time (and who understands anything about football, which I accept many don't) couldn't fail to see what a strong player he is. Intelligent, cultured, committed. And I think greatly valued by Klopp, which is why he has signed him up for the long term.

He is one of those players who is perceived as being on the way out every time a new player is spotted or signed. New signing Keita ... where will Henderson fit in? Fabinho signed from nowhere... it will be Henderson that makes way. What nonsense.

He is the person that Klopp builds around and relies on. Looking back to Klopp's first full season and the fantastic start that we made, it was a new way of playing; three midfielders, three attackers in theory, but in practice it was Henderson as an anchorman and then five other players just doing whatever they wanted.

He was the closest thing to a quarterback. I remember seeing it on TV for the first game against Arsenal and not being able to work it out. It was only when you were sitting there at

Anfield watching the game that you could see this five-player madness all anchored by Henderson.

There have been times when Can filled in well in that position, but he was only ever marking time until Henderson was back from injury. He knew that and that is why he is off at Juventus.

Henderson had a great World Cup. While the media talk about Kane and the emergence of Pickford as a goalkeeper, the best player throughout the tournament was Henderson, and while I don't really give a shit about how England get on, it was good to see him have a good tournament and begin to get the recognition he deserves... That he isn't the captain of England is both a mystery and a disgrace.

This season so far, despite only coming back late from the World Cup, he has been an essential player to bring on late and make games safe. His three substitute appearances have been a masterclass in coming into a game late and being able to stamp your authority on it from the off, which is down to his intelligence and his ability to be a controlling influence.

Good for you, Jordan.

Tuesday 11th September 2018

Bloody international week. No entry in the diary, not a lot to say as the normal world of football comes to a crashing halt, just as we were getting some momentum, and we have a week of meaningless international football. Absolute pain in the arse.

This week is the introduction of a new international competition called the Nations League. I haven't the first clue how it works—every time someone comes on the radio to talk about it I just drift off. From the relative high of the World Cup, the whole idea of a national side playing has gone off a cliff; it just doesn't hold any excitement.

I spend the week concerned that we will have players injured—Gomez, Henderson and Trent are all playing for England and I think if we lost any of them at the moment it would be a blow. Some bright news is Robertson has been made captain of Scotland. While I don't really care about Scotland and I don't think I could name more than three or four in the squad, it's good news for Robertson who has been fantastic for Liverpool since he broke into the side.

It was a strange start for him last year. He was very much unheralded and coming in on a low fee there were no real expectations on his shoulders. Moreno actually started the season really well having been on the fringe for a whole year. I think the majority of people expected him to leave, but he started like a train and it would have been harsh to drop him. Robertson had a couple of games and looked solid enough, but the momentum really was with Moreno. Then he was unlucky to get injured and Robertson stepped up—and what an impression he made, a solid defensive player with an ability to get forward and play a great cross into the box.

But more than that, he was committed, a no-nonsense player—the type of player the crowd loves and gets behind. I think my abiding memory of last season will be that run he made against City at Anfield in the Champions League where he ran the length of the field pressing

every pass, all the way back to their keeper. He nearly scored too… It would have been one of the great Anfield moments.

Spurs away is the Saturday lunchtime game—starting to get excited for that now.

Friday 14th September 2018

This international break is only actually a week off football but it seems like forever. Well, I've managed to survive it and now the proper footy is back in spades.

Starting with Spurs tomorrow we have seven games in the next three weeks and it's a really testing run. Four games in the premier league, three of them against top six teams, the start of the Champions League group stage with two games and a game against Chelsea in the 'Whatever the hell it's called now' cup for good measure. It's a real test for the red men over the coming weeks.

After winning the first four in an impressive controlling style using virtually the same team every week, this is a completely different challenge and I think it will give a real insight into the depth of this squad and how far it can go. It will also give us an insight into how much this is a 'squad' of first team players or whether there is a genuine second string. My own feeling is we have a squad of 20 first teamers.

There are 11 that have played all the games so far, and then in addition we have Clyne, Lovren, Matip, Moreno, Fabinho, Henderson, Lallana, Oxlade Chamberlain, Shaqiri and Sturridge. The question is how many of those players have to be playing before you regard the side as weakened or second string? I think you could play almost all of them and still have a strong side and that is what a squad game is all about. Beyond that list there is Solanke, Origi, Jones, Camacho etc. That's where the second string is coming in.

So, over the next seven games, we are going to see how interchangeable this team is with weekend and midweek games piling up on top of each other. The 12 points from the first four gives us a great base to start from. The Premier League has to be the focus. I would love to think we are going to win all of the next four games (we are!), but I think you need to start by thinking how many points you want to be on by the end of this run of games.

I would be happy if we were still averaging 2.5 ppg. That means we would need to be on 20 points, which means we need eight from the four games. Two wins and two draws. Unbeaten—that would be nice. Of the four games, the home game against Southampton is a must-win. That has to be seen as the easiest of the four games, but it is the type of game you have to take the points from. Beyond that, there are Spurs and Chelsea both away and then finish the run of game with Manchester City at home.

I think I would be happy with a win and two draws from those games. It would mean we haven't lost ground against any of our immediate rivals. Of the three, the one to win is against City. How good would that be.

Saturday 15th September

Another game and another win. Spurs away, which is a big one. Fifteen points from five games and still perched on top of the league.

Family life meant that I didn't get to watch the game. With a number of big games coming up I had to take one for the team and miss this one. But I got to listen to it on the radio, which isn't a bad thing. I love listening to the game on the radio and seeing the game in my mind's eye. It's an amazing skill these guys have to describe in such a way and keep you hooked on a game.

So much better than TV commentary, which I always feel is driving someone's agenda about what you should think about a game that is being played out in front of you. I love so many things about Five Live but football commentary is one of the real highlights.

Wijnaldum scored a scruffy header that only counted through the goal line technology and then Bobby Firmino poked one in. It all seemed rather comfortable until they nicked one three minutes into injury time and the last three minutes were very tense in the car as I listened beyond the commentary for the final whistle.

All the plaudits in the radio going to James Milner for his contribution through the game. He played in the middle with Gini and Keita. Amazing to think Henderson isn't getting a game, but I imagine they are saving him for the Champions League game on Tuesday night. The squad depth is going to be really tested in the coming days and weeks

Sunday 16th September 2018

Actually, not quite top of the league. Chelsea scored four at Cardiff, which puts them top on goal difference.

Disappointing but doesn't take away from the maximum points we have accumulated. To be fair, we should be top, as we had enough chances to absolutely batter Spurs. A really solid defensive and midfield performance but we had a handful of good chances that you would expect us to score.

Mané and Salah were a bit selfish and hesitant in front of goal, which I'm sure Klopp won't be happy with, when there were clear passes available for both of them. Sounds overly critical but you can be when you are consistently winning and playing well. Every detail can be looked at and if those two can improve their team play then we will begin to see the fluency going forward that hasn't happened yet this season. Hopefully against PSG on Tuesday.

Going to be really interesting to see who he picks for that game on Tuesday night. It's a massive game. PSG are the top seeds in the group, have some of the best strikers in the world and will be a big test.

I wonder whether Firmino will play. He had a really good game yesterday but then took a horrendous poke in the eye. The picture of it makes you wince, with the defender's finger in up to his knuckle. It's a miracle the eye didn't get gouged out the socket. Just from the picture you've got to think it must have hurt and he is going to miss the game. Maybe time for Sturridge or Shaqiri to step up.

In midfield, I think he'll bring back Henderson but difficult to say who makes way. Milner has been outstanding and was a real bonus for the Champions League last year. I think Klopp actually saved him in the league for the CL whereas this year he's played every game so far.

Wijnaldum has had a great few games too, topped off with a goal yesterday. He has the energy to keep going in these games and quietly keeps the team ticking if Henderson is playing the defensive midfield role. Keita is a massive talent, hasn't quite hit his peak yet, but I want to be there at the game when he does. He's going to be explosive.

So who does he pick? My shout would be Henderson, Milner, Keita. That's harsh on Gini. In my mind he's the one who goes in this type of situation and will be back for the league game on Saturday. Who knows, maybe he is lining himself up for a player of the season role.

Either way can't wait. My Klopp T-shirt being cleaned, taken my red-and-white gazelles out of the cupboard. It's all in the preparation!!

Tuesday 18th September 2018

European match night. PSG tonight under the lights at Anfield. Train into town, few beers and then watching the mighty red men take on Neymar, Mbappe and Cavani. I'm a bit excited.

The day requires some planning. Trying to work from home without anyone realising there is a Champions League game is tricky. Fate has stepped in to help. I recently had the snip and I received an appointment for today to hand in my final test sample. So as well as having a legitimate hospital appointment, I have also had a legitimate wank! Happy days.

Around that I then build sufficient workload and enough well-placed emails and phone calls to ensure that no one suspects for a minute I am actually out on the piss for a few hours before the game.

Not normally one to worry about what I'm wearing, I have planned ahead to make sure my red Banana Splits Bingo T-shirt (which passes for more than a passing resemblance to Jurgen Klopp) and my knitted red-and-white Gazelles are clean and ready to go. It's a European night after all.

Sitting in the station, my night is mapped out before me. Working out when the rest of the lads are meeting in the pub, I have even had a lucky break in getting the earlier express train. It's all just going in my favour.

Meeting up at the Wetherspoon pub at Lime Street, which has become our regular drinking spot before the game. The idea of Wetherspoons is normally enough to turn anyone off drinking, but that has been overcome by two things: the Wetherspoon app and Table 230, which when brought together create the ultimate drinking experience (for a man in his mid-40s who doesn't get out much).

The app is a thing of wonder. You sit at the table, order the drink on your phone and it arrives. Simple. Effective. Ultimately horrendously destructive. Three minutes it takes. Three minutes from pressing a button to the drink being served to you at the table. No queuing, no talking, no interaction, no dealing with money. Just pushing buttons, waiting and drinking. (The money is taken through PayPal, but that is a mere detail.)

It's wonderful way of getting incredibly pissed in a short space of time. From getting to the pub to leaving you don't have to move. The people around me are as pleased with the app as I am so the rounds mass up one after another. Another tray of drinks... Who bought these? Who cares? Get another one in. You leave the pub with as much money in your pocket as when you went in. Coming out of your account directly is just a numbers exercise. The night is free.

And Table 230. Definitely the best table in this pub and possibly the best in Liverpool for the two to three hours before kick-off. Tucked away upstairs, it sits in its own alcove, surrounded on three sides. A high table surrounded by stools that are attached to the wall. It's the type of table you could run a military campaign from. A war table. A table to rule the world.

The sense of disappointment when the table is occupied is palpable. You have to sit at a normal table. And a normal table when you have been planning on sitting on 230 just doesn't cut it.

Currently on my way through Widnes, ETA is about 5.30, which gives us just over two hours to shout at each other. That's generally what happens at table 230 ... before staggering out to roll into a taxi and all being well arrive at the ground just seconds before a ball is kicked.

From there, the 90 minutes of football is a drunken blur. Tactical analysis is out of the window, that's not what this is about. It's about shouting yourself hoarse and calling the opposition players cunts. There's something special about calling some of the top players in the world cunts. Something strangely satisfying. Anyone can call a premiership player a cunt. It's easy. It's almost lazy.

But to call a top player a cunt is different. I've called some great players cunts. Ronaldo (not the fat one, I haven't had that pleasure), Rivaldo, Kluivert. It just kind of rolls off the tongue. I'd say I'm almost a natural. Tonight it's going to be Neymar. I can almost picture it now. 'Neymar, you cunt!' Amazing.

I see it as the duty of the supporter and the crowd en masse. To create a positive atmosphere and unwavering support for the men in red while simultaneously creating an absolute shitstorm of abuse for the opposition that leaves them quaking in their handmade boots. At Liverpool, I think we do it better than anyone in the whole world.

***

Rabid and marvellous. If there was a better game in Europe tonight I would love to see it. What a game. What a fucking game. I've legged it back to the station. Made the train home. I'm breathless and sweating and I don't know where to start. What a game.

We won and we deserved to win. We were outstanding throughout the game. Two goals conceded doesn't give a fair reflection of how good we were in that game. Conscious of having a game of two halves like Leicester and conscious that I need to be writing about this I emailed myself at half time. Just in case I was too pissed to remember what had happened in that first half. Just two words ... rabid and marvellous.

To be fair, my brain has cleared, and I have sobered up pretty quickly and I know what I meant by that. I meant that the crowd was rabid, and the team were marvellous. But you quite easily turn that round. For times in that first half Liverpool were nothing short of rabid.

For the first fifteen minutes of that game the intensity from the Liverpool team was rabid. After ten minutes I said to my mate, 'How on earth can they carry this on?' They were frightening. They had to take a breath in the end, didn't they?

But then another immaculate cross by Robertson and point-blank header from Sturridge and they become rabid again. Rabid. Force a foul in the box. Penalty. Two nil. We were incredible. The crowd were incredible. We were all incredible. And marvellous. That was the word in my head... Marvellous ... so much so I had to write it down.

The second half was tactical. More tactical. More thoughtful. Less intensity but thoughtful and controlling. We controlled the game at 2-1.

As much as the threat of PSG sat there, it never broke through our control. A flash of brilliance from Neymar where he scoots through the midfield and you just think wow, but beyond that he barely kicked the ball. A goal just before half time that they didn't deserve and should have been stopped by the referee. Second half, a blip in the defence where Neymar lays on Mbappe and an injustice at 2-2 is on the cards. That could never have happened.

Injury time and Firmino hits one from the edge of the box. 3-2. There's an outlet of emotion around the ground but it's more about justice than winning the game. We got justice for the quality and the pressure. Jesus, we were so good.

All through the team. Robertson's crosses, Wijnaldum thrusts of pace, Milner's work rate, VVD's calm control. We were brilliant. All the things I talked about before the game happened. Beer and banter. But right now, that performance and that game have sobered me up. Rabid and Marvellous.

Friday 21st September 2018

I've called a sicky. It's something I very, very rarely do but today I have. Dropped the kids off, been to the gym, few errands to do and now a Maccas. To hell with them. Sitting here with my Big Mac and fighting for positive thoughts to overcome the negative ones surrounding my work situation. I need to detach myself from them.

For the last 30 years, football has been my escape from problems. I've never wallowed in football problems. I always see football problems as an opportunity; that bad results or bad players are temporary and brighter times are around the corner. At the moment, we are in the brightest of times and thoughts revolve purely around how brilliant Liverpool are, what a pleasure it is to watch them and how we must be the luckiest fans in the world.

Some people can't be happy. Some people never are. The bell-end who posted on Facebook how bad Liverpool had been in the second half about PSG. Turns out he posted that at 2-2. What sort of person does that? We concede a goal, we've got ten minutes to score – and we look like we really want to – and this dick gets his phone out to post on a public forum. Whatever happened to getting behind the team? Some people just bewilder me.

Saturday 22nd September 2018

Another game. Another three points on offer. Home to Southampton today in the league. Three o'clock kick-off on a Saturday. A rarity. I can't remember the last one. I used to love three o'clock kick-offs. The routine around them. I loved the routine. Of course, that routine used to evolve over time, a small change here or there. A different person, a different parking space, a different pub but you kind of knew what you were going to get.

That's disappeared in recent years. Lunchtime kick-offs (which I despise), teatime kick-offs (which I love although can't remember too many games through the drunken blur of an afternoon drinking), but the three o'clock home game has become a rarity and therefore a bit of an oddity.

Still buzzing from the game on Tuesday ... a 'big game'. With other big games to come in the next few weeks there is always a danger that the likes of today's game are taken for granted with the focus not quite there. My betting habits certainly testify to that. Today is the sort of game where you bet on a 5-0 win and come away with a 1-1 draw. The expectation is that you will roll over the team in front you. Premier League cannon fodder. But it doesn't always happen.

Looking at the development of the mental side of this team over the past couple of seasons and especially in the last few weeks, I don't think that Klopp will allow that to happen. It doesn't stop it happening in the stands though.

I wonder who gets a game today. Two big games in the last seven days and another four to come in the next 15. A league cup (I'm calling it the league cup and I don't care) on Wednesday night too, which is another chance to rotate, but I guess we will see a couple of new faces today.

I'm dying to see Shaqiri get a good run; see what he can do for more than 15 minutes at the end. There also has to be point that Fabinho gets a look in. And Keita missed out on Tuesday too. It's almost an embarrassment of riches at the moment, all keyed up and ready to play.

Just got on the train. To say it's full is an understatement. It's a disgrace really. Every carriage jammed tight. A network without investment. Poor management leading to industrial action leading to a woefully lacking service.

Deep breath. 20 minutes to Lime Street.

***

Liverpool win 3-0. It's a fairly mundane game, an easy win. It's six wins out of six and it means we haven't been complacent ... we've been professional and put away a fairly average side.

Shaqiri got his start, which I had been hoping for. He was

included as part of the midfield three rather than the front three, which opens up all sorts of possibilities... I had expected him to be a replacement for one of Mané, Salah or Firmino so to see him as an additional creative and attacking option to that is a great option at home. Supported by the work rate of Henderson and Wijnaldum there is space and opportunity for that creativity too.

The bet I put on him scoring went out the window as there was an own goal from one of his efforts and Salah scores a rebound of his other. They took him off at half time, which pretty much pissed on my chips. From a wider perspective, I should hope that he wasn't injured but that wasn't my primary thought as they ran back on for the second half.

Rather than the Wetherspoon pub with its app and its wonderful table 230, the lads elected to try a new bar on London Road called the Liverpool Port Bar. What a shit pub. A money laundering hole if ever I saw one. We used to go to the Picture House, which had some character, dank smelly dark character but character nonetheless. This place today was awful.

'Themed' around the idea of Liverpool as a port with cargo crates as decoration and stripped back tables and benches. The biggest insult was the installation of a container along one wall. They obviously haven't cottoned on that containerisation was the death knell of Liverpool as a port in the '60s; the place was some designer's nightmare, a historian's nightmare ... everyone's bloody nightmare.

I don't know what Whaley and Noel expected from the place but it wasn't delivering anything. They were the only people there when I walked in and we were eventually joined by some London Road locals in their 60s, one of whom fell asleep.

They were determined to stay there based on the obvious look of distain as I walked in. I suppose at the end of the day it's a boozer that serves booze, but it would be nice to have a table that didn't move every time you leant on it as a minimum requirement.

I'll sit in table 230 on my own in future ... although I would miss the banter of two pissed idiots.

Monday 24th September 2018

Dropped points from the rival clubs puts us clear at the top of league after six games. United drew at home to Wolves and Chelsea drew away at West Ham on Sunday so we pull further clear of both of them. It's not just that we win; we need others to fail too.

I read through my comments after the game yesterday. I think mundane is a bit unfair. Routine might be a better description of a performance that was utterly professional and controlled. It would be damning and unfair to call any of this current team mundane given the level they are playing at and the intensity required to do so. This is a wonderful team of hardworking players.

It's funny when you look at back at teams you thought were great at the time and in retrospect there are always a couple of weak links in there, the players that explain away why they didn't actually win anything. When I look at this team now, I wonder who those players are going to be because I can't see the weak ones.

There are great players in there throughout. What is really exciting is the number of players

who are still young and learning... Trent, Gomez, Robertson, the players that will form the spine of the team for the next decade. They might be the ones who don't progress or reach their potential, but at the moment I just don't see it. The two full backs are on another level, the best in the league and possibly the best in Europe.

The consistently good performances that they put in are

staggering. The danger with that consistency is that people potentially start taking them for granted. That would be a travesty.

Salah scored on Saturday, a tap in from a Shaqiri rebound ... but there appears to be talk of him being off form. The pressure these guys must be under to have that level of analysis and criticism over every move. This time last year, there were questions over him, did he have the killer instinct and was he a strong finisher?

We played City at about this time in the season and for the first half hour of that game we absolutely battered them ... only one team in it. Salah missed a couple of sitters, opportunities he certainly would have scored from later in the season, and the questions about his finishing ability were asked then.

He then went on a fabulous run of games in the Premier League and Europe but was getting visibly tired towards the end of the season. A disastrous Champions League final where he is literally wrestled out of the game and a summer of pressure with the hopes of Egypt on his shoulders and he has every right not to be on top form.

To be honest, I don't think he's playing badly; he was unlucky on Saturday with this gorgeous little back heel that would have gone in for him on another day. What he is doing is occupying the mind of the opposition's defence; always looking for him, worried about where he is and where is going to appear from next.

His threat is as big a weapon as his actual play at the moment. It creates indecision; it creates space, which the rest of the team are taking full advantage of. It's a team game and far from being a prima donna superstar, he is an integral part of the team. If we keep winning, I'd be quite happy for him not to score for the rest of the season.

We are now three games into this seven-game testing stretch and, so far, we have been outstanding. Outstanding in a professional, get-the-job-done kind of way rather than an unstoppable football force blowing away everything in front of them way.

Chelsea in the League Cup on Wednesday, before playing them again at Stamford Bridge on Saturday. A double test. Their manager, Sarri, has come out yesterday and said they are not on the same level as Liverpool at the moment. A bit of toffee I think Paisley used to call it. They will be well up for both and we need to continue that steely professionalism.

Tuesday 25th September 2018

More awards for Mo Salah last night. It was the inaugural FIFA Best Awards, which replaces the Ballon d'Or, a big awards ceremony in London hosted by Idris Elba. I watched bits of it but it was so amateurish it made your stomach tighten. God it was awful.

Absolutely no rhyme or reason to the awards. Salah was shortlisted in the top three for player of the year alongside Ronaldo and the winner Modric. But he didn't get into the team of the year ... Hazard did. How does that work? It wasn't just Mo Courtouis from Chelsea was named keeper of the year but didn't get into the team if the year either. That went to De Gea.

What Mo did win was the Puskas award that goes to the best goal. He won it for his goal against Everton where he curled it in from the right corner of the box. Now, it was a great goal – against Everton, which made it even better – the celebration alone puts it up there, but I don't think it's the best by a long way. I don't think it was even Salah's best goal of the season. How it came ahead of Bale's goal in the CL final or Ronaldo's in the semi I will never know.

So, in summary, they were a pile of shit.

Wednesday 26th September 2018

First defeat of the season as we go out of the League Cup to Chelsea. Gutted as we had the game in our hands and lost it in the last ten minutes. One nil up and then went down to a dubious equaliser and a stunner from Eden Hazard, who really is a wonderful player.

I'm disappointed but would rather take the three points at Chelsea on Saturday in the league. I'm disappointed because I honestly thought we were going to win forever. As ever my dreams and expectations are brought down with a mighty bump. At the end of the day this isn't a priority for us. No one died.

Massively changed teams for both, but when I looked at our side I didn't think it looked so bad. And to be fair they weren't. They didn't have the fluidity of the first team, but I guess half of them haven't kicked a ball yet this season so what can you expect? First half disjointed. Shaqiri out wide was peripheral. Didn't get involved in the same way as Saturday. Sturridge off the pace.

Chelsea had the best of the first half, but then we came back into it with some good chances. Some good defending but you can see the difference between our first-choice defence of 18 months ago and the one we have now. That may be harsh as they are all a bit rusty. Moreno made Moses look good and was a liability through the game. Fabinho looked like he was struggling with the pace of the game. Keita looked good in flashes.

Second half we started much better. Sturridge had a chance almost from the kick-off, which he missed and will have nightmares about, rounding the keeper and then overbalancing to put the ball wide of an open goal. It was a good job he scored later or that would have been his and everyone else's abiding memory of the game.

His goal was a good one but created by the pressing of Milner who won the ball back in the corner. Don't know where he gets his energy from.

We had other chances but didn't take them and therein lies the tale. We needed that extra cushion and just couldn't get it. From the second he scored, Sturridge looked tired and I'm surprised he stayed on the pitch. Firmino came on for Mané but played wide rather than central. They brought on Kante and Hazard who made the difference and they pinched two goals, the first debatable, the second a worldie.

There was a flurry at the end to equalise, but Chelsea were a strong and well organised unit. Shaqiri had a better second half, he's quick and nippy and a bit like a jack in the box, but there was a lack of quality in the final ball and decision making. You want him to do well because he looks so up for it, but at the same time he was a bit frustrating with lack of delivery in some good positions. You could see Klopp was frustrated with him at the end of the game.

Never mind, we move on. Our general positive direction is the opposite of the problems over at United, which is moving into meltdown. They got knocked out of the cup at home too, by Derby, but the comedy gold is coming from the standoff between Mourinho and Pogba who are having an increasingly public spat. Pogba criticised the playing style after the draw at the weekend, Mourinho publicly says that Pogba will never captain the side again.

Yesterday, they released a video of a training ground spat, which is just priceless. Mourinho has obviously said something that has provoked Pogba's reaction. It's not an angry reaction, more a 'why would you say that to hurt my feelings' reaction. I would love to know what Mourinho said to get the reaction he did... My money is on 'Your dab is shit.'

It has created a media storm, it's a standoff between the two of them and everyone is picking sides ... a battle for control of the club. If it was Liverpool (and after years of turmoil, thank God it isn't) then you must back the manager, but Pogba is a big commercial draw for them and I would say Mourinho is on his last legs anyway, so it really could go either way.

Friday 28th September 2018

End of the week. Sitting in the curry house waiting for my take-away. Trying not to think about Brett Kavanaugh being elected to the US Supreme Court despite being a piece of shit. Instead I'm thinking about the football tomorrow and taking our revenge against Chelsea and the three points.

I am confident Klopp has learnt more about Chelsea than they learnt about us and he will be working on it with the squad. There will also probably be eight or even nine changes to the team from Wednesday – on both sides – so it will be more about which team can execute their manager's strategy better.

It's amazing to think that the five at the back who played on Wednesday are all now second choice. Eighteen months ago, they were just about the first choice five (Mignolet, Clyne, Matip, Lovren, Moreno), although when you look back, they only actually started together on the one occasion as a starting five (research!).

Last year, Clyne was out of the team for the whole season virtually with a back problem (I don't believe that by the way) and the season before that Milner was first choice left back while Moreno was being rehabilitated from being an idiot.

Nonetheless that is the perception, that they were our best players in those positions, and you can now understand the concerns around the shaky nature of the defence, which in essence was our key problem.

Klopp has addressed that. He's spent world record fees on two players to sit at the heart of it but has managed to surround the two of them with a trainee, an absolute steal (Robbo) and with the form of Gomez so far this season, a centre back with so much potential he could be at the heart of the defence for the next ten years.

The difference between the two units is like night and day, not just on the pitch but also in the minds of the players and the supporters. The worry is not there in the same way.

I think from the team that played on Wednesday only Mané and Milner will be retained. The stronger defence will return; the front three and then I think Henderson, Gini and Milner. Hard-working, strong, dependable midfield. Milner written off for each of the last three seasons but coming back stronger each season.

Saturday 29th September 2018

Half time and we are a goal behind at Chelsea. Team is as we thought, back to full strength with the three workhorses in the middle. I actually think we have had the best of the half overall, but Hazard pops up again to score midway through after some lovely passing play from Chelsea in midfield.

They have had breaks a few times but VVD and Gomez have been quick to tidy up. Liverpool seem to be able to get the ball to the edge of their box quite easily and find space, but their defence is so organised across the 18-yard line it's impossible to find any space in the box. The three upfront aren't quite finding each other and firing.

The Chelsea manager, Sarri, is relatively unknown in this country but there are some experienced players in that side and he has them playing really well. They remind me of the Chelsea side a couple of years ago with Conte, watching them close down every passing angle and even if they are happy to have Liverpool in certain areas with the ball then the next pass is always a struggle.

***

What a goal ... what a goal ... what a fucking goal. Daniel Sturridge ... what a goal!

Minutes to go and a goal down. We have struggled to break down their defence. We have passed and passed and passed around the edge of their area but been unable to break through their organised defence. I'm on the couch, a few beers in, wondering where it's going to come from—and he hits it and what a glorious goal.

It was like an electric shock. Christ Almighty, what a goal. The way it floats over the keeper and into the goal is just gorgeous. The margin is so tight you think the keeper is going to tip it over with every replay angle.

We salvage a point. And while it's disappointing not to continue the winning league run, a goal to salvage a point in the last minute is like gold. I think a point there against that team will be a great point by the end of the season. I was really impressed with Chelsea. We had chances to win it. Shaqiri should have scored from a cross from Robbo and Firmino had a header cleared off the line. They had chances too. Alisson made a couple of great saves.

A great game between two very good sides. We both drop points, which lets City in and they are back at the top of the league on goal difference (+18 after seven games).

And of course, United have been beaten again, which only serves to make my Halloween departure prediction for Mourinho even more perceptive.

It's not going to be the walk in the park that I thought a week ago, but nothing worthwhile ever was, was it?

Interlude 3 - First Game

My first game is a series of impressions in my mind. From the impressions and a little bit of detective work I can piece the game together and get the detail that I can't possibly remember. I was five. There are things that have stayed with me all these years, things that I will always remember as part of my first match-going experience.

I went with my dad. As far as I can remember that is the only game I ever went to with him. As I came to realise later, he wasn't really interested in the football so taking me to my first game probably wasn't a big thing for him.

It was my Grandad who always took me to the match after that and sure enough it was my Grandad who got the tickets for this game. Row three of the old Kemlyn Road stand towards the Kop End.

It was a midweek game or an evening game at least. I remember my mum telling me to wear my pyjama bottoms underneath my trousers because it was going to be cold. It was Grandad who had suggested that.

It was against Wolves and Sammy Chung was their manager. I can remember my dad pointing him out as he sprinted across the pitch in one of those slim-fitting tracksuits they used to wear at the time. It was orange. I think Wolves used to call it Old Gold.

And I remember the Kop. I was mesmerised by the Kop. We were sitting in neat rows in the stand but the people in the Kop weren't in neat rows and didn't even seem to be sitting. They were sort of moving around, moving from side to side, swaying, swimming. There was a steam coming off the Kop as it swam around. It was alive and pulsing.

And they were singing. And they all knew the words and sang them at the same time and seemed to know when to sing at the same time. I think I probably watched more of the Kop than the game. Every time they sang I watched because I couldn't work out who had told them all to sing.

And at half time there were a load of letters across the hoardings at the front of the Kop and they put numbers next to the letters.

And I remember Dalglish. He was my hero and I saw him play for the first time. He had number 7 on his back. My dad pointed him out the first time and then after that I knew where he was all the time. I want to think there was a point where he kicked the ball and took the feet from under the referee and he fell on his arse. And everyone in the crowd cheered. But I don't know whether I have made that up.

And that's what I remember.

Looking through the records, I have enough to find the game. It's the Sammy Chung clue that seals it. My first game was in the 1977/78 season. Liverpool were the Champions of Europe for the first time and were about to become Champions in Europe again. My first game was watching the best team in Europe. How lucky was I!

It was a midweek game, actually part of the Christmas programme of games on the 27th December. It was their second game in two days, which seems barely believable. They had played on Boxing away at Nottingham Forest. The day before. That seems like madness now but was probably how it worked at the time.

What makes it even madder is there was only on change between the games. Ten of the team played in both games. Harder times. Harder men. I knew this used to happen in the 1950s and '60s when everything was in black and white, but the idea of these modern day footballers, the champions of Europe, playing two games in little over 24 hours seems bizarre. Particularly when put in the modern context of managers whinging when they have to play two games a week.

The team that played reads like a who's who of Liverpool folklore: Clemence, Neal, Jones, Thompson, Ray Kennedy, Hughes (c), Dalglish, McDermott, Heighway, Fairclough, and Callaghan. David Johnson was on the bench. Jimmy Case had played the previous day and come off for Callaghan in the fourth minute. The rest of them just got on with it.

It was pretty much the team that played in Rome the previous May. Keegan had departed to be replaced by Dalglish, and Tommy Smith, who scored in the final, was coming to the end and had been replaced for the most part by Thompson. By the time the next European Cup final came around the following May, Alan Hansen was in place. Souness also arrived shortly after this game and he was in the first eleven by the time they beat Bruges at Wembley.

It was a team that had been in development for years. Paisley had taken the strong team he inherited from Shankly and brought new players in. Phil Neal was one of them and it was Neal who scored the only goal of my first game, a penalty. Quite a controversial penalty as it goes. Their keeper saved it to begin with, but Keith Hackett, the referee, said that the keeper had moved prior to the kick. It was retaken, and he scored. I didn't remember that part.

I doubt very much whether there is even a recording of the game. The post-match report talks about the manager and the players questioning the referee decision. At the moment, where we stand on the brink of the VAR revolution, it's seems strange that we couldn't have watched the penalty and the alleged movement of the keeper from any one of ten angles.

The win left us in fourth place behind the eventual league winners, Forest, Everton, and Arsenal. Emlyn Hughes felt they were getting into form and the other teams around them would be worried. We would creep up the table in the second half of the season, but Forest were too far ahead. They won it by seven points, which is a lot in the days of two points for a win.

It would be the start of a rivalry between the two clubs that lasted until about the mid-'80s. As I grew older and became more conscious of the football, Forest were probably the biggest of our rivals. They were the team who were up there; Clough was the mouth that people wanted to close. He had done an incredible job with a small provincial team (having done similar in the early '70s with another small provincial club, Derby).

It never occurred to me that Forest weren't one of the 'big clubs'. Difficult to imagine we were fighting it out for the title of Kings of Europe when you look at where they are now.

I don't think I went to many (any!) games after that one. I certainly don't remember them. I never went to a game with my dad again. That was a one off. The game made an impression on me. I had got the bug, even if I wasn't going back.

In an age where the coverage of the football was restricted to the people who went to the game, newspaper match reports and Football Focus on Saturday lunchtime, there wasn't the saturation of football content we have now.

Merchandise was rudimentary. Apparently, Kevin Keegan was one of the first to have his own fan club—and he ran that himself! Keegan passed me by, my hero was Dalglish. But in comparison to nowadays, I had very little. I had a Liverpool kit with a 7 on the back. It had Hitachi on it, so was probably a little bit later. I had the Kenny Dalglish album, too, and I must have read that back to front so many times. My mum knitted me a little red bear, Teddy Dalglish, complete with a pin badge with a picture of Kenny himself.

The thing I remember more than anything is a mug that used to be at my Nan and Grandad's. Celebrating the 78/79 league win, the mug had photos of all the 14 players in the squad. Shit, low resolution photos, like they had been copied out of the Echo. On every visit to their little house, I would go to the kitchen, get the mug off the hook and name the players, pretty much the ones I had seen that night at Anfield. But I never went back for a while.

OCTOBER

Monday 1st October 2018

Beginning of October and we are tied at the top of the league with Manchester City. We play them next weekend at Anfield. I love it when that happens.

I remember back in John Barnes' first season. It was QPR who were the pace setters that season and we played them in the league in October. Going into the game, we were three points behind them, although we did have games in hand due to problems with the Kop at the start of the season.

We battered them 4-0. It's one of those games that went down in folklore as we decimated the team at the top of the league—they still show the John Barnes goals now, picking up the ball on the halfway line with a half pirouette turn and dancing past their defence before slotting it in. What a game.

I would love it to be that one-sided again this time around, but I don't think that will be the case. The game against City last season was special. Two unstoppable sides at the height of their powers. And for a 20-minute period in the second half, Liverpool went beyond unstoppable—they were frightening, just frightening.

It was loud and breathless in the Kop, we were exhausted, never mind the team. It was one

of the few games where I have had to drive when I was thankful that I hadn't had a beer, so that I could take in the intensity of the game without that alcohol haze.

It was disappointing not to get the win on Saturday. As the eternal (hopeless) optimist when it comes to football, I am always disappointed when we drop our first points of the season. I always start thinking we are the best team in the league (even when I know we aren't) and there is a good chance we will go the whole season not just unbeaten but winning every game.

I have this idea that each game is independent of each other and we generally go into each game as favourites (or at least a 50/50 chance) so why can't we win every one? I am usually disappointed at some point in August, I sometimes make it through to September and I honestly thought this year I wouldn't be disappointed at all. This may be why Bet365 send me so many friendly emails!

At the end of the game on Saturday a draw was like a win. The game was lost or as good as, and I was resigned to thinking about losing, about losing top spot in the league and then thinking ahead to the tough game against City next week and what happens if we lose two in a row.

And what happens? Sturridge pops up to score the goal of goals. I think (to be fair to me), I have been very upbeat about Sturridge from the start of pre-season (go and check back!!) so not only has he done really well scoring two in two games, but I am vindicated in my unwavering support.

The build-up won't really start until after the Champions League games this week. We are playing Napoli away on Wednesday, which I am thinking will be a tighter game, a more strategic and tactical one than some we have seen of late. This will be the sixth game of this seven-game run, I think a draw would be good enough. A chance to play some of the rest of the squad making sure that we have our strongest team available and firing for the weekend.

Tuesday 2nd October 2018

So after watching football all my life and having a season ticket at Anfield I tend to think I understand the game. The level of tactical analysis in the media has grown so much in the last ten years and is all very interesting, but up until now I still rate my own ability to understand what I am seeing before my eyes (when sober at least), but I have seen something on Facebook this morning that tells me that I need to go back to school.

'Sturridge's xG for his goal was 2.6%. What a magician.'

What the hell is that all about? Through the podcasts I listen to, those at the geekier end of the spectrum have talked about xG but I haven't up to this point been interested enough to find out what it means. I don't think I'm the only one. There are a few people asking, and the guy has now explained it. It means from where Sturridge was with the ball in the last minutes of the game, there was a 2.6% chance that he was going to score—basically it would go in once in 40 attempts.

Now, I think that's a load of shit because I was at Anfield last Wednesday and in the last minutes of the Cup game against Chelsea, Sturridge hit a very similar shot, from a very similar position (in my mind's eye at least), which beat the keeper and clipped the bar. So, in effect, he has scored one in two or 50% xG.

And from my couch on Saturday evening, the way I jumped up and started shouting and dancing around, I would put that goal at one in a million. These statisticians don't know their arse from their elbow.

I think sometimes the statistical analysis takes something away from the game. That game on Saturday was amazing, two very strong teams going head to head, giving it their all and producing some incredible football in a great spirit. To break that down into percentages seems wrong somehow.

The big smiles and embraces between Sarri and Klopp said

it all and should be the bit we remember. Certainly will be for me.

Wednesday 3rd October 2018

Sixth game out of this block of seven. Champions League game away at Napoli. Half time and it's 0-0.

It's a stuttering stunted performance so far ... going forward at least. At the back we have been solid and not really looking like conceding a goal. Gomez great again, the back two so solid that Robertson seems to be operating as a left winger! But going forward we can't seem to get any attacking fluidity. Napoli seem to be sitting back and absorbing the pressure on the edge of their box. Happy to let Liverpool have the ball there.

One of the primary reasons for that is Koulibaly who is like a big mountain of a monster at the back. None of the front three can get anything out of him, and on a couple of occasions he has charged forward with the ball like a steam train.

Only change to the side was Keita coming in in place of Henderson, but he went off after 15 minutes. One of those times when they just decide to sit down in the middle of the game that you know is serious. No replays of any particular incident, he just looked like he had a real problem with his back going off on a stretcher.

Henderson came on and spent the first 10 minutes charging round like a steam train himself, probably so he wasn't too far behind Milner on the distance covered stats.

***

Full time. Beaten 1-0 by a last-minute goal. We go from being unbeatable to three games without a win.

Napoli had by far the better of the second half and probably deserved to win, although I thought we were going to hold them out. Liverpool just fell asleep at the end, lost their players and conceded a late goal.

Liverpool didn't really push forward enough and it looked like he was happy with the draw. We took on a lot of pressure in the middle of the half and he brought Fabinho on with 15 to go, which shored things up a bit. It was strange ... as he brought Sturridge on with a couple of minutes to go, you could see him telling the team to focus, to hold on, but they just lost that concentration.

Within a week everything changes. This is your typical knee jerk I know, but two defeats and a draw seem a million miles away from turning up at Anfield with seven wins out of seven. Have we been found out? Do teams know how to nullify our threat?

And then the injury crisis. One player down and the whole of the midfield turns on its head. Last week, it was how are they going to get a game? Right now, it's how bad is Keita? Is Fabinho ready? Are Gini, Milner and Hendo going to burn out? Lallana's never bloody fit. How long before Ox is back in training?

It's City at the weekend. Who'd be a supporter?

Thursday 4th October 2018

The day after Napoli. Still disappointed that we lost, but more with how we played. It's incredible that a team with so many outstanding players can range from being unplayable all the way down to bang average.

On reflection, they were poor last night. It's not about waiting for them to click, that suggests that they were playing OK and just needed things to run for them. I don't think they played well. I don't want to take anything away from Napoli; they were a good side and thoroughly deserved to win.

We shouldn't underestimate the European teams who are

not Barca, Real, Bayern etc. It's an easy and an arrogant mistake to make. Napoli played well and also improved through the game. There was only one team that was going to win it in the last half hour. I thought we were going on to hold out for a lucky draw, but in the end, they got the goal and the reward they deserved.

God, I feel so boring saying that, I'm supposed to be blinded to that type of thing and be totally pro-Liverpool, but sometimes you have to accept that teams are there to compete and win, not just be put on a plate for us to destroy.

The bright side is the understanding between the three players at the back. Allisson was brilliant again last night and inspires confidence through the team—light years away from Mignolet, not just in his goalkeeping but in his whole dominant persona. In front of him, VVD and Gomez are excellent, especially Gomez who seems to be coming into his own as a potentially world-class centre back.

Keita is apparently out of hospital and returning with the team—that didn't look likely last night as he was strapped to a stretcher on the back of a golf cart. He could even be in the running for a place on Sunday. I think it will be Milner, Gini and Hendo myself, but a fabulous option for the bench.

In the midfield, I was pleased to see Fabinho come on in an hour of crisis last night and he certainly stemmed the attacking flow of Napoli and restored some semblance of cover and control—even if, ultimately, we lost the game. I can see him coming to the fore after the next international break.

Saturday 6th October 2018

Saturday night. Waiting up for *Match of the Day* with a large glass if whisky. Want to see the coverage of the United game as the soap opera over there intensifies. They played Newcastle in the teatime game, with reports circulating that Mourinho is getting sacked after the game whatever the result.

I was out with the family but monitoring the score and they were two down within ten minutes. There would have been something really special about Benitez beating him and him losing his job.

They came back in the second half and eventually won with a last-minute winner from Sanchez. It will have bought him a fortnight. I still think he'll be gone by Halloween. Not sure whether I want him to go or not as he really seems to be happy to self-destruct and take the club with him, with seemingly no one else around with the balls or the influence to stop him.

The media coverage of the whole thing is bordering on hysterical, the pundits and ex-players being wheeled out for their twopenneth. Scholes was on *Five Live* yesterday morning with the least insightful conversation I have ever heard in my life. Because it's Scholes, that makes it worthwhile apparently. If you heard a bloke saying the same in the pub you'd tell him to shut up and fuck off.

I don't know whether I want him to go actually. The confusion and distrust he is creating is damaging the club and the longer he stays, the more damage he creates. The list of potential replacements continues to grow and not one of them would inspire me. At the top of the list is Zidane, who is very Hollywood, but you wonder what he would make of the average squad and turmoil around him.

I've put a fiver on Sam Allardyce to replace him and have resurrected my old #prayforallardyce hashtag. That would just be the ultimate pick. I started the hashtag when Allardyce was in the running for the England job a couple of years back. I thought it would have been priceless to have him in charge but didn't think for a single minute it would actually happen, so I didn't put any money on it. All my dreams were answered when he got the job but was gutted I missed the 33/1 odds. It won't happen again.

Sunday 7th October 2018

Big game today. City at home. Aside from the traditional big games of United and Everton, which have all the history and everything that goes with it, this is the biggest game of the season by a long way. Apparently one billion people around the world have access to it.

Seven games in and the two teams are joint top of the league... City just nudging ahead on goal difference. It's also the last game before the international break and what a psychological kick it would be to be top going into that.

The games last year at Anfield were immense. Played at 100 mph, they were breathless. I think the league game was better than the Champions League game a couple of months later, but we comprehensively beat them in both. At the time of the league game they were unbeaten and seemingly unbeatable. Talk about immovable objects and irresistible forces.

Today's game is the same day as the Giants are visiting Liverpool. Two world-class events in the same city. The place has a real buzz about it.

I was going to drive. Last year, I drove and was pleased I did because the quality of the game was so extraordinary. I could take in every moment and the atmosphere was such that it didn't matter if you were sober or drunk. It was just rabid in there. Rabid fury from the stands, from every single person in the ground, willing on the red men.

It amazes me how that rabid fury can simultaneously drive on the reds while negatively affect the opposition, but that seems to happen on these occasions. They are all in the same cauldron, but it affects the two teams differently.

Pulling into Lime Street. Come on!

***

Well, after all the build-up to the game of the season, we walk away from the ground with a goalless draw. The fever pitch I anticipated didn't happen on the pitch or in the stands.

Both sides pretty much snuffed each other out and from the middle of the second half you felt like both of them had settled for a draw. I can't remember a decent chance for either side ... other than Mahrez's missed penalty with five to go, which is still in orbit and will probably collide with Chris Waddle's penalty from Italia 90 sometime in 2026.

Klopp moved around at the back and put Gomez into right back, with Lovren returning to centre back. Degsy had a good game alongside the ever imperious VVD, and Gomez played well and was solid, but he looked like a fish out if water on the right and we missed Trent's attacking ability. When the team was announced, we wondered whether he was going to a three at the back, but no, it was 4-3-3 as usual.

The game was more workmanlike, cagey. I thought in the first half they might have been saving themselves for a lung-busting second half but ended up with much the same ... defensively dominated and cautious ... a battle of two midfields.

That might suggest it was a poor game; it was anything but. With two teams of that quality on the pitch, the football was excellent. It was more a game of chess in the middle of the pitch rather than end-to-end attacking brilliance.

Gini again was the man of the match with a level of control and domination in midfield that is making him indispensable this season. Henderson too, had to be at the top of his game. Milner went off injured in the first half, replaced by Keita, but I felt like we were missing a player for the battle, he always seemed peripheral and not there to fight for the team.

Feeding off a cautious game, the crowd was muted too. Thought we'd lost in the dying minutes when the penalty was given, and there was a brief moment of thunder when they missed it and we saw a chance to steal the game, but even that subsided quickly.

An early season draw, no one giving anything away, a safe point.

Monday 8th October 2018

It's the next international break and as we face two weeks without proper football, there is plenty of time to reflect on how we have done and then plan the next block of games.

Overall, I would say we have done well from the seven games in the block. First and most important, we are still unbeaten in the league. In this block we won two and drew two, beating Spurs away and drawing with Chelsea and City, so we have done well against our immediate rivals.

Supplemented by a good 3-0 win at home to Southampton ... the game that we had to win. It leaves us with 20 points from the first eight games, a solid 2.5 points per game. We are currently sitting third in goal difference, with Chelsea and City both unbeaten and on 20 points.

Just behind them on 18 points are Spurs and I think interestingly Arsenal, who started off with two defeats against the big teams, to be all but written off as a season of transition post Wenger. They have quietly put together a string of six wins, against the lower teams admittedly but doing it quietly and efficiently. United trailing behind with 13 points. They came back from 2-0 down to beat Newcastle on Saturday, which has given Jose a stay of execution.

We are right up there and ready for the next block. We are well ahead of where we were after eight games last season, which also finished with a 0-0 at home, then to United. We were sixth after that with 13 points. What is really interesting is the goals for and against when comparing the two years. Last year, we had scored 13 and conceded 12, thanks to shipping three at Watford and five at City.

This season we are doing better in both. Scored 14 against the backdrop of people saying we haven't clicked up front. I think this is a fair observation; we are certainly missing something, although my suspicion is it is a lack of creativity in midfield, which is cutting off supply to the front three, that is the main culprit at the moment.

We need someone who can break forward and provide a devastating run or a killer ball. Last year, we had Coutinho to do that, whereas this year, our midfield has been solid and controlling rather than creative and penetrating. We are certainly missing Oxlade Chamberlain and Lallana. Keita hasn't reached a comfortable point where he is dominating games, but hopefully that will come.

The big difference is the defensive record with only three conceded, five clean sheets and, really importantly, never conceding more than a single goal in any game. That is testimony to the defensive stability of the defensive unit but also the solidity of the midfield that is in turn affecting the creativity up front. You can't have it all I guess.

Sunday 14th October 2018

International week—what a pain in the arse. The whole weekend with no proper football. I've yet to find anyone who is excited at England playing, but then I don't socialise with right-wing hate groups.

Not only does the football not happen, but the 24/7 media circus that surrounds it goes quiet too, so I don't have much beyond my own thoughts. There has been some coverage this week of Klopp's third anniversary of being the manager, which has been interesting.

There wasn't a revolution when he arrived, but there has been an evolution ever since—in every aspect of the club for me. There is stuff going on off the field obviously, the opening of a new stand and the corporate business that goes with that, a never-ending line of brands who are signing up as official sponsors—none of them major brands but secondary names who are attracted to the glow of Liverpool and Klopp, probably with brand managers who are Liverpool fans, taking the opportunity to spend marketing budgets on getting to see the game in style, when in reality the money would be better spent elsewhere, but it gets signed off all the way up the line as directors and CEOs line up the idea of a European night at Anfield on the piss. It's a gravy train and everyone is having a dip. (That went off track!)

Overall the club seems to be in a healthier commercial state and that has happened at the same time as we start to realistically and consistently challenge in the Premier League and Europe.

The evolution on the pitch has been slow, thoughtful, premeditated. At times too slow for a lot of the fans, loyalty shown to players when many would have moved them on (Hello Dejan Lovren and Loris Karius), not enough signings and turnaround of players. At other times, the changes have been quite brutal (Karius again) and swift (Coutinho) and incredibly ambitious (VVD).

What we haven't seen is a percentage approach to overhauling the squad, buying six players in the hope that a couple will work, which seemed to be happening under Rodgers. We have a seen a deliberate strategy to work with the players in the squad, improve them and be loyal to them where they have responded to the challenge, farm them off where they haven't and then invest heavily in players who are (or are approaching) world class and will make a difference to the first team—Mané, Keita, Salah, VVD, Alisson, Ox. Stronger team, stronger bench, stronger squad—built over a period of three years without massive upheaval.

I remember in his first press conference he talked about winning this title within three years—he has clearly had it in his mind that it would go like this from the start.

The biggest change though, is not the squad of players, they can come and go. It's the feeling of the club. It's the feeling of the players and the team they create; it's the feeling of the style of play, more joyous, more fun. It's the feeling the manager creates around the club. That it's a serious business but it's not that serious.

He has created a swagger, but not a cocky swagger. More of a swagger of self-confidence, of self-belief, of knowing that the right things are being done as part of a process to become the best. Increasingly it's a swagger that says we are difficult to beat and as we swagger further, then it will turn into invincibility.

Beyond the feeling in the club, there is a feeling amongst the fan base, a feeling that we are back and don't think about messing with us because we are Liverpool and I'm not sure I can remember that feeling in that way in all the time I have followed Liverpool—not in my adult life anyway.

Even looking back to the successful years of Houllier and Benitez, I don't believe we had this feeling. For Houllier, we were in the shadow of the United and Arsenal teams and the success we had, although good, was always peripheral to the big battle for the league.

By the time Benitez took over, followed by the mess under Hicks and Gillette, the fan base was fractured, some supporting the manager come what may, others disliking him and attacking him whether we were winning or not. It was almost the club's own Brexit battle—neither side willing to budge an inch on what they saw was the right thing for the club.

It was horrible, it brought fans up against other fans, it became more than the game itself, arguments and bad feeling put paid to what should have been a golden era. Benitez built a phenomenal squad against all the odds – that 2008/09 side had some of the best players in Europe – but all this against a backdrop of bad feeling between owners, managers, media, but most importantly between the fans and ultimately it cost us the league.

You might argue that if we had won the league that year, it would have cemented Hicks and Gillette in their positions to destroy the club even further, so it may be that the bad feeling that destroyed the short-term challenge for supremacy actually saved the club in the long run—I would certainly argue that. It was our great escape.

But the feeling now is one of positivity and it's marvellous. I sit in the middle of the Kop and am surrounded by (mostly) guys who have been there since we got our seats in 1994—that's nearly 25 years. These guys were around my age, had been through the preceding era of dominance and success and were desperate to see it again.

The period after the 2009 season was a bleak time, the football poor with the exception of the Suarez seasons, which brought the team back to life. The anger and resentment was still sitting dormant in the crowd, it didn't take long to raise its ugly head at the game. That feeling has gone.

It's great to see the faces in the Kop again, the same guys all in their 40s and 50s again look like they are back in their teens. Smiles, hugs, jokes—it's a day out again. The camaraderie has returned. The joy has returned. The pride.

And I think the players can feel it—they can feed off it. The idea that the Kop is a twelfth man has returned—we are winning these games for the red men. We should be, I'm knackered after some of these games!

I'm writing this as we sit proudly at the top of the league. The joy has returned, the early season enthusiasm that in recent seasons has, if not disappeared, been at least tempered is so far unbounded.

I'm 46 and I could be 16 again. I can see a situation where we go unbeaten for the rest of the season, where we have the competition won by late March, allowing us to focus on completing the Champions League double. I am a believer again.

The match is a great place to go again. There was a time when it wasn't the case and people were going just because they always had. It was a habit rather than an occasion. I think that has changed as part of this evolution.

Better players, some of the best in Europe now, a more exciting, flamboyant and risk-laden style of play, a confidence and professionalism that emanates through the team. We are here to win, and the fans are there to win too.

For a few years, the match was a nervy place to be. If we didn't start well, the crowd became nervous and we entered an ever-decreasing circle of poor performance and frustration. This has changed. The level of support has increased, not quite unquestioning support yet, but we are slowly turning into believers—Klopp was right, the buzz is back, all round commitment.

Wednesday 17th October 2018

The international break is finally over, and I can come back out of hiding. Klopp has said this week that this new international format is pointless, and he is absolutely right.

No one has got the first clue what is going on with it, little mini leagues and now talk of promotion and relegation ... absolute nonsense. While the games themselves seem completely irrelevant, what is concerning is the number of injuries we seem to have accumulated over the break and how that is going to affect the team for the weekend.

It started during the City game when Milner went off halfway through the first half. He looked like he had been carrying something prior to that and given how much he had played in the preceding weeks (combined with, dare I say, his age) then he was probably in the category of the walking wounded. Sure enough, the reports are that he will be out until the end of the month.

Over the course of the last few days, we have seen a number of players coming home early from the internationals with injuries. Salah scored a goal from a corner (shocking keeping) in his match but was then taken off injured and sent home. VVD played against Germany at the weekend but was then withdrawn from the next game due to the rib injury he has been carrying.

Mané has fallen and broken his thumb, which ruled him out and sent him home. And then, last night, we find out Keita was taken off during his game, which is worrying given what happened at Napoli when he was stretchered off with a back problem, only to be available again on the Sunday.

That means we are potentially five players light for the weekend. Of course, this is the point in the season where we need to be rotating the players and I have confidence that we can put out a strong enough side to win the next couple of games, but it would be nice to be rotating the squad rather than having players out with injury.

Football squads are very strange things. You can be playing well and worry that some of the squad are not going to get a game, which is a problem. Then you lose a few of those players and you worry that team has been severely weakened and we should have invested more in the squad when we had the chance.

With VVD out, I have every confidence that between Gomez, Lovren and Matip we can field a decent partnership at the back. Gomez has come on leaps and bounds this season, arguably player of the season so far, and combined with one of the other two should provide sufficient class.

The midfield is a bit more problematic. If we take a pessimistic view, we are already beginning to look light. Henderson and Wijnaldum have been immense so far this season, but I wonder how many times we can keep going back to them without some rotation. Milner is out for a few weeks, which may be a blessing if it gives him some rest.

Keita with another injury question. I have also heard this week that he hasn't learned the language, which is more of a concern for me. He signed for us over a year ago, I would have thought he would have been having lessons almost straight away, so he would have a decent grasp of the language by now.

On a basic day-to-day view, it means he can't communicate with the rest of the team. I have never seen a Liverpool team who have a better understanding of how the tactics work... It is really noticeable when someone steps into the team and they are not up to speed.

Keita has looked like that to me ... someone who is not in step with the rest. With such a strong setup Klopp is not going to build a team around him, so he has to learn and how can he do that if he can't understand the instructions? The fact that he hasn't learned the language really concerns me and if it's true it is a question over his professionalism.

I don't want to damn the guy at this early stage, but the last thing we need is someone in the squad who doesn't have the same professional ideals as the rest.

Fabinho has been in the background so far. It thought he did well when he came on against Napoli, so maybe he is ready to start coming in at the base of midfield. Henderson and Gini have been solid there so far, but Fabinho behind them may release them forward to provide that link with the front three that we have been missing in the last few games.

Gini scored a great goal for Holland against Germany at the weekend, pushing forward from midfield into the box. That could be the surging influence we need. Henderson can also be an intelligent player going forward if needed.

We are missing Oxlade Chamberlain who I am assuming is

out for the season and Lallana doesn't seem to be able to get a run of fitness, which is a shame as he is an intelligent player going forward and supporting the front three.

It could be that we see Shaqiri coming into the midfield. He did that against Southampton and played well in the first half but was then brought off at halftime, no doubt incurring the wrath of Klopp for not following defensive instructions. Against the weaker teams, I could see the defensive solidity of Fabinho and Henderson sitting behind Shaqiri and the front three ... a bit of 4231.

Up front, we need a realistic back-up solution for the front three, as they can't play every game. Working out where Sturridge and Shaqiri can play, do they need to be a direct replacement in the same setup, or can we manoeuvre the formation to better incorporate them?

And then, of course, there are the two forgotten men— Solanke and Origi. I'm guessing Origi will just go, but Solanke looks like he has potential. He just isn't going to realise that potential if he doesn't play. We need to look at Klopp's ability to revitalise and reinvent players.

Friday 19th October 2018

The football is back tomorrow—thank God, it's been forever.

Following the international break and my concern over multiple injuries, it looks like Salah and VVD at least are back in full training, which is a relief. I think the power has shifted considerably from the national teams to the clubs in recent years so at the first sign of any injury, they are too shit scared to use them and just send them back to the clubs. That has obviously been the case with the two of them—they must be wrapped in cotton wool the whole time.

No sign of Mané with his broken thumb or an update on Keita, but it's a relief to know those two are at least available, even if they don't get to play—it might be best to give them a week to recuperate before putting them in.

The next six fixtures to come look a lot more straightforward than the previous block of games. As much as a pain in the arse these internationals are, at least they break the season into manageable chunks where you can set expectations.

Following the next international break there is a long and testing period right the way through to the end of February—the spine of the season if you like. It would be good to start that run of games in a good position in the league. Last year, following the heavy defeat to Spurs, we went on a long unbeaten run through that winter period, so hopefully the reliance on a specific part of the squad so far will allow us to use the squad more fully again this year.

This chunk of games has Huddersfield away, Cardiff at home, Arsenal away and then Fulham at home in the league and then the double header with Red Star Belgrade in the Champions League. After getting beat in the League Cup we actually get a rest for one of the midweeks, which will give us an advantage over our rivals.

We go into the games with 20 points from eight games, level with City and Chelsea. That's 2.5 points per game, which is a good return given who we have played so far, and we're still unbeaten, which is so positive. I think if we could continue at that rate and still be on 2.5 ppg by the end of this run I would be happy with the return.

That's three wins and a draw—on first look the obvious one to get a draw is Arsenal away. Looking at how they have been playing and in good form with their manager I think a draw at their place would probably be a good one.

The other three games look very winnable but even saying that I feel like I am laying down a curse! We had such a good run last year and then stumbled against Swansea away—so we have to ensure we are not complacent (which I don't think we will be) or have one of those games where no one is firing. Cardiff and Huddersfield have yet to have a win, which is always ominous.

As for the Champions League games against Red Star, people say we need to look at the other teams' games and work out what we need from there; I don't agree with that—I think we focus on our own games, try to secure as many points as possible (I think we will get six) and then have a look how the others are doing after that.

I say we'll get six, but that is the most assuming and arrogant comment ever—I know nothing about how they play, strengths weaknesses etc. So far, they got a draw against Napoli and then have been beaten 6-1 at home by PSG, although that has the shadow of match fixing rumours hanging over it—one of their directors had money on a five-goal winning margin (allegedly!!).

Saturday 20th October 2018

A strange place to be writing this tonight. I'm at the Nou Camp. Front row of the top tier right behind the goal. The Liverpool game has just finished and we have beaten Huddersfield 1-0. I know that Salah scored. I know that Lallana, Shaqiri and Sturridge started, but beyond that I don't know too much (anything) about the game.

I am in Spain so have no way of watching it, no way of listening to it. I followed the first half on Twitter in the hotel room and then have walked down to the ground watching my phone for updates. Watched the last (very tense) ten minutes in my seat here on the Bet365 app where they show who is passing to who. Was sure we would concede at the death.

But we won and now I can concentrate on what is going on in front of me. We are in Barcelona for Ange's birthday and she booked a hotel about 10 minutes' walk from the Nou Camp.

You can see the stadium from our hotel room.

I didn't think for a minute that Barcelona would be at home if you could get a room nearby, but it turns out they are playing Sevilla who are second in the league. Barca are only third so it's a big game.

I'm here on my own. And I think the reason is quite simply I want to see Lionel Messi play football in front of my own eyes. I want to see Suarez and Coutinho, I want to see them batter Sevilla after the final in 2016, but most of all I want to see Messi.

In years to come Messi will be held in the same group as Pele and Maradona. No one else has broken into that group in 30 years, but Messi will, he'll be held in the same esteem. He's in his 30s now, he won't go on forever and it was just too big an opportunity to miss. I feel like I'm doing something really special.

Fifteen minutes to kick-off and the place is filling up quick. I have been here before; I came to watch Liverpool here in 2001. We came without tickets and sat with the home fans for a very dour game.

The team have just finished their warm-up. Messi gets this big cheer every time he kicks the ball. Taking potshots from the edge of the area, he gets an ovation when one goes in.

The commercialisation in the club is at a different level. Liverpool have moved forward in recent years but they are still way behind this. Coutinho is everywhere. His picture is in everything. He is clearly the next in line to be the leading global superstar. I am pleased for him and to be able to say I have seen him play.

And Suarez too. Probably the most exciting player I have ever seen at Anfield. I get to see him too, and I believe I have a special connection with both of them. That they are 'ours'.

They're coming out. They're singing the anthem. Goose bumps.

***

Half time. Barcelona winning 2-0 and I have seen him. And he is as good as I imagined he would be. He sets up Coutinho in the second minute for the first goal. He runs onto a brilliant Suarez ball and scores from the edge of the box in the thirteenth minute. And in the 23rd minute he is subbed off after what looked like quite an innocuous challenge. He dominated the game and then he was gone!! I've seen him play. I've seen him score. Boxes ticked.

It's a very different match going experience to Anfield. It's less raucous, more civilised. There must be 90,000 people here tonight, but they don't generate the noise you would expect. The stadium is vast but is open like a bowl and the noise must just float into the air. No roof to hold it in, it doesn't echo and reverberate, and it loses the intensity.

I have a magnificent view of the game, though, and can watch it in a very different way. In the Kop I am twenty rows back. The whole game is foreshortened, difficult to see shape and formation. I've had that view for 30 years now and can follow the game and understand it from that perspective.

Where I am tonight I have a helicopter view of the game. I can see what 4-3-3 actually means, where they stand, where they run. It's like watching a live game of Subbutteo.

The quality of the players and the play make it an absolute privilege to watch from this angle. Coutinho is at the heart of everything. Suarez is still the same old Suarez (although he has lost a bit of pace from when we used to watch him). Dembele came on for Messi and is a star of the future, amazing pace and ability to run with the ball.

I'm waxing lyrical here and you would think I watched Wigan Athletic most weeks. Liverpool would have these, match them toe to toe, take them on and beat them. We are so lucky because at the moment we are watching football on a par with this. We shouldn't take that for granted.

Sunday 21ˢᵗ October 2018

Sunday evening. Still in Barcelona, which is a beautiful city.

The game finished 4-2 last night. Suarez got a penalty in the second half, which gave me a bit of a kick. The hero of the second half was the keeper Ter Stegen who pulled off two double saves that were beyond belief. At crucial times he kept them in the game. Success is not all about scoring goals.

By all accounts Liverpool didn't play well, couldn't get any fluency but still got the win. They were solid at the back, kept a clean sheet and have set a new record with only three goals conceded in nine games. I assume that's a club record not a world record.

Klopp has come out and said the focus on the defensive solidity has affected the attacking fluidity. You can't do everything. Success is not always about scoring goals. (Did you see what I did there ... albeit it a rather clumsy and obvious way?)

Six clean sheets and three goals from nine games is a great start. Mourinho's Chelsea kept 25 clean sheets and conceded 15 in a 38 game season in 2004–5, which is phenomenal. Our ratios are actually better, but we have a way to go yet.

Wednesday 24ᵗʰ October 2018

Back from Barcelona and into work, although an early dart is planned to get to the Champions League game against Red Star Belgrade tonight at Anfield.

The focus has flipped in the last day or so from the Premier League to the Champions League. We are top of the Premier League, level with City. It's a close run thing ... after nine games there are only two points separating the top five teams. Of the top six, there's only United not keeping pace with the rest. They drew 2-2 with Chelsea at the weekend, Chelsea managing to salvage a draw with an injury time goal ... so they both lose points. City gave Burnley a 5-0 thumping, Spurs won by a single goal and then Arsenal beat Leicester convincingly on Monday night.

Arsenal are going to be interesting this season. With a new manager replacing Wenger, this was always going to be a year of transition for them. They played a couple of the top teams for their first games and had no points after two games but have now gone on a run of seven wins to be right up at the top. Aubameyang seems to be coming into form and the manager seems to get a lot more out of Ozil. Liverpool play them in a couple of weeks so it will be a good test for both sides.

But tonight, it's all about the Champions League. This is the first of the double header against Red Star, supposedly the weakest of the group. Liverpool should be looking for six points out of these two games, and, until they are over, not even worry about what PSG and Napoli have done to each other.

Henderson and Keita are both injured. Much has been made of Fabinho in the press today and it looks certain that he will start tonight. For a £40m player, you would assume that he would walk into the team from the start, but Klopp is always very guarded with his players when they join the squad and he won't unleash them until he is sure they are ready.

Last year, it was Robertson and Oxlade Chamberlain who were in a similar boat, not getting near the team until this time of year. They both signed quite late so it's understandable that they maybe hadn't had a full pre-season, but they both had Premier League experience.

For Fabinho, he joined really early so I can't imagine he hasn't had that pre-season training to ensure full fitness. But he has come from the French League and I assume there is a jump in the pace and ferocity of the game. He has Champions League experience with Monaco, so I am hoping he will slot in quite nicely tonight.

Mané is back from injury, although there appears to be some competition for places across the front three and one of the midfield places potentially. Shaqiri had a good game at the weekend and will be keen to start. Lallana also had his first start since the beginning of the year so he could be in contention too.

Aside from Fabinho, I think Salah and Firmino will definitely play, and then the other three forward spots could go to any one of six players. It's a great problem to have.

In defence, we thought those places were written in stone, but the self-proclaimed best centre back in the world (or one of them at least), Lovren, has returned and staked his place with some solid performances. Will he get the nod over Gomez or will Gomez move across in place of Trent? Again, it's a difficult but very welcome call to have to make.

***

Brilliant performance by Liverpool. We beat Red Star Belgrade 4-0. An efficient and controlling performance, almost from the start.

Fabinho introduced for (almost) his first game and he was outstanding. What a player. Once again, Klopp has kept a player in the background until he was sure he was ready and Fabinho didn't let him down for a single second. Strong in the well-timed tackle, good passing range, happy to win the ball and then pass it on, able to push forward with power when running with the ball and popping up in the box on occasion too. I thought he was excellent.

From my spec in the Kop it looked like the team were playing 4231. Fabinho and Wijnaldum holding in front of the back four, Shaqiri, Firmino and Mané all playing behind Salah who was up on his own. It was difficult to tell at times as they were all so fluid.

Firmino was playing deeper than usual; he looked like he was controlling the game from midfield for chunks of the game. Shaqiri, was buzzing round all game, linking things up, he had a great game too, and got an ovation when substituted.

Lallana and Sturridge both came on toward the end and both had chances to score but the most noticeable thing was the creativity they both brought to the game when they played. What a bonus to have players like that to bring on when in form.

Gini was terrific again; playing in the holding role, he manages to add an air of dynamism to the midfield in what would normally be a screening role. He was man of the match again for me, despite the great performances from Fabinho, Shaqiri, Robertson, Gomez (how quick is he!).

I suppose it would be rude not to mention the front three in all this; after all, they all scored! Salah up on his own, great for him to get a couple of goals to get him some momentum, Mané was quiet and the most peripheral of the three... He missed a penalty but then popped up at the end to slide one in, but it was Bobby Firmino who caught the eye from a little bit further back.

Some of the short passing play in the second half was breath-taking. They have obviously been doing back flick practise this week and there was a prize for who could do the best. Even Albie Moreno was getting in on it at the end.

For all of my salivating, Red Star were a poor side, who brought little to the game, but Liverpool had them in complete control. It's another win and another clean sheet.

Thursday 25th October 2018

Still buzzing about the game last night. This whole midfield thing is a real quandary. How can we have so many good players?

Fabinho starts last night and is just outstanding, like nothing else we have. He reminded me of Patrick Vieira, which is about as big a compliment as I can give. Everyone's been questioning why he hasn't had a game so far, but again Klopp has got it right and hasn't put him in the team until he is ready.

Everyone thought Gini would be on his way at the beginning of the season with all the new players, but he has stepped up and for me is the player of the season so far. Milner is improving with age and Henderson is still the best midfielder in the squad.

Keita has been thrown in too early but will come in to his own in the New Year and now, to add to the confusion, Lallana waltzes in waving his hands and saying, 'Don't forget about me!' If Oxlade Chamberlain was fit, we'd be writing to the FA to see if we could change the rules to 12-a-side.

It is an amazing piece of man management to keep all of these players happy and motivated. It's difficult for 'normal' people to understand the level of motivation of these guys. I imagine and hope that they all want to be playing every week, so how can they be happy? How does Klopp generate a level of respect amongst the squad that they can accept that some of them just won't play and have to wait for their chance? And then, when they take that chance, they still might be out the following week. With all of that competitive tension, it's a wonder that this squad looks like they're having the time of their lives.

The cop out answer to that is we'd all be having the times of our lives if we were paid £100k a week, but I really don't think it's as simple as that. These guys are the best, at the top of their game and have got there by being super competitive and focused. They have an animal-like instinct to win, have been brought up to win and you can't take that out of them, shed loads of money don't come into the equation. So how does he take that singular view and turn it into a team view? That's what the best managers do particularly now in an era of 25-man squads—and I honestly believe we have the one of the best managers in the world.

I don't know how I've arrived here... I was going to write about 4231 and reminisce about Rafa. Let's see if he plays the same formation tomorrow and I'll have another go at a Rafa love-in next week.

Saturday 27th October 2018

Another Liverpool win and we go top of the league again, at least until City play on Monday night. Ten games, still unbeaten with 26 points. Today we beat Cardiff 4-1, which sounds over-whelming, but the score is no way a reflection of the game.

There will be some criticism of the team I think as they didn't really hit the heights. There is an expectation that at some point we are going to absolutely steamroller a team and with a goal after about 10 minutes today, that looked to be the case. Salah scored from about six yards, at which point it is fully ex-pected that we rip this team a new one.

I can't remember a half where we had so much possession of the ball without really being incisive... I think the easy term is sterile domination, we had that in spades, but at half time it was still only 1-0.

Second half wasn't much better. Cardiff had next to nothing to offer, but Liverpool aren't quite clicking together. It may be a different formation, new players coming in... We had Fabinho, Moreno and Lallana from the start today; can't put my finger on it, but until Mané scored the second with a bullet of a goal, it was difficult to rest easy.

Neil Warnock had said this week that it was virtually im-possible to beat this Liverpool side at Anfield. Now Warnock is a gobshite, but this is probably about the truest statement he will make all week, even if in his addled mind he thought it was actually some form of reverse psychology. But with about 10 to go, they manage to go up to our end and score and for a few minutes Anfield is concerned.

Concerned that we have had all this dominance for nearly 90 minutes and haven't put this side to bed, that we are going to lose two points to this team that lacks all the qualities Liverpool have in abundance. But then we step up. We step up and score two in the last 10 minutes to make the game safe but also give the impression this was some kind of tour de force. It wasn't.

Shaqiri gets his first goal, thoroughly deserved after his substitute performance and the energy he has put in over recent games. And then Mané gets a second. Within all of this, Mo Salah, only a fortnight ago being written off as a one-season wonder, scores another goal and gets two assists.

We are top of the league. After the same amount of games as last year, we have 10 more points, scored a couple more goals and conceded about a dozen less ... just four against so far. So while there may be criticism that we haven't blown this team away, I think we need to be thankful that we have won again and that this more solid, less flamboyant approach is bringing us more points than we ever had before.

There can be an arrogance amongst supporters. That we will win every game and that we should be winning it handsomely and in a creative style, which makes us the envy of the football world. An arrogance that other teams don't have the right to win, forgetting that although there is a massive disparity between the resources and ability of the teams in the Premier League, these are still the 20 best teams in the country with millions to spend on players from around the world. I think we need to be careful that we don't become like spoiled children and begin to bemoan a win because it hasn't been delivered in Corinthian style.

We should be thankful for every win and every point, thankful that we got that win without hitting the heights ... never taking this marvellous football team for granted.

Monday 29th October 2018

Sad news over the weekend, which puts football into perspective. The Leicester City owner, a Thai businessman, died in a helicopter crash as he was leaving the ground after the game on Saturday evening. He died along with the two pilots and two of his assistants. There is a massive outpouring of emotion for this guy who invested so much time, money and passion into the club.

What Leicester achieved a couple of years ago in winning the Premier League is unheard of, a 5000/1 shot at the beginning of the season. A year before that, they were marooned at the bottom of the league with 10 games to go and no one gave them a hope of staying up. Two years before that, they were in the Championship, missing out on promotion in the play-off final.

Over a six-year period, this guy created an environment in the club that took them from just another club to champions of England, playing in Europe. It's a modern-day fairy tale. You couldn't make it up.

In a league that is currently dominated by half a dozen teams, who have so much more resource at their disposal than the rest, the Leicester story gives everyone hope. Liverpool are fortunate that they are in that top six and, although we haven't been in direct contention for the title in recent years, we always feel we are in the ball park, always a season away with the right signings, the right approach and a fortuitous following wind.

But for the vast majority of clubs and fans, they will never break into that group, short of an Arab investment group coming in and transforming the club—but that isn't always a given.

There are loads of people who have come into football in recent years, multimillionaires, billionaires who adopt clubs as their own little plaything, not really understanding how it works, not really investing correctly, just hanging in for the payoff in the long term. I think a few of these could die in a tragic accident and people wouldn't care—for some it would be a blessing.

By the sound of it, this guy has been different. He has listened and has built the club with the right people. He has invested wisely, he has been involved with the fans, he has donated to local hospitals and universities—he has contributed to the club and the community. He buys the whole ground a pint on his birthday for Christ's sake!

That's not to say he hasn't had a little good fortune. The year they won, he clearly benefited from the top teams being in a state of transition – and Spurs being bottlers obviously – but fortune favours the brave and I don't think there is a single person who would begrudge that win—for most football supporters he made the impossible possible. It's a sad loss.

Tuesday 30th October 2018

Manchester City beat Tottenham 1-0 last night on what was a disgraceful pitch and all of the teams have now finished 10 games - we find ourselves joint top of the league.

The league is like two leagues at the moment—the top six (I suppose I have to include United even if they are off the pace) and the rest, which vary from average to downright poor.

For me, the key to winning this league is first and foremost beating 'the rest'—that's 28 games or 76 points up for grabs and, on a single game-by-game basis, I don't think there is any reason why any of the top six shouldn't be beating any of 'the rest'. Some games will be more difficult than others obviously, but the gap in resource and class suggests that each one of these games should be a walkover.

And when it comes down to it, three points is three points and that's all you get whether you beat United or Huddersfield. (Yes, I know there is the whole six-point argument for your direct competitors but that kind of disrupts my flow for now—so leave it).

After you've beaten the rest, it's essentially a mini league between the top six and whoever can get 20 points from the 30 on offer wins the league. Last year, City won both leagues – the top six and the rest – they beat everyone, while we didn't fare as well against the top six and also lost a few cheap points (Swansea away?).

What's great about having a top six is the number of games between those teams – 30 in all – and this season there are only eight match days where there isn't a clash between two of the top six. That means someone is losing points almost every week.

There has been a top six clash for each of the last four weeks and there will be for the next seven weeks—all the way to Christmas. That is someone (us or a direct rival) losing three points every week – and in the case of a draw that's four points lost between them – even better!! In the other eight weeks of the year, the top teams play the rest and it's very rare that all 6 win—only once a season for the past two years.

Last weekend, it was Arsenal's turn to drop points against one of the rest—a draw against Palace, which drops them two points and takes them away from those at the summit. They are the real bonus games when 'the rest' take points off our rivals.

This weekend, the top six clash is Liverpool against Arsenal—it's massive. This is where getting knocked out of the League Cup has its advantages—we have an extra few days' rest while Arsenal have to play tomorrow night. Time to get some work done on the training ground!

Interlude 4 – Central League

My experience of the match through the early 1980s was limited. After my first game in 1977, I don't think I went to a first team game for about six years. All the way through junior school, my exposure to football was probably about the same as any other kid at the time.

I supported a team, just like most of the other kids; everyone knew your team and you knew everyone else's. A lot of kids got a kit for their birthday and I was no exception. A red Hitachi kit at the end of the '70s, a white kit with the red v neck collar after that, then a jump to the shiny yellow kit with the red pinstripes—the team version had Crown Paints on the front but mine didn't.

Every year, the same kids would have the Panini sticker album and spend every playtime doing swaps. The ability to remember who you have 'Got' and who you have 'Not got' at the speed we used to shuffle through the packs astounds me know, when I can barely remember what day it is or the reason I have just picked up my phone! We also all had an encyclopaedic knowledge of every player in the league and the Scottish league (although their stickers were only half size), encyclopaedic in terms of height and weight at least.

Kids were aware of the league and results, but there was no internet, little coverage on TV, so knowledge of the game was filtered and wasn't the ever-present news cycle of today. Our experience of the game was different—we actually played the game! And we played because we wanted to, not because our dads wanted us to be spotted as the next up-and-coming star.

Lots of the kids played for their school team and also a local team. That was where the engagement with the game happened. Unemployment was rife in the early 1980s and we used to have unemployed dads come and coach us, good players, ex-professionals. We used to play school matches every week and when we weren't training, we were out in the road playing 'three and in' or ' sixty seconds', or going down to the park, jumpers for goalposts and all that. That was your football apprenticeship, learning to play and playing as much as you could, after school or in the holidays, with anyone you could find who wanted a game (and had a ball!).

As for Liverpool, in much the same way as many of the professionals come through the reserve side to learn the Liverpool way before being let into the first team, my first regular matchgoing experience at this time was through the Central League. Liverpool used to win the Central League more regularly than they would win the league and I went to so many games with my Grandad on the bus—it was how I got into the habit of going to Anfield.

The Central League game used to play on Saturday afternoons at Anfield when the first team were away. Grandad's season ticket would get us in free of charge and we would sit in his seats in the Main Stand. They only opened the Main Stand for these games and you could sit where you liked, there were just a few hundred at the game. The place was eerily empty, and any noise would bounce off the inside of the stand, the claps echoing like the twang of an elastic band.

It was the reserve team playing, but you got to see the first team players if they were coming back from injury, which was really exciting, or the new signings who weren't quite ready for the first team, such as Rush, Whelan, Nicol, and Molby.

I saw so many of the players, but it was more about sitting and watching and understanding the game. You didn't get carried away with the atmosphere of the crowd; it was a more clinical experience and gave an insight into how the game works. It sounds very purist of me, but a lot of the blurts who watch the game now and don't know how to go it without a TV commentator should be put through the apprenticeship I had.

NOVEMBER

Thursday 1ˢᵗ November 2018

Big game on Saturday – Arsenal away – a big test for both sides to see where everyone is up to. I had kind of discounted Arsenal for this year, after 20 odd years of Wenger, they have brought in a new manager and I thought this would be a 'year of transition' (that old chestnut).

For me, Arsenal had a really good selection of players in midfield and going forward but were dodgy at the back with Cech well past his sell by date. They had a poor start but also an unfortunate start in that their first two games of the season were City and Chelsea so they were without a point after the first two games.

Since then, they have been playing 'the rest' and have had a run of eight games against the lower down sides in the division, quietly racking up the points—seven wins and a draw, which is a good return and leaves them only a few points off the top.

It looks like Ozil is playing well and back on form and I have just seen some data where they are ranked top in terms of distance covered by the team. Now, that doesn't win any trophies in itself but it does say they are working hard, covering the ground, something for which Liverpool have become renowned since Klopp took over. So potentially we have two hard-working, attractive and skilful sides coming to head—it should be a great game.

Last year's game was bizarre. Last game before Christmas and we had been on a roll. Having dominated the first half, we missed chances and ended up going in 1-0 up. We went 2-0 up early in the second half. I thought to myself, *That's it, we're safe,* and I took the opportunity to go for a piss and get (another) beer out the fridge. I got back to find us drawing two each and watching them score again.

Mistakes at the back, compounded by an absolute howler from Mignolet, I think that was the end for him—two games later he was dropped for Karius and hasn't really been seen since.

Firmino scored shortly after but by that point it was to get us back into the game on level terms rather than taking it out of the hands of Arsenal. It was the perfect example supporting the narrative of Liverpool being weak at the back.

Within 10 days, we had signed VVD and Mignolet was consigned to history, so to an extent it was something of a watershed game for us. Now, nearly a year on, it will be interesting to see how we have progressed.

I'd love to win, I always love to win, but I would maybe take a draw, in fact no, what am I talking about? I'd take a fucking win—we are Liverpool, Klopp's Liverpool, let's beat them.

Saturday 3rd November 2018

A 1-1 draw away at Arsenal. A great game. By no means a bad result but disappointing that we gave away a late goal. Arsenal were a good side, their manager has got them fired up and although we had enough to win the game, a draw was a fair result. Far from being a team in transition, Arsenal looked like a strong side and will be up there in the top four on that performance.

A point at the Emirates will prove a valuable one later in the season. We are still unbeaten and go back to the top of the league, at least until City play Southampton tomorrow, which you would expect them to win.

Liverpool returned to 4-3-3 today after experimenting with 4-2-3-1 for the past couple of games. It was probably the right decision to give a little bit more solidity in the middle as Arsenal had a strong midfield with their new guy Torreira being a little ferocious dynamo in the middle.

Fabinho didn't look up to it at all. Having had a couple of good games at the base of midfield, he seemed lost and off the pace today. Henderson's star became a lot brighter in his absence. He is so strong and controlling as the point man in a three-man midfield, allowing the other two midfielders to push forward and feed the three up front. That position really is the point of leverage on which the whole team turns. Fabinho looked lost and, as a result, Milner and Gini had too much covering to do to keep control of the game and the front three didn't get the service and support they needed.

I'm probably over-egging it there. We still had the best of the game, but we weren't able to properly control and dominate. We will need to persist with Fabinho, but it will be a case of finding the right formation and the right opponents. For games of that pace and class, we need Hendo back in the middle.

Monday 5th November 2018

Sometimes I yearn for the days pre-internet and pre-social media. When life was simpler. When you just went to the match and then to school or work the next day and people chatted about the football and then the week went by and people went to the football again.

Or people went to the pub after the game, talked about the game, watched the game on *Match of the Day*, read the report in the next day's paper and then waited for the next game to come around.

It was no less exciting. You could enjoy the game, form an opinion based on what you saw, listen to others' opinions based on what they saw. Agree or disagree, have favourite players, have players you didn't like. Life went on.

Since the start of the Premier League, we have moved steadily away from that. The PL is a product of Sky and with it comes a 24-hour news cycle. The PL pretty much dates to the advent of the internet for the masses in the early '90s. The growth of news on demand, chat rooms, user groups.

Then, from roughly 2005, the growth of the smartphone and social media. And for most of that time, Liverpool have been mainly frustrating, mainly not challenging and as these channels grow so has the amount of whinging. The growth of technology has taken the whinging from the pub/school/workplace and put it everywhere. Everywhere so you can't get away from it.

I think one of the key differences is when you were listening to opinions in the pub/ school/workplace, you knew the person and could weigh that opinion on how much they knew about the game. Had they been to the match? Had they just read the paper the next day? Were they just repeating what their dad had told them (had their dad been to the match)? etc. etc. etc. It was up to you to decide whether a person with an opinion knew what they were talking about or whether they were a dick.

And conversely, you had to think about your opinion and stand by it. You wanted people to value your opinion, to be seen as someone who went to the match and understood what they were talking about.

But now not only is there opinion everywhere, you can't get a sense of who the people are and whether they know their arse from their elbow.

Why am I ranting?? Since the final whistle on the game on Saturday evening, and probably ten minutes before that, the wave of social media opinion is overwhelming. It was a 1-1 draw at Arsenal, a better-than-anticipated Arsenal. I think the common phrase is 'heads are falling off' and it would appear that heads have fallen off everywhere.

How bad a performance it was … midfield are awful … don't look like scoring a goal. Where is the perspective? Granted, I didn't think Fabinho played well, he looked out of his depth, but this was his first game against one of the top sides. We got an away draw against one of our rivals. It's a good point. It's a shame we didn't hang on for the win, but no one needs hanging for their goal, it was a good move, converted brilliantly against a defensive line that was otherwise immaculate.

Since the advent of social media, it has been a forum for criticism and I think now we are doing well, either people don't know how to break the habit of being critical or are being hypercritical because of the high bar that has been set by City, Chelsea and, to be fair, ourselves.

We have won eight of our first 11, drawn the other three against top six rivals, and conceded only five in the process. IT'S A GOOD START, EVERYONE.

Come May, if we don't win the league I will leave myself open to criticism (they're on social media, what else are they going to do) that I wasn't pushing hard enough, that I was too forgiving.

We are third currently on 27 points. We have played more games against our top six rivals than any of the others. We have five games against 'the rest', which takes us through to mid-December. In that time, all of the other top six have to play the top six teams TWICE. Plenty of time and opportunity for dropped points elsewhere, as long as we can keep winning.

I know the answer to this. Spend less time on social media and more talking to people whose opinion you respect. Rant over. Red Star Belgrade away tomorrow night.

Tuesday 6th November 2018

Back to the Champions League and tonight we have the second part of the double header against Red Star Belgrade. It's a crucial game really and one that Liverpool really need to win to reduce pressure on the upcoming games.

Red Star are the weakest team in the group and as such we need to be taking six points off them. We got the first three at Anfield against a fairly weak team. If we can get the second three tonight, it keeps us at the top of the group, safe in the knowledge that either Napoli or PSG (or possibly both of them) will drop points when they play each other later on.

From there, we just have to work out what we need from the last two games—PSG away and then finally Napoli at home. It's a tricky group as any two of the three teams could go through. We want to be getting those three points tonight to ensure we don't have to be getting them in the final games—at that point we want to be concentrating on the leaguegames.

The most interesting piece of squad news is that Shaqiri hasn't been taken along with the squad. Shaqiri is from Kosovo, which was formerly part of Serbia, now independent but not recognised by Serbia as a national entity. It appears that Shaqiri moved to Switzerland during the Kosovo war with Albania. During the World Cup this summer, Shaqiri scored for the Swiss against Serbia and made the Eagle symbol from the Albanian flag. It got him into a lot of hot water with the Serbians and with FIFA.

Shaqiri played in the match against Belgrade at Anfield, but as there were virtually no away fans there was very little reaction. It sounds like if he had have played tonight there would have been murder, so Klopp has taken the decision not to take him at all—a common-sense decision based on the perceived security risk.

I have to say I am not an expert in Balkan politics and

probably don't understand the depth of feeling and potential re-percussions of him playing, but my initial reaction is one of dis-appointment. Not that he won't be playing (there are plenty of other games ahead) but that we have had to make this decision based on political pressure. It surprises me that Klopp has bowed to this pressure; that he has let outside influences affect his squad decision—I feel like we have let them win before we have even got on the pitch.

We are Liverpool, we shouldn't be dictated to in this way. Shaqiri is one of our boys and we should take him and protect him. It sounds like he has accepted the decision with good grace—a practical and common-sense decision if ever there was one. Hopefully we can win without him and he can return at the weekend with a good performance. Just disappointed—don't like being told what to do by anyone!

***

Never take things for granted. We got beat 2-0 by Red Star in a hostile atmosphere. Two goals conceded in a frenetic first half and then unable to break them down in the second half. Sterile domination. All of the ball for the whole half but unable to break down a committed defence. We played poorly but, to be fair to Red Star, they played out of their skins and were a wildly different side from the one who played at Anfield a fortnight ago.

It was a six o'clock kick-off so I had to listen to the first half hour on the radio. The ground was loud. Commentator said the loudest and most intimidating he had heard. That came across the same later on TV. When they scored the first, the background noise of the stadium went berserk. Again for the second.

From what I saw of the first half, Liverpool struggled to put passes together. They managed a couple of chances, but in the main there was no fluidity from midfield into attack. We missed Henderson again. Second half, Firmino came on for Sturridge. We had all of the ball in midfield but couldn't get past a six-man defence. We never looked like pulling it back.

So now it's a dog fight. Our saving grace tonight is that Napoli and PSG drew again ... they both dropped points. We have six points alongside Napoli, PSG a point behind. We have to play them both, first of all PSG away and then Napoli at home to finish the group. My mind can't compute it at the moment, but a rough stab says we need a win and a draw.

They both have to play Red Star. I would have said that is an easy three points before tonight, but having seen them play at home, I have changed my mind. They got a draw at home to Napoli too, so PSG could be in for a tough time.

Whatever we need, we have made it harder for ourselves through a poor, toothless performance.

Wednesday 7th November 2018

Wednesday morning and I'm more disappointed with last night's defeat than I was straight after the game. Normally it's the other way round. I've seen enough defeats to wake up next day and think it's only a game with another one around the corner to resurrect ourselves.

This morning, I am thinking about the manner of the defeat and whether this is a truer reflection of how we have been playing in recent weeks. In the shower this morning, I did the mental gymnastics of what needs to happen in the group from here on out. I always seem to do this in the shower—take it as my time to work out the mathematical combinations of the upcoming games. In the 13/14 season, it was ridiculous the amount of time I spent in there.

Assuming both Napoli and PSG beat Red Star (which is a fair assumption but not a foregone conclusion) we can still qualify in any one of three ways. First, if we beat PSG away in the next game we are through. Easier said than done. Next, if we can get a draw with PSG and then beat Napoli at home, we go through. Again, it's tough. The final option is beating Napoli by more than a single goal at Anfield. That's a big ask, too, but exciting—imagine the atmosphere in Anfield for that game if we needed to beat them by a couple of goals, it would be like Olympiakos in 2005 all over again.

I'm sure there is another scenario where Red Star get on a roll, win both their games and qualify top of the group—it's not impossible, but I think I would have washed away down the plughole trying to work out those options.

It was a poor performance last night. A few changes to the team with Matip, Lallana and Sturridge coming in, but that shouldn't affect our ability to win, to compete. 'We should play our strongest team,' people shout, but we can't do that every game. We have 20-odd players and we need to be able to substitute them in and out of the team. The perceived top 11 can't play every game.

As it goes Sturridge missed a sitter at 0-0, which would have changed the game completely. I thought it would have been better to bring off Lallana at half time rather than Sturridge. He (Lallana) didn't seem to be in sync with the front three, seemed to be overlapping, sharing the same spaces. Once Red Star had gone 2-0 up, they were happy to hold out and that is what they did. Liverpool barely created a chance in the second half, so it wasn't even a close thing. They stifled us moving forward from midfield and we had no way around it.

I think that is the bigger concern in the medium to long term, we are not fluid enough at the moment if teams want to come and park the bus—we don't have a way through. I won't use the Shaqiri not playing excuse, it's a team-wide thing and not down to one missing man.

We turn to Fulham at the weekend—I'm not going to say an

easy win as that flippancy is not serving us well. We should be able to beat them is more respectful and more how we should be talking. (Whatever!)

Friday 9th November 2018

Friday afternoon. Working out best way of getting an early dart from work. I hate Friday afternoons.

Fulham at home this Sunday. It's a twelve noon kick-off, which is a shit time to have a match. I can only think it's the TV that is dictating the kick-off time.

Too early to get out and have a pint before. From my experience, the early games on a Saturday always have that vital bit of atmosphere missing. No one is quite up for it. Having it on a Sunday is even worse.

I've got a pass for the day but that requires the others to have one too, and because of the stupid time there are other commitments at this time. Drinking isn't much fun on your own.

I'm researching the other part of the book at the moment. All the matches I'm researching are a 3 p.m. Saturday kick-off. Easy. In this day and age, they should be relaxing the restrictions on televising games at 3 p.m. on a Saturday. They used to spout out that it was all for the good of game, but I don't think that applies anymore. Any protectionism around the game has been eroded away by the power of Sky and the other vested interests. The only good of the game they care about is making money out of it.

There used to be the same protectionism around major sporting events; that they had to be shown on terrestrial TV. The FA Cup final, The England Cricket Test matches, The Open. They've all moved on, each piece of sporting traditional sold out ... for a lot more than thirty pieces of silver too.

If they can all go, then the supposedly sacrosanct no screening of the 3 p.m. Saturday KO can go too. Play them at the same time and televise them. You can watch these games in Australia and the US at the push of a button. Every other pub on the high street is showing them on one dodgy stream or another. And if there's no pub locally, then you can watch on your laptop anyway.

All being held up by some archaic law. Get it changed. It's ruining my weekend!

Sunday 11th November 2018

A safe home win for the red men today at Anfield. 2-0 against Fulham. It's another three points ... not sure what there is to add beyond that.

It was a game that never really got going. The 12 noon kick-off didn't help, it felt like the crowd had other things on its mind. With a crowd of 50,000, I think there is a requirement to drink about 100,000 pints of lager before the game (on average) and there just isn't time before a noon kick-off. So it was like a bloody library in there.

Considering Fulham are bottom of the league, I didn't think they were too bad. In the first half they cut through three times and were unlucky not to score. Eventually they did but it was ruled offside. While they were still celebrating, Liverpool took off down to the other end and scored—brilliant piece of opportunism. As it turned out the Fulham goal wasn't offside at all. Tough luck, we had one disallowed at Arsenal last week, they all have to take the rough with the smooth.

Second half was a one-sided affair, Shaqiri scored well from a Robertson cross. Beyond that we had all the possession, some good chances, but it was never going to be a mauling. I think would have been harsh on Fulham.

What I did notice was the work ethic in the Liverpool team. I don't know whether they had a rocket after the defeat in Belgrade, but you could see an uplift in the effort level, which is to be admired. Trent is having a difficult time at the moment, heavy touch, things not falling for him, but you couldn't fault the effort to overcome it. Good on you, lad. I'd put Salah in that boat too.

On the other side, I thought Robertson was terrific, the ground he covers and the pace he covers it at is immense. Always there for the overlap, always there to support and the number of times his persistence pays off and he comes away with the ball makes you really pleased for him. A hard worker getting his rewards.

Shaqiri is fast becoming a fans favourite. And I think he knows it. He's like a little windup toy and every time he gets the ball, he just comes alive. He took his goal really well and the crowd loved him for it and the celebration.

City beat United so we are still two points behind them, but Chelsea and Arsenal both dropped points to 'the rest'. We're still up there; it's another important three points.

Monday 12th November 2018

It's the end of the next block of games and we have another of these bloody international breaks. This is the last one before Christmas and following this break there is a long slog of 11 games in 39 days.

In the Premier League, I am really pleased with the progress. In the four games in this little block we won three and drew one—the draw being away at Arsenal, which is a pretty good result. Mid-November and we are still unbeaten despite the perception we are still not hitting the heights of last season.

A quick year-on-year analysis says it all. After 12 games, we are eight points ahead of where we were a year ago. We have 30 points, that's 2.5 per game. Despite not firing on all cylinders, we have scored a goal more than last year and conceded

12 goals less—just five in 12 games.

We have managed to beat all of 'the rest' and have only dropped points to our top six rivals. If that isn't progress I don't know what is. We are two points behind City who are also unbeaten. It's going to be a tough season and the goal is going to be staying in touch with City for as long as possible. It will be demoralising for them to be winning all these games and still not being able to shake us.

I was out on my bike at the weekend. I overtook this guy on his bike and was pedalling away into the wind only to realise about a mile later that this guy was slip-streaming me (tucking up right behind my wheel and letting me do all the hard work into the wind).

Me being me, I wasn't going to let him overtake me again, so I carried on doing all the work. By the time I got to my turn-off a couple of miles later I was shagged, I turned off and this cheeky fucker was tootling along without a care in the world, giving me a cheeky wave.

Liverpool need to be that cheeky fucker, letting City forge ahead, taking on all the pressure of being unbeaten at the top of the league and just tuck in behind their back wheel. Waiting for the moment when they are all knackered from the wind in their face. We've just got to be in the right position to strike.

As for the Champions League, ultimately that has been disappointing. A formulaic win at Anfield should have led to a follow-up in Belgrade but we were caught out there last week by a hostile crowd and a pumped-up well-organised team.

Losing that game was costly. It means that while trying to keep pace with City in the League, we also need to pull out a couple of top-class performances against PSG and Napoli.

These should have been the cruisy games, where we get to put some minutes into the lesser players in the squad. We don't have that luxury now—it's going to be do or die. They are going to be big games—a win in Paris would be awesome, but I think it is more likely going to come down to a winner-takes-all game at Anfield. And losing that game will be worse than getting knocked out—the Europa League, which is the last thing we need.

Our next two home games are Everton and United, both at 4 p.m. on a Sunday. They're weeks away but I'm already excited. Yesterday I said the Anfield crowd needed 100,000 pints of lager to get up for a game. God knows how many will be consumed ahead of those two.

Friday 16th November 2018

Emotional day today and really caught me out. People on social media referring to Sir Kenny Dalglish. I thought that was strange as it had been announced ages ago. Didn't realise this was the day he was actually being knighted. I found the video and have to say it was a tear in the eye moment.

Kenny Dalglish is my first and only football hero. He signed for Liverpool just before my fifth birthday and is the person I have always associated with Liverpool. He is Liverpool.

I probably wasn't old enough to fully appreciate how good he was at his prime but he was always there ... the first game I went to in December 1977, the abiding memory is seeing Dalglish play.

Right through early school, Dalglish was my hero, and I have grown up with him and his achievements. At 13, I was there when he won the double; my first years on the Kop were watching him as a manager and the amazing team he created with Barnes and Beardsley.

I saw him in the aftermath of Hillsborough, shouldering all that responsibility, and I can remember like it was yesterday the day he resigned, when the pressure of that tragedy took its toll.

I was there the day he won the league with Blackburn at

Anfield and can remember how happy the crowd was that he had won, even if it wasn't our team.

And then all those years he was away, knowing at some point he would come back. I remember when he did come back. Living in Sydney and going out in the early hours to find a pub with other fans where I could celebrate the return of Dalglish.

Today he was knighted by Prince Charles and I can't express how proud I was. Proud of Kenny (Sir Kenny), proud of the club and city he represents. I know there is a school of thought that says he shouldn't accept it, that it's a sell-out. I don't subscribe to that at all.

This is recognition of his achievements and his contribution. Recognition by an establishment that has fucked this city over time and time again. He has broken through that, risen above it and got the recognition.

This is recognition for the city, for Bill Shankly and Bob Paisley who should have been knighted but never were; recognition for the people and their families who suffered and died at Hillsborough. It's recognition for the people who supported them. It's recognition for us all.

Even if this recognition is from an establishment that we don't recognise or respect. It says to me that we have stuck two fingers up to that establishment, we have stuck together, and we have won. That establishment have had to look at us and, however grudgingly, recognise what Liverpool have achieved, and Kenny Dalglish is the symbol of that achievement.

As I was driving home today, I had a very weird moment. I was thinking about Dalglish and that recognition, I was thinking how the next step is the upcoming trial of Dukinfield and the rest and how the fallen at Hillsborough and their brave families will finally get a semblance of justice and how that will lift a weight from the shoulders of the city.

At the precise moment I was thinking about this, I looked at a row of bins lined up on the pavement (it was bin day), and a bin with 96 written on the side was standing there, shouting out at me.

It struck me that this is undoubtedly our year; that this is the year when we have had our recognition, that this is year when we will we get our justice and that this is the year we become champions again.

Of course, that sounds like a jump, and, to be honest, as much as I want us to be Champions, if we have to wait for that then so be it. If this is the year we get recognition and justice, then we should be content.

Thursday 22nd November 2018

Football back this weekend. It's only a fortnight but it seems like forever. Did it always seem to be this long or is that we are riding this crest at the moment and we are just desperate for the next game?

As per usual, I haven't been following the international football. Apparently, both England and Scotland have been promoted ... promoted to where I really don't know. What I have spotted through the week is how well the Liverpool players have played, and while I don't like them playing, risking injury, taking energy from their legs, I am really pleased for them that they are doing so well.

When we look across the international games, I wonder if any other top clubs have as many players at the top of their game. Salah scoring for Egypt, Trent for England, the monster Van Dijk for Holland, as well as Robertson captaining his side to promotion. We should be proud of them all.

The further good news today is Sadio Mané signing a new five contract alongside Bobby and Salah. Players can see the potential and want to play. Bring on Watford for the weekend.

Saturday 24th November 2018

Back on the winning trail. We beat Watford 3-0 away. It's a great win. It's a fist pump win. That's where we are up to at the moment. It's not ecstasy, jumping up and down. It's a fist pump ... job done.

It's a bit early for this. This is only supposed to happen at the 'business end' of the season when all that matters is the result. It's not even bloody December yet. I didn't see the game live. Listened on the radio. They had a good strong team out considering the big game against PSG on Wednesday. Still not playing well. Still not clicking.

The idea that this is a two-horse race kicked in when City scored two early in the game at West Ham and their game was effectively won. To get to half time goalless was a worry.

We were better in the second half, the goal from Sarah eased things and then Trent sealed it five minutes later. Bobby put one in for good measure at the end. Fist pumped. Another three points. Come on.

Chelsea have been beaten for the first time tonight. Spurs beat them. United drew at home to Palace and are now too far off the pace to come back. God knows how I'm going to cope until May if it carries on like this.

Sunday 25th November 2018

Another massive week coming up. Away to PSG on Wednesday night and then the blueshite on Sunday. The season is escalating itself to a level that I can't remember previously. Do we always have so many must-win games?

Another professional performance yesterday. Three goals, three points, clean sheet. The only downside to the day was two yellow cards for Henderson, which means he misses the derby next week. The internet fume is off the scale. I'll only be upset if Milner isn't available next week. He'll be perfect for that game.

It means Hendo can play again in Paris. We need to win that game; it's the need-to-win games where I feel like we have really stepped up over the last couple of seasons. I feel like the squad have the character and the belief over and above any other team who wants to step on the field with them.

Yes, we have all the ability and pace in the world but it's that winning belief that makes the difference. It's not the end of the world if we don't win. It just means we need to beat Napoli at Anfield in a couple of weeks, but it would be good to put this to bed and show the rest of Europe where we are at this season.

I'll talk about the Blueshite later; we've got bigger fish to fry before then.

Wednesday 28th November 2018

Big game tonight. PSG away in the Champions League. It's one of the games to get properly excited about.

Not just a game between two heavyweights but a game that affects whether one of those heavyweights progresses to the last 16. It's not quite last chance saloon, but the result tonight has a massive bearing for both of them.

After defeats to Napoli and Red Star already there is more riding on this for Liverpool than I would have hoped. A win against Red Star would have almost put that through, but now we require a win tonight or against Napoli in a couple of weeks.

This is where we have to prove what a good team we really are. I keep saying Liverpool haven't clicked yet this season, but I've been thinking about that and I'm not sure it's right. It's fair to say we are not attacking with the same fluency as we were last year, but at the same time we are a tighter, stronger, more robust unit and in the league we're unbeaten having only conceded five goals in 13 games. That's some going by any stretch of the imagination.

It's not that we haven't clicked; we're just playing a more controlled and controlling game. We are comfortable within ourselves and if we are not quite playing that gorgeous attacking football that we saw at the second half of last season then so be it as long as we are taking the points and moving closer to the league title.

Tonight is massive. I thought if we won we were through, but the radio is saying that is not quite a mathematical certainty. If we win it certainly puts us out of reach of PSG, but then it's dependent on the other game in the group where Napoli take on Red Star.

Radio also saying Neymar and Mbappe are doubtful after injuries last week. I think that's a load of shit. Toffee as Paisley would say. Whether they play or not, I don't think I would swap them for our front three.

Guessing tonight we see who are real first 11 are. Who he trusts to deliver when the chips are down. I can see the front three supported by Hendo, Milner and Gini. Strong and reliable. Big game!

***

Half time and we've got out of jail a bit there with a Milner penalty at the end. PSG winning 2-1 and have been dominant throughout that half.

The look on Milner's and Henderson's faces before the game told its own story. They were so focused, both in a world of their own ... and some of the tackles Milner has thrown in have been solid to say the least. Both Di Maria and Neymar (he and Mbappe both started of course) have certainly felt it.

PSG had all the half. First fifteen they were all over Liverpool and the goal was inevitable but helped by some lazy Liverpool defending.

From 20 minutes, Liverpool managed to get out of their own half, but the midfield three were solid without providing any ball up front... Salah was isolated and Mané was anonymous. From this point, we had the ball but susceptible to the break, which in the end, came from a combination of Neymar and Mbappe to make it 2-0.

Veratti in the middle has been really dominant, controlling things and bringing the forwards into play, although he was lucky to stay on for a shocking late challenge on Gomez.

At 2-0 we are out the game, thinking about what we can do to resurrect things. Maybe Shaquiri or Keita to provide that link between the middle and front three. But then out of nowhere a penalty; great run from Mané brought down on the edge of the box and Milner converts.

Now were back in it. In with a chance. We've taken all their hits and are still in touch. This is where the character comes in. Stick with the same eleven and see what we can pull out. If we can pull this back, it might even outweigh the fact the Steve Macmanaman ruins every game he commentates on.

***

Full time. Finished 2-1. Better in the second half but can't really think of a chance to score. Buffon plays for them now and he barely had a thing to do in the second half. I think PSG held back, they never really looked like they were looking for a third goal. They were happy to sit back and were organised enough in defence to nullify any threat from us.

Midfield was poor I thought. Too flat, with no one breaking that line forward and feeding in the front three. As solid as they've been, they have played a lot of games already this season and probably need to bring in Keita, Shaqiri and Lallana over the next few games to provide a cut through.

The game was ruined in the end by all the PSG playacting,

but I guess that is their prerogative in the position they are in.

It means we are still in it and it is all down to the last game. With other results, Gary Lineker has just done his best to explain what we need to do to qualify. It was previously to win by two clear goals, but now we can win 1-0 as well. In fact, any win except 2-1. I don't know to be honest. I don't care right now.

We've lost all three away games in the group so if we qualify it's bloody lucky. What I do know is the next game at Anfield is going to be amazing. Nothing short of amazing. It's a cup final. It's everything. We'll have to play better than we did tonight, we'll have to be at the absolute top of our game. Napoli are a good side. What an atmosphere it will be ... one of the great nights in the making.

I nearly missed it. The club dropped the ball with my Napoli ticket last week. It's a long story but on Friday afternoon last week they had sold my ticket (MY ticket) to someone else and the game was sold out. I played hell and managed to get one from them, but until it drops on the mat I won't be happy.

Friday 30th November 2018

Derby weekend. Everton at Anfield. People may think otherwise, but it's the biggest game of the season. When you start your football following life being told that this is the biggest game, it's hard to shake; instinctively this is the biggest game, even when you know that, nowadays, Everton are a mid-table bag of shite not realistically in the same league in the modern game. They are a relic.

There are grown men with kids at school who have never seen Everton win a trophy ... it's literally a generation ago. I can't remember the last time Everton beat Liverpool... There are probably bluenoses out there who have it tattooed on their back.

It's like a cult. Where I grew up it was probably 50/50 blue and red. As I've got older they have disappeared out of my life, when you meet one you feel in some way superior. You can't say it, but you definitely feel it. A little upturn at the corner of your mouth that they don't even know is there. You're a red; he's a blue. You're not crass enough to mention it. You just know it. Inside.

The first one I went to was the one in late 1984; Sharpe scored the goal at the Annie Road end that beat Grobbelaar who was wearing a peak cap. I was distraught. As we walked out the Main Stand, Uncle Arthur told me not to worry, I would see us lose others. It may have been the first time I had seen Liverpool get beat.

At the time, we were European Champions; they were on their way to winning the league. We were the best two teams in the country, probably the two best in Europe. Not like that now. We've been short of that level and they are shite. Nothing but shite.

I don't see any bluenoses anymore. It's a shame I don't get that pleasure to rub in how totally abject they are. Richarlison cost £50m... I'll just throw that in.

Everything I'm hearing on the radio today is how they have the best squad in a while ... more pace, more balance. Silva is keeping his head down but slowly building momentum. He doesn't like the limelight. I didn't realise, I hadn't heard much about Everton so I just assumed they were as shite as ever. Another mid-table side living in the past.

Midnight now, beer and whisky, thinking about the derby. Four p.m. kick-off Sunday. It will be carnage. Madness. I haven't talked about the deterioration of the friendly derby. It's horrendous. The bitterness and fume of the blues fuelled by the indifference and arrogance of the reds.

It's a five-pint match at the weekend, for the entertainment of the masses, they are happy for fifty thousand scousers to get bladdered all afternoon. It will be fucking carnal in there. I could write five hundred words on the midfield and football strategy, but who cares? People will be thinking about blood not strategy.

Interlude 5 – Becoming a Regular

I started to go to more matches in the 1983/84 season and it built from there—always with my Grandad. Probably from the age of six or seven, I used to spend to so much time with him. Sitting on the top deck of the bus, driving round Liverpool, pointing out the buildings he had worked on before the war. Back and forth, back and forth across the Mersey on the ferry, not getting off on the other side because then you had to pay. And, of course, going to the reserve games.

By the time I was ten or so, I started to go to a few more games, mostly cup games, and we would sit in the Kemlyn Road. Not just any old games either—the easiest way in nowadays is in the early rounds of the League Cup. It was none of that, quarter and semi-finals of the European Cup – Benfica, Austria Vienna, Panathanaikos – these were big games, and we always seemed to score four!

The one that really sticks in my mind of the Kemlyn Road matches wasn't a European game but an FA Cup 3rd round game against Newcastle. There was so much hype around that game. Played on a Friday night, it was the first time Liverpool had played Newcastle in the Cup since the final in 1974 and much was made of it. Now, for me, 1974 was a lifetime away, but for the adults it was only ten years and relatively fresh in the mind.

For the Newcastle fans it was revenge and they brought thousands of fans—like I'd never seen before. They filled the whole Anfield Road. Black and White and so noisy. The Kop rise to it and it is the first game I truly remember for the atmosphere in there on the night being anything out of the ordinary. Looking at the records, there were only thirty-three thousand in the ground, but there was definitely an edge.

Before the game, there were so many Newcastle fans in the concourse of the stand—faces painted black and white on many of them. I was there in my bobble hat and scarf and there was a loud, good-natured air of rivalry between the fans.

We battered them. Four nil. One-way traffic by all accounts. Our team, on their way to a treble that season, is like a list of well-known household items: Grobbelaar, Neal, Kennedy, Lawrenson, Nicol, Hansen, Robinson, Lee, Rush, Johnston, and Souness. Whelan was substitute.

Newcastle were led by Kevin Keegan, supported by a young Beardsley and Waddle, with McDermott making a return. They never made an impression. Johnston scored two and set up another. It was more like a demonstration game according to the report.

The newspaper report of the game talks of skirmishes after the game and that was my abiding memory of the night. As we walked down the stairs after the game there was a crowd of Newcastle fans, the same ones we had joked with before the game with the painted faces, waiting for us—an ambush. I remember being scared, watching the Liverpool fans jump into it, shouting.

My Uncle Arthur, in his fifties then I guess, helped me and Grandad into the toilet; then, as the fighting followed us, he bundled us through the streets and the alleyways behind the Kemlyn Road until we ended up crouched in the shadow of the wall, in one of those little courtyard gardens on Skerries Road. Fighting going on all around us. The old couple in the house let us in, they gave Grandad a whisky, as he sat there shaking. It wasn't always like that; in fact, it was never like that, but that night and the painted faces stick in my mind.

At the same time, I was making more regular trips to league games. The old man who sat next to my Grandad in the Main Stand, Joe Gittens, was dying and I got his ticket when he couldn't make it. So started the ritual of going to the game.

I loved the ritual. Get dropped off at Grandad's, watch Football Focus, get picked up by Uncle Arthur and my cousin Alan, a Scouse tearaway who had followed Liverpool all over Europe for the last ten years and had a story for every game. We picked up our Gary, my cousin's husband, on the way and the five of us would go to the game, me sitting in the middle of the back seat of a little Ford Fiesta listening to the chat going on around me. Always football and politics.

This was the time of Thatcherism and specifically of the miners' strike. Sitting in the back of that car was an education in left-wing working-class politics. The talk of the threat of the dole, of shift patterns and overtime, of scabs was a million miles away from home.

At home, we were Conservative. My dad was Conservative, and I think that drove my mum's view too. We had the Daily Express delivered every morning and I would read it cover to cover before school, back to front obviously. We were relatively well off, focussed on our education and going to university from an early age – that was never in doubt – and very much the aspiring Thatcherite family.

The miners' strike was a crunch time. It absorbed the country, which was pretty much at war with itself, much like now with Brexit. Everyone had a side, and no one was for changing. At home, I would watch the news with my dad, who called the miners for everything, cheered on the police and the Nottinghamshire miners for wanting to break the picket lines. Driving to the match, Thatcher was the devil, the police were bastards and the Notts miners were scabs.

It was a confusing situation for a 13-year-old but instruc-

tive. There were never open arguments in the family about it but a brooding disquiet between the two sides. Pretty representative of the country as a whole I guess, especially when it all came to a head.

DECEMBER

Saturday 1st December 2018

Midfield, midfield, midfield. Reading the reports from the press conference yesterday and everyone is talking about the midfield. Not creative enough, not enough attacking fluidity ... as if the football we played through the second half of last season was the same as we played in the first. It wasn't. We weren't good in the first dozen or so games. We got hammered a couple of times ... fours and fives.

Don't people understand he has changed the approach? He has improved the defence and that means providing more security in midfield and that means they can't do everything. After 13 games we have 33 points and are unbeaten. Last season we had 23 points at this stage. Last year we he had scored 25 and conceded 18... A year on it's 26-5.

People want it all ... that's probably harsh. People who watch the game understand. It's the press looking for a story, an easy narrative. Drives me mad.

Sunday 2nd December 2018

Derby day. The gods are conspiring against me, but they shall not prevail. Half four kick-off, which in itself is absolute madness from a public order point of view. The plan had been to get to the pub by about half twelve and go from there, but there is a delay at every turn and it is eroding my drinking time.

I have made all the necessary sacrifices for the game. I've driven to some games, even missed one of the home games in order to get good boy tokens in the bank and I thought I had enough. I thought putting Christmas lights up in the rain last night was the final masterful sacrifice, until I couldn't unknot the lights, snapped the cable and had a little paddy!

So as I leave the house today, having run round this morning doing errands, there is a quiet fume going on in the house. Asking what time the kick-off is and then looking theatrically at the clock as if to emphasise the number of hours I will be away from the family.

I will not let the mind games defeat me. It's like water off a duck's back today. As I left, I said loud and proud, 'I know you don't all really care about the match, but it's the derby, it's the biggest game of the season and it's going to be amazing.' I'll say similar in a fortnight when it's the United game at the same time!!!

So I have conquered the mental and psychological. Now to conquer the physical—actually getting there. Taxi is twenty minutes late. Phone the taxi company, they don't care. He eventually arrives. I know why he's twenty minutes late when I see how bloody slow he is driving.

I tell him I am trying to catch a train that I would have got if he'd been on time. Does that speed him up? Does it buggery. Telling me about QPR winning the league in 1977. No they didn't. He was convinced. Liverpool won the league in 1977, I'm literally writing a book on it!

Get to the station. Train delayed. Of course it is. I should be thankful it's running at all. Check Whatsapp and it looks like the others are having similar issues. It eventually rolls in. Two carriages that look like they date back to the 1970s. Broken Britain!

I think the only consolation is I am now part of a successful

Guinness Book of Records bid to get the most people into a train carriage —we should all be really proud, even the guy next to me with intolerable BO. I can type what I want in front of him as, by the look of it, there is only a remote chance that he can actually read. He stinks though. Really rancid.

It's all part of Derby Day. Can't wait to be in there. The primal nature of the crowd on Derby Day. They used to call it the friendly derby. Holding hands across Stanley Park. I can remember it actually so it's not that long ago. Nothing like that now. Probably since they last won a trophy ... 23 years ago.

The talk is they are playing better. That their manager Silva has put some pace back into the side and they are playing well on a good run of form. Liverpool need to come out fighting. Putting the Paris game behind them and getting on the front foot. The past couple of years have been full-blooded Allardyce type games. There's a chance this one will be less blood and thunder and more passing and movement.

Henderson is out after the red card last week. Midfield looked flat on Wednesday. Needs a different dimension. I am thinking that one of Keita or Shaqiri will play with Milner and Gini behind them. We need something to break their lines, put them on the back foot. Maybe this is the game where Keita announces himself.

Into Lime Street. Jesus, this guy stinks. Come on, Liverpool.

***

Merry Christmas, Everton. We beat the blueshite with a bizarre 96th-minute winner.

I don't quite know where to start. I'm still waiting for someone to call me and tell me the goal was disallowed. What a crazy moment. The place went absolutely berserk. I went berserk but at the same time was looking at the linesman and referee and fourth officials or anyone who was going to say the goal didn't count. I have seen the replay. It was bizarre. Somewhere between Pickford and the cross bar the ball has got loose and Divvy has jumped in.

It's conceivable that will be the last thing Divvy ever does for Liverpool, but he will be forever a legend. I believe Klopp went wild. I haven't seen that yet, too busy looking for someone to disallow it. What a moment.

The game was a good one. Everton played well. You can see a good side with potential in there. At the same time, they never really threatened and were never going to score. Never going to break through our defence. It was a battle in midfield. Gini and Fabinho both played well as did Shaqiri, supporting the front three, but again we lacked the fluidity between the two groups. No service from back to front. Firmino isn't helped by playing behind Salah. It kind of negates his impact.

That's the heavy analysis. The upside is we beat the shite in about the 96th minute with a lucky goal. There's no better type of goal at that stage of the game. The luck overwhelms every rational thought about the fair result. Ha, ha, bollocks to them. We won!

Monday 3rd December 2018

The day after. The inevitable hangover has taken its toll—I accelerated into whisky as the night went on and am feeling it today.

It can't dampen the high from yesterday's win and more importantly how it came about. I have watched the goal a hundred times and still can't figure out what Pickford thought he was doing. The shot from VVD wasn't a shot at all; it was a wild scuffed swing at the ball that ballooned away. The ball was going out—was going to hit the top netting.

At worst, he maybe needed to push the ball backward to ensure it was going out—he wasn't being challenged, he wasn't under pressure. It looks to me as if he has tried to catch it and in the process has brought the ball back into play.

It's a car crash – a slow motion car crash – and it's hilarious. For every derby game I have been to where we have outclassed and outplayed them and battered them, this is the best of the wins. To take it away from them in such an unfair and grotesque way after 96 minutes of play is just priceless.

For the few seconds after the ball went in, the ground was just pandemonium. Everyone just went totally nuts. I have to admit I was looking around a little nonplussed waiting for someone to disallow it, while at the same time jumping on whoever I could find and being jumped on at the same time. I haven't seen such a reaction in ages. Everton plus injury time plus goalkeeping mistake was too potent a combination. We all just went mad.

I didn't realise until last night that Klopp had run on the pitch and the fume that has been created amongst fans and media alike. What nonsense. High drama on that scale and they get prissy about a guy running on the pitch to celebrate. They want to sort their heads out. He's been charged with bringing the game into disrepute today—on the same day that Spurs fans are throwing bananas at black players. There needs to be some sense of scale.

This is where the games come thick and fast now. Burnley away on Wednesday. Don't talk to me about being tired.

Wednesday 5th December 2018

While I'm not generally a fan of the effect of social media on how we follow football, I have to say there are some crackers around following the derby at the weekend. I think my favourite is the Everton fan who has filmed himself in the run-up to the goal, presumably to record the scenes when Everton manage to get a goalless draw.

Focussed on his face, as he holds his phone in front of him, you can see the blue flare going off just behind him (at 0-0!!), you can hear the sarcastic oooh's from the Everton fans as VVD slices the shot from the edge of the area and the aaah's as it bounces off the bar. And then you just hear the crowd go crazy as the goal goes in. His face changes. For a split second, he looks in doubt at his phone, as if the phone is going to tell him the truth in some way. In that moment, he looks lost. That look is priceless.

We move on. There is a full programme of games this midweek, part of the football marathon up to and through Christmas. Half the games were last night—City won again, that is the only result of note and leaves us five points adrift with tonight's away game against Burnley in hand.

Burnley were arguably the team of the season last year, punching far above their weight and qualifying for Europe. This season they seem to have reverted to type, in the relegation zone and struggling, partly caused by the terrible start to the season as they played a long list of Europa Cup qualifying matches.

It's a tough game though. Cold, miserable and raining in the place that God made last. It's the start of four tough games in little over ten days. Bournemouth away at the weekend, Napoli at home in an absolute do-or-die game and United at home next weekend.

There will have to be some rotation in the squad. There were some tired bodies out there against Everton and they were resorting to mental strength to win the game in the end.

Henderson can come back in after suspension; Keita needs to be tried out at some point with a run of games. Fabinho needs a run too. Upfront, it looks like Mané has an injury and Firmino looked spent on Sunday. This is where we need to look to Shaqiri, Sturridge and the hero of the weekend, Origi—clearly on a hot streak.

At the back, it looks like Clyne is completely surplus to requirements, but we need to get some game time for Lovren, Matip and Moreno (please God not together though) to give the first teamers some kind of rest.

***

It was seven changes in all and it brought a 3-1 win against Burnley tonight, coming back from a goal down. I listened to the game in the car. Alexa can do many things but she can only play digital radio, which hasn't any radio commentary so it was into the car to listen to it on good old Radio Merseyside on FM.

First half was slow going, not a lot to report. Liverpool had the best of it but didn't have the cut through. Second half they started better but quickly conceded a goal. Milner pulled one back shortly after, followed by Firmino who had come on as a substitute with Salah.

Shaqiri scored the third in injury time, which was an absolute peach. Just watched it on MOTD. Liverpool defending a corner, Alisson makes an incredible save but fails to clear the ball, which bounces around the Liverpool box. Alisson scoops it up on the touchline and immediately runs to the edge of the box to release Sturridge, gorgeous little dink up to Salah, another one touch across to Shaqiri who hits it first time from the edge of the box. End to end in three touches—beautiful football.

Keita seemed to have some good flashes in midfield. The only downer in the night seems to be Gomez going off on a stretcher in the first half. We don't need to be losing players at this point in the season.

A 3-1 win, another three points keeping us in touch with City, we even pulled a goal back against them tonight. Chelsea got beat, Arsenal and United drew ... lots of dropped points.

Unbeaten after 15 games, 39 points ... that's 2.6 ppg. Bournemouth away next ... need to keep up the momentum.

Thursday 6th December 2018

Something different today. Something I need to write about because it's real and it affects my view of everything, absolutely everything.

Over the past few months my wife has been struggling with a sore shoulder and rib cage. She has been to GPs and got second opinions from other GPs; she has been to see specialists ... muscular skeletal specialists, rheumatoid specialists. She has persisted when they have told her there is nothing wrong; she has been for MRI and CT scans. She has pursued this and become increasingly anxious. She has done this on her own while I have been at work and without worrying the kids, letting them live their carefree life.

Until this week when they found an abnormally large cyst in her ovaries. Until this week when it has become very real. When we reach an absolute crossroads. The possibility of it being cancerous.

She has been beside herself for the past couple of days. Can't think straight. Can't sleep. Can't stop crying, except in front of the kids. She has been helpless, and I have been helpless, waiting for her appointment with the specialist this afternoon.

She has feared the worse, feared that she would die, feared that the kids would be left without her. She's been tortured. And I have tried to be strong, tried to tell her that everything will be OK, tried not to let her see how terrified I have been, thinking I would lose her and the kids would lose their mum.

The specialist at the hospital could see the fear on her face (and probably mine) as we walked in today. And he was marvellous, objective and yet caring at the same time. Talking in detail both dispassionately about the evidence in front of him and with great compassion to the people sitting in front of him.

The evidence suggests that the cyst is benign. He thinks it

isn't a problem. My wife is too scared to take it in; he talks to me in the hope that I can better absorb what he is saying. He is not giving us the all clear, there are more tests to be done, but the evidence is pointing in the right way.

As we drive home, I think about priorities and perspective. I am writing a book (I'm not quite writing a book yet, I'm keeping a diary that may one day become a book) and I am fixating over football players and points per game because it has meant everything to me for the past 40 years.

I am yearning to win the league, something I haven't seen since I was a spotty teenager as if it is the be all and end all. The be all and end all is where I was today, with my wife, holding her hand. This doesn't mean that I'm going to stop writing; it doesn't mean I'm going to care any less about my red men and Klopp and the elusive title. I think I just wanted to stop and remember and record where it sits in the grand scheme of things.

Resume normal service

Saturday 8th December 2018

Match day again. Today it's Bournemouth away. They had a really good start to the season but have fallen off in recent weeks and are firmly mid table.

I thought when I started writing this that I would be covering the ups and downs of the season but so far it's only really been ups and is becoming a little repetitive maybe. Every game is a must-win game and I'm really happy after every win.

The reality is every game is a must-win game at the moment. We have had a record-breaking start to a season – Liverpool's best ever with 12 wins and 3 draws – and most seasons we would find ourselves comfortably at the top of the league, but this year we find ourselves running almost head to head with City who are two points ahead of us. Every time they win, we need to win to keep pace, making sure we are not falling away and dropping into the pack below to contest fourth.

We have been in that group for the last few years and the odd loss is part of being in that pack—just as Chelsea lost to Wolves the other night. If we want to be in that elite race for the title, we can't afford that anymore. We need to win every game, especially when we are playing teams outside the top six.

I think it will be a tough game today, but Bournemouth are a good footballing side so the games are generally open, free flowing and high scoring. We need to get our noses in front—that will make the difference.

It's tough in the context of the run of games too. Everton last Sunday (still laughing!), tough at Burnley mid-week, and then the mammoth challenge of beating Napoli on Tuesday – an all-or-nothing game – and then United at home next weekend. That context demands using the squad to the full making sure we are getting as much out of every player, ensuring they are ready to drop in seamlessly if they haven't been playing regularly.

As I type, my phone has literally just made a trumpet sound and I think, *What the hell is that?* It's the Liverpool team being announced just as I was about to speculate on who is playing. The app I follow (Forza) had sent it through as a 3-4-3 but have changed it to a 4-3-3 mid-sentence.

Fabinho has been put into right back with Trent on the bench. Matip retains centre half in the unfortunate absence of Gomez. No sign of Lovren anywhere. Keita gets another game in midfield next to Milner and Gini (Hendo on the bench). Shaquiri in a front three, Mané on the bench.

It's becoming a strong squad, there are no overt weaknesses in the side and there is a strong bench with lots of attacking option—Sturridge, Origi, Lallana alongside Mané, Trent and Hendo.

The only weak point at the point where I have concern is

centre half. Gomez went off the other night and will be out for six weeks with a fractured leg (fractured doesn't sound as bad as broken). That's a big loss as he has been exceptional alongside VVD this season—sometimes looking the senior of the pair.

My concern is not with the quality of Lovren and Matip, they are both excellent players although not as consistent as Gomez has been. It's more about their inability to get a run of games, one or both always seems to be injured or unwell and that puts pressure on the squad. VVD has played every game so far and, at some point, he is likely going to drop off in form a little or, worse, get injured. He needs to be rotated as much as the rest of the squad as he didn't have the best injury record before joining us.

Where is the opportunity to do that in the next six weeks? Playing Lovren and Matip isn't the end of the world but I am concerned about having them both fit at the same time and if anything happens there is a drop off to the next player.

The positive (there's always a positive) is that Gomez will have had a mid-season rest out of the limelight and will hopefully be able to come back in February for the remainder of the season. We just need to hope we get this vital win on Tuesday and are still in touch with City, so there is all to play for by then.

***

A resounding 4-0 win at Bournemouth earlier today. They said he was a one-season wonder; they said he wouldn't hit the heights again. Today Mo Salah scored a hat-trick and is currently the joint top scorer in the league with 10 goals.

I'm writing this with 20 minutes to go and Chelsea leading by a goal to nil against City in the teatime game. We are currently top of the 'as it stands' league and deserve to be there.

The start we have made is outstanding. In league history (that's all league history not just the Premier League), there are only three better starts to a league season... Spurs in 1960/61 (for the kids, they won the double that season), Chelsea in 04/05 and City last season. It's an outstanding start.

Liverpool were so assured today. A few changes made but were always in control. Salah scored from a rebound in the first half (77 mins... Chelsea 2 City0!!! David Luiz header). Some may say he (Salah) was offside, so he added another two in the second half so no one could complain. His pace and control running onto through balls is outstanding.

A joy to watch ... although for some reason he seemed to have a really serious face on after all three of them. It's a serious business I suppose. The other goal was a rather bizarre own goal from a good Mané cross.

(I am distracted here to be fair ... still 2-0 to Chelsea).

Liverpool played as close to a 442 as I have seen in ages. Gini and Fabinho in the middle, Keita on the left, Shaq on the right. Firmino playing Kenny to Salah's Rush. Milner made the sacrifice and moved to right back.

Liverpool looked in second gear for most of the game. VVD and Matip tidy at the back so not a lot got through. What did get through was stopped by our magnificent man in pink. Alisson is majestic and I think this luminous pink kit adds to the majesty. He looks absolutely enormous... God knows what Shankly would have called him.

At one point he ran out and made a headed clearance, which was nothing short of awesome. Just like they did with Ronaldo's overhead kick in the Champions League last year, they are going to have to stop the frame and measured how high he was in the air when he connected with the ball. I honestly think he was nine feet in the air. It was phenomenal.

Imagine seeing something that size coming at you dressed in shocking pink. I think I am developing a man crush ... another one, I already have one for Klopp, but I think this new one is more based on lust!

Eighty-nine minutes. Still Chelsea winning 2-0. Normally at this stage City would be threatening to score, but although they have most of the ball, they don't look like getting through. It's reminding me of the closing stages of our game at Stamford Bridge, when they were so organised and we couldn't get through ... until a wonder-goal from Sturridge. Into stoppage time now and City would need two of them.

That's it. Full-time and we are top of the league. Where we belong, we have been professional throughout, machine like. Not only are we a point ahead of them, we have taken six goals off the deficit too ... only eight goals in it now. That's a significant gain.

When they interviewed Milner after the game today, they said we were top of the league TEMPORARILY... You can stick that up your arse right now!

Sixteen games, 42 points, 34 scored, just six against. Top of the league. Outstanding. COME ON!!!!

Monday 10th December 2018

Still there, top of the league.

I was thinking about this yesterday as I was walking the dog. I've been buzzing to be top of the league, but I had a think around the whole thing yesterday and I have decided to wait a little before I let this go to my head.

Of course, we should enjoy being there, but now we are in the headwind and City are sitting on our back wheel, ready to strike. We've got a tough few league games coming up. Of our next five games, three are against top six sides, which are going to be tough.

United next week and whatever form they are in, they are always bastards. They are likely to try to nullify the game next week, play for the draw, take out all the sting from the game. And then you just know he's going to bring on Fellaini for the last ten minutes. That's going to be a long, uncomfortable game (potentially).

We've also got Arsenal at home before New Year, who haven't been beaten in over twenty games themselves. First game of the New Year is the head-to-head clash with City.

I think until those games have all been played I'm just going to sit on this top-of-the-league thing. I think I must be out of practice. As a kid I would just take it in my stride, it was always happening, it was where we belonged. For the past few years we have been yearning to get back to the top on a consistent basis.

Now we are there, I'm absolutely terrified we won't be able to hang on. We've got half a bloody season left yet. I'll be old before my time.

Let's wait until we've played 21. See where we are then.

Tuesday 11th December 2018

I say massive a lot, normally as in 'Massive game'—it's my go-to word. There's a point where you can use it too much, where it doesn't mean anything anymore. Tonight is colossal, gargantuan; I'd go so far as to say elephantine.

It's Napoli in the final group game of the Champions League. It's the game that I looked at in September and thought, *I hope there isn't too much riding on that game.* Well there is—at this point in time, it's monumental.

Through poor away performances (in a tough group) we go into tonight's game with our destiny in our own hands, but requiring one of a number of specific results, while at the same time avoiding another set of specific results. We shouldn't be in this position, but we are, so we need to take on the challenge in front of us—it's going to be mass ... err, titanic!

Tonight, we need to win either 1-0 or by two clear goals—2-1, 3-2 is no good to us. It's essentially a repeat of the Olympiakos game to get us out of the group stage in 2005. I have no idea why we need those scores; I have heard talk of head to heads and goal difference but I have no idea really, just what needs to be achieved on the night.

It all assumes that PSG are going to beat Red Star in the other game, which I don't think is nailed on at all. Belgrade is incredibly intense, and the superstars of Paris may well falter. If PSG don't win then it doesn't matter about the score at Anfield—as long as we win.

So excited for the game and the atmosphere in there. The club made a mistake with my ticket, so I am further back in the Kop tonight and due to a few other things happening, I am having to drive when really it's a five-pint match. I've had to make a tactical sacrifice with the alcohol, which has bought me a bigger session at the weekend for the United game.

I say it's a five-pint game, but the heated fervour in the ground on these games can negate the need for alcohol—the atmosphere itself is intoxicating enough. I had to drive to the City game in the Champions League earlier in the year and the advantage is you get to be as raucous as all of those around you and still get to follow and understand the game—though don't be looking for any greater analysis of the game afterwards.

The game is so big becomes it comes at an absolutely pivotal time in the season and also in our wider development. For this season, we have just reached the top of the league and we need to continue the momentum in the short term. Champions League progress brings that momentum, the idea that every game is a big one, every game has to be won.

The alternative tonight if we don't go through is we end up in the Europa League, which I think is worse than crashing out altogether. Europa League brings Thursday night games and the Thursday-Sunday conundrum—no one likes it and without a having a lot of evidence I will brazenly say that it affects our chances in the league enormously.

It affects fans' ability to drink as much before the game on a Sunday, which in turn affects support levels, which in turn reduces the level of performance on the field. The teams in the Europa are difficult to get excited about in the same way, the trophy isn't as good, what else do you want me to say? The Europa is a bad option.

From a longer-term perspective, not qualifying affects our momentum. Last season we broke through, first of all into the group stage then into the knockout phase, and the romance of the club took us through to the final. We are a club who should be in the knockout stages, we enhance the competition by being there, our supporters deserve to be there, they enrich the competition and bring a desire that the other clubs just can't match. To not qualify tonight would be a travesty for the competition and would be a shame for the club and its support.

But we can't just expect to go through based on who we are—we need to go through based on the points we collect and, so far, we haven't collected enough. We've been outstanding at home, PSG in particular was an incredible performance, but have been lacking away from home tactically. We need to ensure we don't repeat that mistake tonight.

***

Talk about living on a knife edge. We've just beat Napoli 1-0 to go through to the knockout stages.

I'm back at the car and just wanted to take a minute to write a few things down. What a ninety minutes of football. Ninety minutes of absolute exhilaration. We had the better of them. We could and should have beat them 4-0 – Mané should have had a hat-trick in the last fifteen minutes – and at the same time the game was tight as anything.

It was two top teams going for it all or nothing. And it ends in the 92nd minute with Alisson saving what should have been a nailed-on goal for Napoli. That's how it looked from our end anyway. What a save. He just made himself huge in front of the guy. The guy must have shit himself. That's the save that kept us in the competition. It was nailed on to knock us out and he was like an imposing giant.

He wasn't the only hero though. VVD is immaculate. He's so in control, so quick, so silky, so ahead of the game. Wijnaldum in midfield was immense. Milner too, but Gini just seemed to be everywhere, stopping things, starting things. He did everything but score and he should have had a couple himself.

Salah was non-stop all game. Getting nothing for much of the game out of Koulibali, he persisted and ran and ran. I thought he'd run himself out. Mané quiet in the first half and got better as the game went on. How he didn't score at least one I'll never know.

We needed a second. Although that didn't matter to them getting a goal, we needed a second to be handily placed for a third. The whole game we were a sloppy pass from letting them in. And while there were a few stray passes they were never getting past the defence. Matip played well too.

It was breathless. I'm breathless now just thinking about it. Adrenaline and high emotion. These are the types of games you wait for. You hate it and love it all the same time. You come away feeling alive. What a feeling.

Fucking hell.

Thursday 13th December 2018

Top of the league and last 16 of the Champions League. I wrote this book to capture the ups and downs of the season, to talk about the agony and the ecstasy of following a football club.

I'm struggling a bit. Where are the downs, where's the agony?

It was an honour to be at that game the other night. I've watched countless games there and I'm not saying it was the greatest game ever (it wasn't), but to see that collection of players, their passion, organisation and delivery, the 50,000-odd people in the stadium were honoured to be there. Even the people who left early.

And while we're on it, what is that all about? Why are people walking out ten minutes early? What's wrong with these people? There's a guy who does it on our row every game. He did it last week at the derby at 0-0 when we're looking for a winner. He missed the greatest (funniest) winner in history. He did it the other night when we are holding out for a win in the Champions League. It's not because he can't cope with the tension, it's because he doesn't want to get caught in traffic or the queue for the bus. What on earth is he thinking?

He's paid £40+ to watch an all-or-nothing game between the top two form sides in all of Europe, which, to be frank, could have gone either way, but either way was going to be an absolutely barnstorming high emotion finish and he walks out to beat the traffic. Sometimes I feel like not letting him past, telling him to sit the fuck down, taking him hostage if necessary. Watch the game, you prick. Unbelievable.

Now we're through, with the draw on Monday, I can look at the options for the draw. I hadn't wanted to jinx it before then. We came second in the group, so we have to play one of the group winners. It's European royalty—Madrid, Barcelona, Munich, Juventus, Dortmund and Porto.

It was a similar story last year, similar line-up. I wanted one of the big teams, I wanted to go to the big grounds and watch us play. At the time, I was still a bit apprehensive about it, that we didn't have the firepower or the experience to progress, so if we were going out, we would go out on a high against one of the giants.

To be honest, I was disappointed when we got Porto even though they were the easiest draw. But then we battered them, and we got momentum and we proved that we could go toe to toe with any of them. That we were up there, and we shouldn't fear who we draw, while they should all be terrified of drawing Liverpool.

This year, I don't care who we get because we will hold our own, compete at whatever level we have to and have as good a chance as anyone.

My dream draw would be Munich. I lived in Munich for a summer when I was at college and it's an incredible city, I went to watch them at the old Olympic stadium, which was a mind-blowing piece of design. Now I want to see them in their new stadium, and despite what I said earlier, I think they are a bit weaker than some of the others.

All the English teams are through to the last 16, which proves the strength of the Premier League at the moment, the same Premier League that we are currently sitting proudly on top of.

Saturday 15th December 2018

What's the first game you look for when the fixtures come out? Its United, isn't it? Yes, you have a scan for the derby, but really United is the game. When are they coming? How long have I got to prepare? When do we need to be on top of our game? Fucking United.

It's tomorrow. And there is excitement and dread in almost equal measure. Maybe not so much dread this year, but, on the other hand, if it's them who pop our balloon and take that top of the league position away from us, then that could be the most dreadful thing ever.

That's how it always is with United. You want to see the game, you want to watch us beat them, but there is always that dread in the back of your mind that they will win. It's always been that way.

I'm looking forward to us beating them tomorrow, looking forward to the feral atmosphere in the ground, but at the same time I'm dreading the thought that they will somehow hold us at bay and then manage to create some way that they beat us. The dread centres around Fellaini; that we somehow give him half a second and he donkeys his way in.

I've been going to United games for 35 years now. I've seen wins, draws and defeats. Ultimately, I've learnt that life goes on, but in the run-up to the game that's forgotten. If we win it will be the best thing ever; if we lose it will be the worst.

City won today, so they are top of the league, but we have that all important game in hand. A game in hand to put us back where we belong, but it's United stopping us. They are bang average at the moment. So many issues riven through the club. They're in trouble. No one knows whether the manager will last another week or another season.

At the same time, we are really moving forward. The squad, the style of play, the determination and professionalism, we are champions in the making and because of that we have everything to lose. That's where the dread comes in. That we could lose it, but, even worse, we could lose it to them. The bastards.

To be more positive, we are beginning to look like we are going to click. At some point, someone is going to get an absolute hiding. That could be tomorrow. Could be.

Sunday 16th December 2018

Match day. On the train into Liverpool for the United game. Nerves.

The nerves need addressing. Three hours of drinking lager at pace should do that. It's a mental time to have the United game. Four p.m. on a Sunday. Just enough time for everyone in the ground to have minimum five pints and fuel themselves up for the annual hate fest.

It's not hate that spills into violence any more. I think we're all past that. It's just a charged atmosphere in there and the bad feeling in the ground is palpable.

I think the nerves today come from having something to lose. For the first time since I don't know when, we are in the ascendancy while they are undoubtedly in the doldrums. But that doesn't mean they can't take our unbeaten table-topping record away from us. If anything, it makes it more likely. That's what I'm feeling anyway. That's the nerves.

I can't bear Mourinho. What a shithouse. In as much as I think Klopp is everything good about football, then this whinging bastard is everything that is bad. It's anti football. It creates bad feeling. It's not what the game is supposed to be about. But he is the one, more than any other, who can squeeze the life and the joy out of a game in the hope of coming away with a point. A dour point. He revels in it. In being the anti-hero. And if he gets his dour point no doubt it will be all about him afterwards. Horrible.

Injuries also create the worry. Matip out for six weeks with a broken collar bone. He'd had a couple of good games and looked like he was going to be a solid enough replacement for Gomez who went out for six weeks a fortnight ago.

We now need to look to Lovren. This isn't a bad thing. He's one of the best central defenders in the world (he said so himself!). The thing with Lovren is he sometimes needs a game to play himself into form. He hasn't had a consistent run since the start of the season and the pressure is on him to have a good game. United targeted Lovren last season. Two goals from Rashford, but it was Lovren who was seen as the weak link against Lukaku.

Trent is also out for a couple of weeks, so we are potentially exposed down that right-hand side. I hear that Clyne is injured but, even when fit, I can't see him getting anywhere near the Liverpool side. I think Milner or Fabinho will be there today. That leaves a space in midfield so we may see a more attacking option in Keita or Shaqiri.

Try to stick it to them. Attack them. Put them on the back foot. I'm only writing this to get myself going. To quell the nerves. Alcohol and aggressive writing. The way forward.

***

One-way traffic. We absolutely battered them. Out of sight. Makes me wonder why I have been so nervous—no need to be, we showed why we were top of the league and they showed why they are struggling. We were imperious; they were a disgrace. Come on, the red men.

Finished 3-1 but was as one-sided as I have seen all season. We were all over them. Better in every department. Our pace and intensity were better throughout and really it should have been a massacre—it was in all but score.

Mané gets one in the first half down at the other end. They had one attack that I can remember in the first half and scored from it—scruffy little goal, don't know what happened there.

Second half, normal service was resumed and we ran all over them, they never laid a glove on us, shit houses, every single one of them. Lukaku sulked for most of the game, probably because playing had stopped him being able to eat for 90 minutes—he's enormous. Fellaini came on at half time, but their team were so anonymous I don't know even know who he came on for; didn't matter, he never got close to influencing the game.

Then Shaqiri comes on and scores two in the last twenty minutes—what an impact from the little man. The crowd love him; he loves the crowd.

We bossed the midfield—this is the game where Fabinho shows himself to be the future of the midfield. Wijnaldum was man of the match for me, the guy just doesn't stop. Milner was out injured and Henderson only on the bench but, even without them, their midfield never came close.

Biggest surprise was Clyne getting a game. I thought he'd been frozen out, done something wrong. He came in from the cold today and played really well given the size of the game and how long he has been missing. It's like an extra man in the squad, up until this point he has been written off as an option. Really positive.

What else to say?? Can wait to see it on *Match of the Day* tonight COME ON, YOU MIGHTY TOP-OF-THE-LEAGUE REDMEN!

Monday 17th December 2018

Sitting in the afterglow of a comprehensive drubbing of Manchester United. It's a good feeling.

I made the fatal mistake of stopping drinking when I got home last night, sat back on the couch for five minutes to quietly revel and rejoice in the win and promptly fell asleep. Out for the count. Woke up three hours later – dehydrated and disorientated – wondering what the hell had happened!!

Been catching up on it all today, matching up the initial impression of the game with reaction and the statistics of the game – the most telling was our 36 shots to their 6 – it really was one-way traffic. They barely laid a glove on us.

Their goal is a bad mistake from Alisson but that's OK because Alisson is our new hero and is easily forgiven—it will never be brought up again, until, of course, we lose a game due to an Alisson mistake and all his past crimes are taken into consideration, but that's not going to happen, not ever!

First time I got a close look at the Mané goal, he takes it so well but it's a wonderful ball in from Fabinho, a piece of delicate precision mixed in with his otherwise marauding display. Is it bad that I haven't mentioned Robertson? Do we just expect these wonders from him every game now? Even Mourinho was heaping praise on him, which says something.

I'm still not going to go mad until after the City game, but we are sitting pretty at the top of the league. 45 points form 17 games, unbeaten and only conceded seven goals. It's still the fourth best start to a league campaign since records began. We are witnessing something here—something big!

The excitement doesn't end there. Champions League Draw today and we got Bayern Munich. The dream tie. Discussing it in the pub before the game yesterday, the unanimous decision was that if we got Bayern we were going and, sure enough, we were the last two names out of the pot.

A flurry of excitement and then the scramble to get the flights. Finding the flights and how quick you can get the details into the screen before they pull the fare and everything goes up. There's no time to be humming and harring about it. Once the dates are announced, it's a question of just looking at the options and going for it. I have already negotiated this as my Christmas present off Ange—she even sent her card details through so I don't even have to ask for the money back. What a lucky man I am—or so she keeps telling me anyway!

Flying out on the Tuesday before the game on Wednesday and then back on the Thursday. As for match tickets, well, that's another question. I will have to remember to be polite to Whaley the ticket monkey.

I'd review the rest of the draw but I don't really care—I'm off to Munich!

Tuesday 18th December 2018

I was a whole seven weeks out, but today was the day the Mourinho got the boot. I thought he wouldn't make it to the end of October and somehow he has managed to hold on, but they have had to let him go—let him go with a £15m payoff!

I have mixed feelings. On the one hand I am sorry to see to him go as every day he was there he was ripping the fabric of the club up more—I would have been happy to see him there indefinitely as it was clear for all to see that the situation was completely unworkable.

He had alienated the senior management who weren't supporting him, he had fallen out with the team who weren't playing for him and he had completely alienated the fan base who just weren't going to support him. It had already become a basket case and every day he was there was going to make it worse. They realised they just had to cut their losses.

On the plus side, it was good that it was Liverpool who dealt the fatal blow, who finally showed up the team at the weekend for the utter mess it had become. Apparently, we hold the record in the Premier League for the team that managers have faced last before being given the boot—11 times in all, it's quite a record.

So now the media circus moves on to who is going to replace him. They have released a statement to say they will replace him with a temporary manager until the end of the season and get a long-term replacement then. At this stage it looks like it will be Solksjaer who gets the gig for the rest of the season; let's see how much late-goal scorer goodwill he gets—twenty years since he was there and the goodwill is ebbing away quickly. Hee, hee.

Today is also the release of the *Guardian* Top 100. I don't know why I'm talking about it here; last year the whole thing really pissed me off, mainly because Firmino didn't even get into it, proving what nonsense the whole thing is.

At the same time, though, I am curious as to who will get in it from our squad following our Champions League run last year. It's a measure of how much our team has improved.

Last year, we had three players in the Top 100. Salah was

22nd, Coutinho was 24th, and Mané was 36th. In addition, Keita and Fabinho made the list, though they were playing for other clubs.

I am intrigued to see who will get in this time round. My guess would be Salah, Mané, Firmino, VVD, Robertson, Henderson and Alisson. Based on how much they have played this year, I think Keita and Fabinho will miss out, but the signs are there that they would be in it if playing regularly.

I also think Oxlade-Chamberlain would have been in had he not been injured. I'm sure Lovren would put himself in there too—he's one of the best central defenders in the world, don't you know.

Today they have released 70–100 and Milner has got in there. I wouldn't have necessarily thought to put him in there, but he has been incredible all year, not the flashiest of players but a solid reliable cog in the team and a potential match winner. To be fair, he was the fulcrum of the team that went to the CL final and for some the first name on the team sheet in that run.

Having seen some of the others in the first thirty, I'm inclined to think the whole Liverpool team should be in there—Wiljnaldum definitely, Trent, Gomez and of course Shaqiri, although I don't think he has done enough quite yet over a prolonged period. I can certainly see us being the Premier League team with the most players. On reflection, I think we'll have eight in all.

My inevitable disappointment with the final results will follow over the coming days, which will then degenerate into basic name calling and abuse at the judges and the selection process—watch this space.

Wednesday 19th December 2018

They have released the next 30 players in the Top 100 this morning. From 70 down to 40. I can feel the bees starting to buzz in my bonnet.

The only Liverpool player in today's list is Alisson at 43. That makes two players in the list so far. Either there are going to be another six players in the top 40 or I'm going to be sorely disappointed!

So far City have seven players listed, Spurs, Arsenal and Chelsea three each. United have a single representative with Lukaku coming in at 41, which is already making a mockery of the whole enterprise.

I have a horrible feeling that Robertson isn't going to get in there, which is disappointing, with Harry Maguire at 79, Kieran Trippier at 72 and Jordan Pickford at 65. There is obviously a bias towards the World Cup this year!

Thursday 20th December 2018

Next 30 players in the *Guardian* Top 100 released today. Three more reds to make five in all. Mané, Firmino and VVD.

Looks like I'm going to be disappointed. Unlikely that Robertson and Lovren are going to be in the Top 10, so it looks like they didn't make the 100. To be honest, I didn't think Lovren would make the list (I think there's probably only Lovren himself who thinks he'll make the list), but the way Robertson has been playing throughout this calendar year, you would think he would get in there. I would certainly put him ahead of Harry Maguire, who is at best an above average central defender.

On this season's form, I think Wijnaldum is also unlucky to miss out. That said, when you look at who's in it, it looks like a list made by bedwetting *Guardian* journalists who only really rate a game and club based on the hospitality provided at half time.

Friday 21st December 2018

Final day of the *Guardian* Top 100. Top 10 revealed and Salah comes in at number five. He's the only one. Lovren misses out (Note – the Lovren thing is a joke, reader). No doubt, as the self-professed best centre back in the world, he will be on to the *Guardian* for a recount.

I think he's been unlucky not to be included in the Top 100, after having played in both the Champions League Final and the World Cup Final (lost both, but that's a side issue). More unlucky is Robertson, who has been world class all year but is unfashionable and I think that counts a lot for the bedwetters at the *Guardian*. Wijnaldum and Trent too.

Klopp must be pleased to have six players in the Top 100, five of which are in the Top 50. It's real progress to have players of that quality in the team. I think more than having them in the side is the others who must all be on the fringes of that Top 100, a squad of 15 really and how they play together, being more than the sum of their parts.

***

Another win and a clean sheet. Good start to the Christmas fixtures as we beat Wolves 2-0 in the Friday night game. Four points clear at the top of the league.

Saying it was unremarkable would be harsh. I think everything this team is doing at the moment is remarkable, if only to make the game look unremarkable. Control—steady, grinding control of the game. Wolves aren't a bad side, they beat Chelsea a fortnight ago, but they never really looked they were competing with Liverpool tonight.

We controlled for the vast majority of the game; they had a 10 minute flurry in the lead up to half time without actually having a meaningful chance, but aside we from that we had the ball and we had the game in front of us. The flamboyance has been replaced by a level of control of a match I haven't seen for many years. Impregnable at the back, dominant in midfield and too many moving parts up front.

Salah was good again tonight. Not just the goal and the assist, it's the constant, incessant work rate to put pressure on their defence throughout the game. They must be physically exhausted and emotionally addled by the end of the game.

VVD got man of the match. He also got his first goal of the season, but it was his serene authority over the game that stood out. There was a moment when I saw him run, but other than that he almost moves in slow motion. He's like Keanu Reeves in *The Matrix*.

I thought Fabinho did well again, from a couple of months ago when everyone was questioning him; he is now putting in solid performances, defensibly solid, while putting in offensive passes that can split a team ... another assist, too, in setting up Salah.

Four points clear. Whatever happens tomorrow we are top at Christmas. Pressure now being on City. What happens to them when it's not going all their way?

Saturday 22nd December 2018

Four fifty-five p.m. They've cracked. They've fucking cracked. City got beat 3-2 at home to Palace. Liverpool won last night and it's the first time any pressure has been put on this team and they have crumbled.

Palace went 3-1 up. I've been out walking the dog listening to the last half hour. All one-way traffic, but they couldn't break through Hodgson's famous two banks of four. I got home before the end of the game and am pacing up and down the garden in the dark. The poor dog's looking at me like I've gone mental. They pulled one back with five to go and I thought Palace would capitulate. But no, they held on.

Four points clear at the top of the league at Christmas. I don't know how I'm going to cope till May. We're not even at the halfway point yet!

Monday 24th December 2018

Christmas Eve. Amongst all the family stuff going on, it's a nice moment to reflect on where we are. When I started writing this, I thought there was going to be a rollercoaster. I thought there was going to be more anguish. Anguish has been in short supply this season so far.

There is a need to create anguish in the absence of real anguish. On Twitter today, I came across a debate about Coutinho and whether Klopp would buy him back if offered. A completely hypothetical situation, created due to a lack of anguish and real things to worry about. Real things to worry about in a football sense that is. The answer to the hypothetical is no, of course he wouldn't. We got £140m for him and have only improved since he left. He's a great player but we have moved forward, moved on.

We continue to win and move forward and it's difficult to write a book and continue to create more and more superlatives. I'm not giving up, this is not me saying I have run out of words, I'm just saying in a normal season there would be far more ups and downs and there would be more words to use, more thoughts to think. As the trajectory is only one way at the moment, my words and thoughts have been cut in half. This is me creating my own anguish now.

We are in the midst of a truly exceptional season. As I only have half the emotional lexicon to deal with, I am going to have to resort to stats to quantify the exceptional. The last resort for anyone.

We are 18 games into the season and have 48 points. We have won 15 games and drawn three (lost none). Against the rest of the league outside the top six, we have played 13 and won them all. We have scored 39 goals and conceded just seven, which is a record in itself. Four points clear of Manchester City and now just five goals behind (from 14 just a fortnight ago). By any standards, this is absolutely exceptional.

The context is a league where the top are breaking clear of the bottom, where the top five are scoring points at an unprecedented rate and the bottom teams are struggling to compete... A gulf has opened up between the haves and have nots. As in society, football is creating its own divide.

Only three times has the leader after 18 games had more than 48 pts (Spurs in 1961, Chelsea in 2006 and City last season). Only once has the 2nd place side had more than 44 points (2012). The team in 3rd has never had more than 42 points and even 4th and 5th have never had more than 37 points (or the two points for a win equivalent) in 119 seasons.

Spurs must be well pissed off. They battered Everton 6-2 at Goodison yesterday and looked like a very strong side. Forty-two points would have them leading 100 times in the past 119 years. Even Chelsea and Arsenal in 4th and 5th would be top of the league in 42 of the past seasons.

Between the top five they have hoovered up all the points from the teams at the bottom. The bottom five teams have a total of 61 points, which is lowest ever after 18 games. To beat these teams has become the norm; to get beat by them is disastrous. Fortunately, we have a 100% record so far.

I've watched some great teams, the Barnes and Beardsley team was the best I've ever seen. In my mind's eye, that team will never be beaten. At the moment, this team is up there with them. That's about the best compliment I can give.

I'm not going further than that at the moment. The lazy media narrative has moved on from 'Not playing as well as last year' to 'but has he won any silverware?' So that's what we need to do now. Win a trophy.

Of all the stats floating round at the moment, there is one that is quite sobering. In the past ten years, the team at the top of the league at Christmas has gone on to win the league. Only twice it hasn't happened and both of them are Liverpool, in 08/09 and then 13/14. So that needs to be the focus now. We need to be in it to win it. It's going to be nerve wracking, but it's going to be worth it.

Libpool, Libpool, top of the league. Merry Christmas.

Tuesday 25th December 2018

Christmas Day. Late now. I have just poured a massive whisky into my prized Waterford hand-cut tumbler (a simple thing of absolute beauty).

With two kids, Christmas Day is a long day. My six-year-old came in at quarter past one this morning to say Santa had been. We managed to put her off till half five when my son came in all excited. It hasn't stopped since then.

Christmas can be a tense time and it has been in the house all morning. Extremely tense, bordering on turning into World War Three at the merest misplaced word. I wasn't holding out much hope, especially with my wife's family about to arrive.

In the end, we had a lovely time. Four hours sitting round a table, eating good food, talking and telling jokes, playing games. It was a wonderful Christmas day in the end, the best I can remember. Just very simple but very heart-warming and memorable.

Its ten o'clock now and all the kids are in bed and all the adults are exhausted and asleep. I'm browsing through Twitter and I find a recurring video of Henderson's party at Anfield for local children. Any other time I would be sceptical of this, but I am seeing more and more of it. Of the team we watch every week who are setting new standards on the field, making a real impression off the field. Hospital visits, school visits, parties for the underprivileged.

I'm going to go out here and say this is about Klopp. This is about Klopp raising the bar about how the team play but also how the club act in a social sense. At this moment I am going to say this is more than PR management, this is an effort for the club to be better people. Klopp is the easy one to get the praise, it could be any one of the team at the club, but Klopp is the figurehead. I'm going to give them the praise anyway because it's Christmas. And I'm a bit pissed and happy.

Wednesday 26th December 2018

The Boxing Day game at Anfield. We tidily put Newcastle away 4-0. What more is there to say?

This team is something special. Without really getting out of first gear against a Newcastle side who had very little to offer, they got to 2-0 and everyone seemed quite happy with the result. We got the win; Newcastle walk away without a serious dent in their goal difference. Lovren blasts one in from ten yards, Salah converts a penalty after he was brought down (the first home penalty for 424 days).

At about this point my watch buzzes, I look and it tells me that City are getting beat by Leicester. The word passes round. City are dropping more points. Other people get the message and pass it round. Within a few seconds, the whole ground knows and erupts into full voice. Liverpool, Liverpool, Liverpool. It's like we've won the league.

The team get the message and proceed to push forward. Another two goals. Shaqiri and then Fabinho. It ends four nil, which is justified based on the gulf between the two teams; Liverpool have quietly put another team to the sword. It's ruthless. It's controlled but it's incessant and it's ruthless. Breaking teams, grinding teams into submission.

City never recovered. They've have lost three games in the last four. They have surrendered a 14-goal difference advantage in a month... We are now level with them. It's not even City who are our closest rivals now. That's Spurs after a 5-0 win.

But at the moment I'm not worried who is in our shadow. I said to a guy as we walked out that we are seeing something special here. It was a bit of an emotional thing to say, a bit wanky I thought as it came out of my mouth. Like I was a *Guardian* writer or something. But he just nodded his head. It's true. Special.

Saturday 29th December 2018

Some context here. I am standing on a train platform at midnight and apart from 90 minutes of football have been drinking solidly all day. (Note – this entry has required some major editing just to make it legible, but I have tried to retain the general thrust of my pissed mind)

Through the first half some football that is as good as anything we have seen for 25 years. Four-one at half time. After they scored it's about the best football you could hope to see. Defensively midfield attacking. Every part. It's an honour.

How dare they have the temerity to score against the mighty Liverpool? How dare they? Very quickly I have elevated myself to the 'how dare they' point.

Today was Arsenal and we battered them 6-1. We absolutely battered them. I was thinking we were in a position that was unrealistic, and we had to be concerned that Arsenal are coming who have been 20 games unbeaten when, in fact, we have torn them apart. That they had the temerity to come to our ground and score a goal is frankly beyond belief.

This piece of work is not about being accepting of our position. Of doffing our cap. This is about being accepting in the moment that we beat this good side. That we weren't just beating them. That we destroyed them.

They scored a goal and it was like a poke in the side just to annoy us. How dare they? Bobby got a couple. Mané chipped in and then Salah got a penalty. It doesn't tell the story. From the point they scored we were about as complete a football team as you have seen.

Today was our Christmas Day out. The lads I have known from school for thirty-plus years. Normally it wouldn't happen on a match day but today it has. Today wasn't supposed to be the focus. But in the end, it turned out that way. What else can we do but marvel at how good this side is?

I'm too pissed to break it down. To work out who had a good game and who didn't. They all did. This is a solid team. A squad. It's formidable.

Monday 31st December 2018

End of the year. New Year approaching. I suppose it's time to reflect on the year and the progress made.

It's been an incredible step forward. From this point last year, where we had a squad coming together, players emerging, excitement being created, we are at a point where we are seeing three years' work coming to fruition, and probably the best Liverpool team since the Barnes team.

This year we went all the way to the Champions League Final, sweeping aside all before us. And after the disappointment of Kiev, we have come straight back and put together a run of results that is unprecedented for this club.

Guardiola said it today... Liverpool are probably the best team in Europe and the world at the moment. He was throwing out some toffee ahead of the City game on Thursday, but on current form he is right, at this moment we are the best.

It could all come crashing down in 2019, the balloon could just pop and we slide down the league as fast as we have climbed to the top. But that is for tomorrow and the days to come. Right now, I am glowing in the reflection of this team who are sweeping aside all before them. They are truly magnificent.

Played 20, won 17 of them, drew the other three. Scored 48 goals, conceded just eight. We have been virtually impregnable since the start of the season. Led by VVD, there is a defensive cohesiveness that I can never remember seeing before.

Combined with that, in recent weeks we have seen the return of the attacking fluency from last year. Salah scoring virtually every game in December (we won all seven games in the month, the first to do that), but now we have the others coming through too. Firmino and Mané, ably supported by Shaqiri, who is undoubtedly the biggest bargain signing of the last ten years.

Individual players have improved—it's difficult to single any one of them out... Trent, Robertson, Wijnaldum, Gomez. The team dynamic has improved, the resilience, the problem solving, and the crushing inevitability of it all.

I feel like I am running out of things to say, of superlatives to describe what I am seeing and the momentum that is being created. You'd think writing about an unbeatable team would be easy, but it's not. Maybe I just shouldn't worry about it and enjoy what I have been waiting thirty years to see again.

Interlude 6 – Season Ticket

Do you know what the last day of the miners' strike was? It's a good quiz question. I do. It is one of those days that is printed indelibly in my mind. It's the 3rd March 1985. A Sunday. I can remember vividly the moment it came to an end. We were all at my cousin's house in Huyton Village.

My Nan was in hospital in Whiston. She was dying. With her at the hospital were my Grandad and her three daughters. The rest of the family had decamped to my cousin's house to wait for the news. It was only ever going to be bad news, Nan had been deteriorating for months, but it was a situation where the whole family gathers together. Uncles, cousins. The only other time we gathered like this was at Christmas – at my Nan's – but the mood now was much more sombre.

Athletics was on the TV; Sergei Bubka was setting new records in the Pole Vault when the news flash came on. The miners had been beaten. It was like another death. It was horrendous. Initially anger in the room. 'Bastards. The bastards.' It quickly turned into quiet disbelief and sadness. One by one, the entire family came into the room to watch and listen to the TV, me perched next to it. Tension. Christ, I can feel it now as I'm writing.

My dad was there. He didn't say anything. He kept his head down. There was a depth of feeling in the room where he knew this wasn't the time to say anything. It wasn't the time to crow. The miners had been out for nearly a year. It would have been a milestone for them to hold out against the massed forces of the state for so long and they had crumbled just before that anniversary. At the time, I didn't understand the significance, but I understood the raw emotion and hurt in that room.

My Nan died the next morning, 4th March. Dalglish's birthday. It's a connection I make every year. After Nan died, I spent more time with my Grandad, staying over at weekends mostly. He was lost without my Nan. She did everything for him and now he was having to look after himself. I'd call him most days and he sounded so sad and empty when he answered the phone. 'Hiya Grandad.' I'd say.

'Hiya Son.' His voice picked up instantly.

I think I was the person who helped him through that sad time. Not in any practical way, just being there for him. We'd chat, mostly about football. He was blinkered when it came to the football. One-track mind. I phoned him after the Heysel tragedy. 'What do you think, Grandad?'

'It was never a penalty.' One-track mind.

Just before the end of the 84/85 season, Joe Gittens, the old man who sat next to Grandad, died. He'd been ill for most of that season and I had used the season ticket most weeks. As was the way, then and now, the ticket was passed to family or friends and I got the ticket. Grandad bought it for me for the 85/86 season and it is my most treasured possession to this day.

There was a running joke at the time that the average age of a season ticket holder was 120. Tickets were passed down. Waiting lists were bypassed and people kept tickets in other people's names. Grandad had his ticket in the name of Robert Clunie since the mid-'60s, bought off a guy who he worked with. He would never have changed his name on the ticket for fear of it being taken away.

All things being equal, I would still be Joe Gittens but for the dreadful events of Heysel and the fire at Bradford that summer, where so many people perished and couldn't be identified.

Liverpool had an amnesty, allowing season tickets to be regis-
tered in the correct names and from the start I had my own sea-
son ticket in my very own name. I was 12, first year of high
school and I was a season ticket holder. That was me, forever.

I always associate that season ticket with the death of my
Nan. Life changed at that point—just a little. While I didn't re-
alise it at the time, it was the start of a series of events that
would bring me ever closer to the football—as both an obses-
sion and an escape.

And what a season to start on this journey. Kenny's first
season. The glorious double winning season. It didn't start like
that. It started under a shadow. Joe Fagan departing in the
wake of Heysel to be replaced by Dalglish as player-manager,
which was almost unheard of. Everton had just won the league
under Howard Kendall and had been deprived of winning the
double by a Norman Whiteside goal in the cup final. Thirty
years of bitterness were about to start with the European ban,
which prevented them having a crack at the European Cup.
Merseyside had the best two teams in the country, but Everton
had the edge.

Just as I was reaching high school, consciousness of local
rivalries, albeit friendly ones, began to take hold. My first game
as a season ticket holder was at home to Arsenal. I still wasn't
allowed to hold my season ticket. Grandad didn't trust me not
to forget it, lose it, or have it pinched. I was given it at the turn-
stile, pulled out the voucher and gave it back to him on the
other side. I wasn't that grown up yet!

The team that day was a continuation of the evolution of the
team that had started under Paisley and had been so dominant
in the early '80s, with a couple of new faces: Grobbelaar, Neal,
Alan Kennedy, Lawrenson, Hansen, Whelan, Molby, Nicol,
Beglin, Rush and Dalglish. Nicol and Beglin were in midfield
that day, but within a couple of months Neal and Kennedy
would move on, Neal bitter about being overlooked for the

manager's job. Nicol and Beglin moved to full back and that would be the team for the rest of that year.

Liverpool won 2-0. Whelan and Nicol scored. I don't remember those details. I do remember the kit though. The first Adidas kit. Beautiful. Even as a kid I loved Adidas (it borders on obsessive as an adult!) and that kit was special. So simple. The crest somehow woven into the fabric and the three stripes on the shoulder. A thing of beauty. Molby wore it best. An absolute giant in the middle, not moving very quickly, but players bouncing off him when he did. What a season that would be. Some would say the best ever. Kenny winning the double on his first go. It ended on a high but coincided with another life-changing event.

JANUARY

Thursday 3rd January 2019

The hyperbole is off the scale. The game tonight is apparently a head to head between the best two teams in the world. It literally doesn't get any better than that.

And who's saying they are the best? The managers of course, but not about their own teams, about the opposition. It's a battle of wits between Klopp and Pep as to who can talk down their team's chances the most, who can dismiss the game and attach the greatest air of unimportance.

Pep started it. Following three defeats in four games and Liverpool's nine-match winning streak, he was keen to heap the pressure of favouritism onto us. Not to be outdone, Klopp has gone back and said that City are still the best despite a recent run of bad form.

And while they throw toffee at each other, the rest of the country is gearing up for an immense game of football. A few weeks back, following City's defeat to Chelsea, I was looking forward to this game as the one we had to hold our nerve to. We couldn't celebrate anything until this game was over and we would get a more realistic view of where we stood.

Since then City have lost twice and we find ourselves seven points clear. We are in a win-win as far as I can see. We can lose obviously, but we are still four points clear. The pressure is taken right off, which will allow us to go at them with all guns blazing. A free hit.

The midfield is a bagful of options. I think he will go for Henderson and Wijnaldum, but the big question is who the third will be. Solidity in the shape of Milner or Fabinho. Attacking options through Keita or Shaqiri. You could realistically perm any three from six and wouldn't be disappointed.

I think one of the thrills for me is that we are the big game. We are the game the whole country is waiting to see. We've been through Arsenal versus United, Chelsea versus whoever. This time it's Liverpool. The team everyone wants to see. Whether they are for or against or just neutral, they want to see my team play. I have had Stoke fans talking to me about the game tonight. They're literally not in the same league, but they all want to be part of it.

That's where it's bigger than the tactics on the field; it's an idea, a dream even. They have elevated themselves in the national consciousness. It's going to be incredible.

***

Half time. I'd say cagey rather than incredible. Incredible still to come. City leading 1-0 through a brilliant Aguero goal on 40 minutes. Smashed it into the near post. Alisson never really had a chance. They stepped it up for the last five minutes, and I'm pleased we got to half time without conceding another.

It's a brilliant game of football. Two quality sides going at it at 100mph. Tackles flying in, four bookings already. Liverpool absorbed all the pressure in the first fifteen minutes and then cut them open with a brilliant move from midfield. Mané hit the post and then a scramble leading to a goal line clearance. Looked like it was in, but only 95% of the ball was over the line. Another 11 mm and it would have been a goal. So bloody close.

City have had the possession, but our midfield is pressing so high, the game is so compact between the back and front line. One mistake from them and we'd be all over their defence, which looks a bit makeshift.

He went for Milner in the end, looking for that midfield solidity. We have that and have sapped their momentum, but I think we need to throw on a more attacking option now. Salah has been coming back into midfield to pick up the ball. We need someone to take the ball forward for him. I would say Shaqiri is the best option.

Don't want to get caught at the back though. Lovren looking like a bit of a liability, booked for a wild challenge and then been burned by Sane a couple of times. Good job VVD is there with his calming influence.

Back out...

***

Well, that's it. Beaten. I know, I know, we are four points clear at the top of the league, but it's like a real kick in the guts. It's a while since we've been beaten in a game, maybe I'm not used to it or don't know how to take it. I'm gutted.

City won 2-1 and overall they probably deserved the win. Bobby headed one in just after the hour and I thought that was our way back in, but we never really came up with another meaningful chance. City snuffed us out. They broke with a counter and Sane scored. After that we just couldn't break them down.

There was a passage with fifteen to go, when we must have put 60 passes together, but it was sterile possession, we couldn't break through their defence. It wasn't so much two banks of four, it was a moving swarm of players, always moving quickly and always knowing exactly where to be to cut off the angle.

To an extent, I don't think we were daring enough with the

ball. We played the safe ball and waited for them to make the mistake.

With the pace we play at, most teams will eventually make a mistake, but these were too good. We needed to attack them more, be more aggressive, more cutting. I think on the night they looked like they wanted it more. After a difficult few weeks for them, that was an impressive performance.

The game was a class above the usual football fare. Not all out attacking, there weren't too many chances, but an absolute master class in tactical awareness and delivery ... from both sides.

No doubt there will be a social media meltdown now, the beginning of the end, the clamour for reinforcements in the transfer window, how we could see it coming, etc. All the shite. I think people need to get some perspective and understand we didn't play badly tonight, we just played a great team and got beat in a very even nip-and-tuck game. Fine margins.

So now to dealing with the loss. Right now, it feels enormous. I don't know whether I was kidding myself into this idea of invincibility. It's not losing a game; it's losing everything we have played for all season.

I know I'm being stupid really. This is about winning the league, not about being unbeatable. Everyone gets beat sometimes and it's about how you come back from that disappointment. City have proved they can do it tonight. It's now up to Liverpool to pick themselves up, dust themselves down and start again.

Friday 3rd January 2019

Thought a lot about the game, the aftermath and our position today and I think my conclusion is I just want to get to the next game.

The game was close last night. A game of few chances and

fine margins, played at a high pace where both sides effectively cancelled each other out and was decided by three outstanding goals. On another day, the same two teams would play out a similar game and we would come out ahead. We missed out on a goal by 11 mm, which boggles the mind. That goes in and the game changes.

We've had a fantastic run of games and in recent weeks have started to hit the heights of last season, only a more solid version of last season. Last night, we didn't hit those heights but at the same time we didn't play badly. We were just beaten by a very good team. That is where it's important to apply perspective.

We are top of the league. Top of the fucking league. Four points clear with 17 games to go. We've played more games against the top six than any of our rivals, just three games left to play against them, two of which are at home. We have got a run of ten games now where the only top six game is United away. Ten games to put together a run.

And that's why I want to get to the next game. To get back on the wagon and begin to put another run of results together. To prove that we can come back from this. To prove that we're champions in the making. We have it right in front of us.

FA Cup third round this weekend. It sounds awful, but I'm struggling to get any interest together for the whole thing. We play Wolves away on Monday night, but I can't seem to get excited about it.

It's the decline of the FA cup. I think it's irreversible. I don't know whether it's an age thing or a decline thing. I could tell you every winner of the FA cup through the '80s but not one from the last 10 years (I could say that of a lot of things to be honest ... living in the past clearly). It's not a thing that sits on the radar. It has become a relic. And as much as the BBC try to talk up the magic of the cup, there is no genuine interest. Certainly not in the way it used to be. The whole enterprise has been undermined and devalued.

The game is an opportunity to play some of the youngsters; more importantly, it's a time we can rest some of the players. Its ten days' rest until the next league game against Brighton, so hopefully some of the key players can rest up.

Transfer news today. Solanke moved to Bournemouth for £17m. It's a good price for an unproven player. He obviously had potential but not enough to get anywhere close to the team. The return of Sturridge and Origi this season has moved him further down the pecking order and it was unlikely he was going to get a game. I thought they might loan him, but if he hasn't been able to make an impression so far, maybe he isn't up to the level we require. Good luck to the lad.

Clyne has also gone out on loan to Bournemouth. Now, a month ago this wouldn't have surprised me at all. I thought he was never going to get near the side again. But then he plays against United and plays well, given we've barely seen him. I thought there might be an opportunity, at least to back up Trent. With Gomez injured and Trent not quite at full pace, I wonder who the backup is. There is always Milner and Fabinho, with Camacho coming through. Maybe it's what Clyne needs; he's a quality player who just needs to get back into the groove.

Monday 7th January 2019

You can stick the magic of the cup up your arse. Knocked out the cup tonight by Wolves in a drab and disjointed game.

It's good to have a squad where you can rotate players in and out and not affect the flow of the team, which we do really well, but when you change eight players at once and the whole shape and dynamic of the side changes then you are always going to struggle.

That's what happened tonight. VVD and Alisson get the night off. Fabinho covers in central defence. Lovren goes off injured after three minutes and we are playing a 16-year-old kid at centre back, assisted by Camacho who thought he was a winger rather than a full back.

Midfield was disjointed. Milner, who is supposed to be the rock, makes mistakes and has no assistance from Keita who was anonymous. Jones had a couple of good touches but couldn't really work out where he was playing. Shaq and Sturridge both poor and apart from a good goal, Origi didn't do much either, although, to be fair, he did keep running.

It was a poor display from what looked like a thrown together team. Roll on Saturday.

Thursday 10th January 2019

Back to the league this weekend and the start of the run-in for the title. Just 17 games left to the end of the season, which will now count down very quickly I'm sure.

We have 54 points, four points clear of City. If they win all their games they can get to 101 points, so our target at the moment is 102. That means we have to win 16 games out of 17 as we stand. That is a big task and there is little room for error.

We come off the back of the defeat to City. That game could have gone either way, there wasn't much in it at all, but the question is how we bounce back for the upcoming games. It's all about the character of the players and the team.

We have played City now, so there won't be any teams as good in the run-in—although they could say exactly the same. There will be tests no doubt, but the key is to be beating the teams outside the top six and so far this season we have a 100% record against them. We have pretty much steamrollered them.

VVD and Alisson were out at the weekend. Rested. But they will no doubt be back against Brighton. The big question is who will play next to them. With Lovren going off injured at the weekend it leaves us without a recognised second centre back and Gomez and Matip are still a few weeks away from fitness.

Does he go out and buy a player? I think not. He tried it with Caulker a couple of years ago, and the lad never got a game other than as a last-minute sub pushed up front to get a late goal (he didn't).

The young lad Hoever was brilliant the other night for a 16-year-old debutant anyway. He looked a real find, but he also looked very young and raw. The assurance that he had bringing the ball out of defence was very quickly offset by him being pushed off the ball and losing possession easily. It's great to know he's there for the future, but he's not ready for the premier league at such a crucial time.

It looks like it will be the midfielders being brought to help out. Fabinho had a good game on Monday at centre back. He is clearly an option. Wijnaldum has also played there before and Henderson sometimes plays so deep he looks like a third centre half anyway.

These are good options who are integrated into the team already and better than buying a short-term replacement who won't get a look-in when Gomez and the rest are back anyway.

But the kick on from that is we lose one of the midfield players. I think Milner needs a bit of a rest to ensure he is fit for the run-in, Keita really hasn't stepped up yet and I don't know whether Lallana will ever be a reliable option again. Ox is back in late Feb apparently, but he won't be able to hit the ground running and we will have to see how the injury might have affected his game.

We are top of the league and we should be enjoying the moment, but now is the time when I seem to be focussing and worrying about squad depth. From having a wealth of players, we seem to be close to bare bones. There is a strong core, but I am worried about the strength in depth once we go beyond that.

We are so close, but the closer we get, the more the anxiety increases. It never used to be like this, did it?

Friday 11th January 2019

Game at the weekend is getting bigger the closer we get. Right through December we had this incredible momentum and looked absolutely unstoppable.

That was brought to a crashing halt against City even if the game was very close and in truth could have gone either way. That's followed by the defeat to Wolves in the cup, which was a massively changed side. But it's another defeat, two in a row, and we desperately need to avoid a third.

I think we need to play – and hopefully to win – just to prove we are still on track, that the last two games haven't interfered with that title winning momentum, that we are still the same team, that we are not a busted flush and that we can get straight back on the bike and carry on going. There is very little room for error and we don't want to make an error and give up this ground at this stage—we need to keep ahead and comfortably ahead.

There are only two competitions left to play now. There are 17 games in the league and as many as we can manage in the Champions League, but seven would be nice. It means we return to a pattern of mostly one game a week for the next month or so—we also get a rest for the 4th round of the cup and there's bound to be a bloody international break in there somewhere.

It means we can get into a nice rhythm where we don't need to worry about rotation. Some will whinge that some players aren't getting a game, but that has to be put to one side as far as I am concerned. From here on in we need the strongest team on the field as often as possible.

Lovren is out, that has been confirmed today, so we are down to one recognised centre back – VVD – possibly the best in the world at the moment but one recognised centre back nonetheless. Fabinho played well there at Wolves and with VVD and Alisson to marshal him, I am not overly concerned.

I think it would be good to give Keita a go at some point soon. We need to see what he can do, see if he can play himself into a run of form so he is another option for the manager. Once he's playing well, then we can use him as impact sub but until he has got that confidence back I feel like we need to be starting him and giving him the freedom to prove himself.

Brighton played well at Anfield as I remember. We got an early goal but couldn't add to it and put the game to bed. My feeling was they were trying to stay in the game as long as possible and threw on the big guns for the last twenty to try to get something out of the game. I also seem to remember an absolutely amazing save from Alisson, which saved the three points near the death.

It's good the game is a Saturday 3 p.m.—no live TV spotlight to shine a light on our need to get back into the groove, just an opportunity to play our game and focus on the result without the media spin.

Saturday 12th January 2019

Back on it. Back on the winning trail. Beat Brighton today with a Salah penalty. One-nil. Professional, controlled, never in doubt. Not the best performance by all accounts but defensively solid, never going to concede a goal and able to defend a slender lead to the final whistle. A game closer to the goal of winning the league—16 to go.

In the shower this morning, I'm thinking about this. I always seem to be thinking about it in the shower. I'm thinking we really need to win and if we don't we are down to a one-point lead, which just isn't enough, and if it goes down that route it's not going to be fun till May. I was in one of them moods. I think it's the wait for a game that causes that mood.

Regular games, regular wins, forward momentum puts me in an altogether more positive mood. First of them was today.

My son's 10th birthday party today. I'm in Flip Out in Chester, which is a God-awful place, with one earbud hanging out my ear listening to the commentary on *Five Live*. I'm actually concentrating on other things and the fact I have an earbud hanging out my ear hasn't gone down well, but I need to be in touch with the game, so it's talking to me in the background.

It's not the most exciting game. Fabinho as expected in central defence. Hendo and Gini in the middle with Shaqiri ahead of them. Front three. It's a quiet first half. 'Tactical battle' they call it on the radio. Radio speak for a shit game.

Second half, it sounds like Liverpool come out faster. Salah wins the penalty and then scores it. Liverpool are tight at the back. First time since March last year that Brighton haven't scored at home. There's a fist pump at the final whistle and the earbud goes in my pocket.

My nerves are settled and I'm looking forward to the next game. We're seven points ahead of City at the moment and they play on Monday, but I'm really not too bothered about that at this stage. This is about us. I'm pleased that we have shown psychological fortitude today. We've shown that we are winners.

Dry January finished this evening on the back of it.

Tuesday 15th January 2019

Bit of a blow today as Trent is ruled out for a month with a knee injury. He had a problem in the warm-up at Brighton but went on to play the game. I assume the two are related.

The pressure and anxiety around our league assault is building at the moment, and it feels like it couldn't have come at a worse time. At a time when everything seems glass half full, my reaction to this is very much glass half empty.

Gomez still out for a couple of weeks. Matip back in training but not match fit. Lovren out for a couple of weeks. Fabinho already covering centre back. We are short in that side of the defence without a doubt.

It's just a week since we let Clyne go to Bournemouth on loan and right now that looks like a short-sighted decision. Clyne hasn't played much, but when he got a game just before Christmas I was surprised at how well he played, and I thought he was going to be a good backup option.

Clyne is an established international (or at least he was) and I'm sure he doesn't want to be a good backup option. He wants to be playing every week and getting back to his old self. I guess he asked Klopp to go on loan and for him it is undoubtedly the best option. For Liverpool now, it potentially looks like a mistake.

It's not as if we are without players. Milner can cover. Fabinho also. We also have Camacho sitting on the sidelines. I can also assume that Clyne was let go because Klopp feels Camacho is ready to step up and in the Wolves game last week he was one of the bright spots. It could be his turn to step up. I think the positive about Klopp is his trust in his players and his ability to bring the best out of them through imparting all of his confidence in them.

We have to trust him. The positive is Trent will have had a month's rest when the Champions League starts again. He'll be fresh as a daisy!

Friday 18th January 2019

Football resumes tomorrow. Home to Crystal Palace. Feel like it's all a bit disjointed. We are only playing Saturday to Saturday, but at the moment I feel like the wait between games is derailing our momentum. Want to play every day and get these

16 games played and won.

It may be disjointed by the shitfight that is Brexit that has dominated the news for two years but has reached a crescendo this week and has ultimately shown the British political system and the people who take part in it not to be fit for purpose. I don't want to get into it here as it has a danger of turning into a rant.

Behind that story and the obscene amount of coverage it has received, the Hillsborough trial has started this week and I think it has gone almost unnoticed in many parts. Not in Liverpool, not to the families and the people who are involved and care deeply and passionately about the outcome, but to the wider population, I don't think this is front of mind.

I have thought about this a lot this week and while at the beginning of the week, I was raging about it, I have calmed down now and think it may be for the best that the trial doesn't start off in the spotlight. The process of justice will be no less vigorous and may benefit from being away from the spotlight of the media and the reaction of social media. There are appeals out there already not to comment as it may affect the outcome.

Its thirty years since Hillsborough. Thirty years and there still hasn't been an acceptable outcome. That those people could be treated like that on the day and their families been treated in the way they have in the years since is beyond belief in a civilised society.

I'm all grown up now and the idea that this could have happened in such recent history absolutely staggers me. While 30 years is a long time to wait for justice, at the same time it feels like yesterday.

At the time, I was 16. Still growing up. Still at school, GCSEs about to happen. Looking back now, I didn't appreciate the severity and enormity of it. This was just something that happened. I think it washed over me, that scale and enormity. I'm sure it did.

It was just one of a number of things that were happening in my life that at the time I took as par for the course but looking back are life changing, largely negative experiences—relatives dying, parents divorcing, family splitting up. It is something a teenager takes in his stride, packing away the psychological baggage to open up later on his journey.

One of the enduring memories of the day was the hug I got off my mum when we got back late that night. I remember that as being a desperate hug. It's the type of hug I would give my son now, when he would be oblivious to the scale of danger he had been in.

It's only as I have got older and watched the progression of the fight for justice over the years that I have begun to appreciate the scale of the tragedy. Last year, I had to go to Anfield for a meeting in the week and I took the opportunity to walk around the new stand and concourse that has been built.

I stopped for a long time at the Hillsborough memorial, looking at it through adult eyes. The thing that struck me was the ages of the victims. So many in their teens and twenties – 'kids' – you don't see that many people of that age at the match now. Where I sit in the Kop, I am surrounded by guys in their 40s and 50s. Such a different experience.

I can close my eyes now and think about the match tomorrow. A normal match just like any other. It's difficult to even imagine that 96 people would not return home from that match. Ninety-six people being crushed to death by a combination of archaic facilities and being treated like animals. And yet, it was only 30 years ago that this could be allowed to happen in our country.

My little boy isn't interested in the football. He's interested in Fortnite and Lego. Part of me wishes he loved the football like I do. I really want to share the joy of this season with him, for him to be as invested and excited as I am. But he's not and actually that's fine.

There would be a point when he wanted to go the match on his own, being all grown up with his mates, and I don't know whether I could stand it. Thinking about that day and that hug that my mum gave me when I got home, I just don't know whether I could do it.

Over the next three months, there will be a process to get justice for those people who died and for the rest of us who survived. I'm not going to do a running commentary on it because that is not what this is about, even though it has the hugest bearing on the club and its people.

In the opening arguments, there have already been suggestions that the fan behaviour was a contributory factor, which makes my blood boil. Leaving that idea hanging there. That idea was firmly put to bed at the inquest. They were just guys going to the match. And some of them never came home.

Saturday 19th January 2019

Crystal Palace at home today.

The next step on the road to winning the league. It's Hodgson, isn't it? Fucking Hodgson. Two banks of four. An absolute fuckwit of a man.

In their quest for mid table mediocrity you really can't tell what you are going to get with them. They struggle and stumble against other mid table sides and then go and beat City at the Etihad over Christmas. So they are no mugs. With all Woy's many years of experience one thing he does know how to do is frustrate an opposition. And with Zaha and probably Benteke playing they also have a threat. A lumbering lopsided threat but a threat nonetheless.

If we can focus on our own game and the way we have professionally taken sides apart this year I would like to think we can brush them aside.

Defensive injuries mean there might be a couple of makeshift selections, but with the preparation that goes into these games by Klopp I am sure each player will look like he was born to play there.

My guess is Milner at right back with Fabinho in central midfield, but I wouldn't be prepared to put money on it. Come on the reds.

***

A win. Another win. We beat Crystal Palace 4-3. Just back in the car and it's bitterly cold. Want to write something down before the rosy glow of another win takes hold and I start waxing lyrical about the reds at the top of the league.

That was horrible. Absolutely horrible. Horrible first half, horrible defending for their goals. Horrible goals by us, spawny goals. Horrible time-wasting tactics by them. Horrible refereeing. Horrible tension. Horrible cold weather. It's a win. It's three points. But they are the horriblest three points we'll get all season. There. I've said it. I can drive home now.

***

A few hours and beers on and I feel a lot more positive about what I have seen today. We won differently today. For five months we have been in almost complete control of games, dictated largely by our defence and ability to keep a clean sheet.

Today was like a game from yesteryear. More chaotic, we didn't have that control in the same way, the defence was shipping goals for fun and the only way to win was going to be to score more goals. We did that today, which was impressive, if a bit unnerving.

We had all the ball in the first half. One-way traffic for half an hour before they pop up and score to leave us a goal down at half time. That bastard Hodgson.

We came out more aggressive in the second half and within a minute we had the equaliser. There is nothing better than a spawny goal sometimes and this was as about as spawny as they get with a deflection to let Salah in, although he did finish it really well, poking it past the keeper.

That is just what the ground needed. We were ignited. It was a second half when no one sat down. Followed up minutes later by Firmino with another deflected goal. I thought we were home but, to be fair to Crystal Palace, they kept pushing and pulled back to 2-2.

We went ahead from a terrible goalkeeping error and then Mané finished it off in extra time, only for them to pull another back at the death. A roller coaster game and that is something we are not used to this season. We have seen Liverpool shut down games, close out the opposition, but Palace just seemed to keep coming.

Milner was sent off for two late challenges on Zaha but that didn't really reflect his game. He seemed to spend the majority of the game standing on the touchline waiting for the ball in attack ... and he got two assists.

Henderson and Fabinho looked good as the midfield pair in a 4231, but the front four looked somehow imbalanced. I think I prefer a 433, but in the current setup the formation seems to leave everyone just out of position. Firmino too deep, Salah isolated and Mané on the wrong side. We won, and we continue to win, so it can't be all bad, but it's just leaving me a bit confused as to how it all fits together.

The fourth player in that line-up today was Keita. He had a poor game I thought. Didn't seem to fit in at all. I was pleased he got a game and am desperate for him to play well and get into form, but he just didn't seem to be on the same wavelength as the rest of the team with the level of desire.

I am disappointed with him so far. He really isn't the player

I thought he was going to be. I thought he was going to be like a bull in a china shop, demanding the ball, dictating the pace of the game, first name on the team sheet.

I realise he has had injuries and that has affected his progress, but he just looked so peripheral today, both in terms of where he was playing and how he was playing. I feel like this isn't his best position. He looks like he needs to be playing further back on the pitch with the game in front of him.

But at the moment, he looks hesitant, not engaged in the game, his body language looks wrong, too nonchalant, and I think he would get lost and overrun if he played in the engine room of the team. He doesn't look in the same game as Hendo and Fabinho.

Pressure back on City now, they play Huddersfield tomorrow to get back to a 4-point gap. In the past few seasons, Liverpool have got better in the second half of the season, that's when the flowing football has appeared. I can only hope that will start soon because the tension today was overwhelming, and I don't know whether I have it in me.

Monday 21st January 2019

A long wait to the next game now. It's the fourth round of the cup this weekend, which we aren't a part of. I'm pretty much fine with that. It gives the lads a chance to regroup, rest and prepare for the final push. I believe they have gone somewhere warm to do that, which is a great idea as it's absolutely freezing and miserable here.

Nonetheless, it leaves us ten days between games. Next game is midweek home game against Leicester. It's part of a full programme of midweek games, which I actually quite enjoy. I think it's that all the teams are playing at the same time and there is a whole selection of moving parts to the evening, following all the results. As opposed to the half dozen kick-off times we have most weekends due to TV commitments.

I think the thing that will sustain me through to then is Klopp's fist pump at the end of the game on Saturday. It was boss. I don't think it's just me who wants him to do this after every game. I think there is a large part of the Kop willing it to happen.

He comes onto the field at the end of every game and gives every player a Klopp hug. I would love to get a Klopp hug. I think more than anything in the world I would just love a Klopp hug. Just once. Just to experience it and then I think I'd be happy. After he's given every one of those lucky bastards a Klopp hug, he generally acknowledges the Kop in some way. Usually just a wave.

Last year, when we beat Hoffenheim to qualify for the Champions League, we got a full-on fist pump celebration. There was clearly a lot in winning that game. As much for him as for us in the crowd watching. Since then we have not had anything full on. The type of thing you see in the videos on YouTube when he was at Dortmund.

But this weekend we did. We got three full on fist pumps followed by a beating of the chest. I for one loved it. The crowd cheers every fist pump but there is a feeling of internal excitement with every one.

A feeling of overcoming an obstacle, of being tested and coming through the other side victorious. It wasn't the best game from Liverpool, wasn't the best defensive performance and on a couple of occasions we looked rocky. But we came through and there was a feeling of relief. You could see that relief in Klopp and that is where the fist pumps have come from. An absolute emotional release.

It had been tense for us poor supporters in the crowd and Klopp was identifying that. That it was OK to be tense, that it had been tough but we had won and we could celebrate. It's him identifying with the crowd and understanding the emotional investment we all have in this endeavour.

The Kop isn't full of kids anymore. The demographic has changed. The people haven't changed. A lot of them are still the same people who were going in the '80s and '90s but those people are a generation older. They have seen us win this thing and they want to see it again and there is a lot of pent-up angst across the group.

But despite being older, Klopp is still an idol to a lot of them. Despite being in their 40s and 50s they are still looking at this guy in the same way we looked at Dalglish 40 years ago, when we were kids.

We are hanging off his every word. Quietly hoping that he is going to come to our end of the ground and acknowledge us and being secretly made up when he does. I think he has the Liverpool fan base in the palm of his hand. Every single of one us willing him on and hoping that he will make us part of the journey.

Or maybe that's just me…

Saturday 26th January 2019

A weekend off for the FA Cup fourth round. Liverpool are away in warmer climes preparing for the game on Wednesday against Leicester.

I've been out tonight but have got back to watch *Match of the Day*. Just enjoyed watching Everton getting knocked out in extra time to Millwall. It's not just getting knocked out; it's getting knocked out by a blatant handball. For some reason there is no VAR at the game despite it being on live TV, and they have missed the worst handball goal you have ever seen.

The fume on Twitter is magical. Looks like Silva is on his last legs.

Tuesday 29th January 2019

Get. The. Fuck. In.

City have bottled it again. They've been beaten and leave us with the chance to go seven points clear tomorrow night.

There is a full programme of games tonight and tomorrow. City had to go first and were away to Newcastle. Twenty-four seconds and they were a goal up. Newcastle are struggling, can't get a win, a good bet for relegation. It was a foregone conclusion.

But they have got back into the game and then won it with a penalty. It's a great result for them, a great result for Rafa, but right now it's an incredible result for us. When we are looking at 15 games to the end of the season and thinking that City can win every one of them, this is a massive boost.

Focus switches to tomorrow night at Anfield and the game against Leicester. It's all very well City getting beat (it's better than that to be fair), but Liverpool have to win their game to go seven points clear.

With all the changes to the scheduling for the TV, there will be a lot of this in weeks to come. City are going to play seven out of the next eight games before Liverpool, which gives them a perceived advantage every week, through the pressure it supposedly piles onto Liverpool after a City win. I think that's a load of shit at the best of times but certainly will be if we can draw seven clear.

There's going to be pressure on every game here on in and for every game the level of pressure will ratchet up a little bit further. Not just pressure from City but pressure from the weight of expectation that every fan is putting on the team. Do they feel it, though, or are they sitting in this little bubble where they are not exposed to the anxiety and tension as it builds?

They've been away for a week in Dubai recharging their batteries, so hopefully they are fully charged and ready to go.

There hasn't been much news out of the camp, until a scare went around yesterday that VVD has been unwell and a doubt.

Now, I don't want to suggest for a single minute that we are heavily dependent on Virgil and we would collapse without him, but the idea of a return to the days of Lovren and Matip when we have a chance to go further doesn't fill me with anything but dread!

Wednesday 30th January 2019

Lovren fit again apparently after his latest injury. We need him because Gomez is out indefinitely at the last report with complications around his fractured leg. Trent out too, and with Milner getting sent off in the last game we are short of options for right back. It will likely be Fabinho there tomorrow; his flexibility is preferred to Camacho who is on the bench.

I think the most interesting thing tonight is Keita being moved back into the two in midfield. This is his chance. We all want him to do well and are finding excuses for him when he doesn't perform. Well, tonight there are no excuses, lad. This is your chance to shine.

Cold tonight. Hat, coat, gloves on. Let's do this!

***

Five points clear at the top of the league, but right now I'm so disappointed. A one-all draw with Leicester tonight and although we are in a better position than we were yesterday, we didn't take full advantage tonight to get the win.

Right up to the last minute, with the way things have been going recently, I was convinced we were going to sneak a goal, but in truth it never looked like coming. In truth, we conceded so many chances at the back and got away with it so many times, Leicester were probably disappointed they didn't get more out of the game, despite all the possession we had.

Overall, I guess a draw is fair. It's the first time we have dropped any points against teams outside the top six this season, which is an incredible record. I am going to games at the moment confident that we are going to win, expecting the team to perform at a level where we take all the points and I think, at the moment, I'm just so disappointed that we haven't lived up to that tonight.

City lost yesterday; we drew tonight. We are a point up in the deal but can't shake those two missing points out of my mind. City play before us for about the next six weeks so that is a psychological barrier we all need to get over.

The pitch looked very wet tonight; the players seemed to be tottering around unable to keep their feet. I had just said that it would be difficult to score to my mate next to me when we scored. Mané slotted one in and the whole stadium was on a high, feeling we were on our way to the win everyone wanted so much.

After that, the chances were few and far between, for Liverpool at least. For what seemed like most of the half, we passed the ball across the defence with the occasional probing pass forward, all as if both teams were happy to play it out at 1-0. Then they had a couple of chances, good chances too, let-offs for Liverpool.

When their goal came, there was a feeling of inevitability about it. Silly free kick to concede from Robertson on the left and the defence totally caught out by a ball over the top.

Second half we couldn't seem to get it together. Henderson ended up playing at right back, but we missed him in the middle. Gini had a good game but wasn't assisted enough by Keita who for the most part looks too timid. He had a better game than the last one from a deeper position, but he really didn't impose himself and looked peripheral for most of the game.

He was unlucky not to get a penalty in the second half. It

was right in front of us; the defender caught him when he was through on goal. It looked nailed on, but the referee waved it away. What I don't understand is if it wasn't a penalty, then the referee obviously thought that Keita had dived ... so why wasn't he booked? For me it was a stonewall penalty, which would have changed the game completely.

He went off in the end for Fabinho and from that point Wijnaldum had a stronger partner and we began to dominate the game in midfield. Henderson stayed out at right back and was targeted by them when they played on the break. They created some great chances and really should have scored.

I thought they were incredibly organised and hard to break down. When they did break, they only seemed to break with two or three players and the rest of the team were very disciplined and retained their shape.

Salah didn't get a look-in; Bobby had some of the ball but was crowded out quickly by their defensive organisation. Shaqiri didn't make much of an impact either. Lallanna came on with Fabinho but didn't really change things.

A lot of it comes down to being short at right back. We had to sacrifice Henderson tonight and he would have had a greater influence on the game in midfield. It's a weakness for us and the loaning out of Clyne looks like a mistake at the moment. He has been loaned out and Camacho isn't ready to come in so we are exposed, which in turn is leading to the sacrifice of our strongest midfield player. Trent needs to get back, Milner will be back after suspension, but we are still exposed in that area.

I will just have to be content with the five-point lead... What a spoilt bastard I am!

Interlude 7 - The Double

It is without doubt the best day of my teenage years. 10th May 1986 is burned into my memory. It was the day of the FA Cup final, where we beat Everton to win the League and Cup Double in the first ever all-Merseyside final. At the time, it was about the pinnacle of domestic football to win the double. Only two teams had ever achieved it before—Spurs in 1961 under Bill Nicholson and then Arsenal 10 years later under Bertie Mee, both well before my time.

Liverpool had won all manner of doubles in the previous 15 years, the league alongside the UEFA Cup, then the European Cup and the League and League Cup double had become a regular occurrence in the early eighties. We even had a treble under our belt, in 1984 winning the League, League Cup and then the European Cup in Rome.

But 'the double' had a sense of mystery and romance about it. Before the league became the hyper commercialised Premier League and the Cup was a valued competition, not seen as a run-out for second teams and a try-out for promising youth players. 'The Double' was a serious achievement.

But as we were in the midst of winning the double, at home we were going through a life-defining upheaval. The week is burned into my mind for more reasons than just a day out at Wembley. When I have boiled it down, it was the week that drew me to the football more than any other, where football became my saviour, in the same way it is now.

It was the end of my first year as a season ticket holder, going along to all the games with Grandad (what a season to start!). I was thirteen, second year of high school, one of the more able kids in school and hard working. Outside of school, I was a swimmer and would be training just about every night after school, as well as occasional mornings. And, of course, football at Anfield every other weekend.

Dad had been working for a couple of years as captain of the cross-channel ferry to the Channel Islands, a high profile and well-paid job that saw him working alternate fortnights. He would be away for two weeks, when my mum would manage everything at home, including my 10-year-old twin sisters, and then we would have him home for two weeks, where we would get loads of time with him, picking us up from school, going out to pubs with great beer gardens, taking me to play golf.

From the outside, and as a kid, it seemed that we had the ideal set-up. My mum idolised my dad and ensured that everything was being managed in the two weeks he was away, so he could relax when he was home. You'd put it in the realms of domestic bliss. And then it all changed, literally overnight.

The weekend before the cup final we were in Morecambe. My sisters used to do dancing competitions and every May Bank Holiday week, they would go and stay in a B&B for a week and take part in competitions at the end of the pier. When Dad was working away, I would go and stay too, but this year he was home and we had the week at home, driving up on the Saturday to watch the girls.

As we drove up the M6 that morning, we started talking about cars and which one we should get next. We always had a new car, a sensible family car, but a nice one—he liked Vauxhalls and at the time we had a sporty Cavalier. He asked what I thought of an Opel Manta, which was like a sports coupe. I said, 'It's very nice but not very practical, we wouldn't all be able to fit in it, would we? We would need something bigger.'

Then he suggested a Chevette, the small model in the Vauxhall range. Even at 13, I thought this was a bit of a come down. I remember thinking they were strange suggestions, but we left it there.

That afternoon, Liverpool won the league. We beat Chelsea 1-0. Dalglish with that goal that everyone has seen a million times, his arms raised and that fantastic smile. It put us clear and out of sight of West Ham in second and Everton in third, who were both still in a with a shout as the games kicked off that day. They would play each other on the Monday, Everton winning to finish the season as runners up.

Two days later, Bank Holiday Monday, the final of the snooker was on TV. We were all home, playing out in the road in the evening. We got called in and could see that Mum was upset. And then it happened, he just announced he was leaving. Just like that, out of the blue. No arguments, no fighting, no tension, just leaving. Everything changed in that moment. Not that you realise that at the time, not that you fully understand the implications, but everything changed.

I remember being up in my room with my mum. I was upset, and she was consoling me, although looking back I was probably consoling her too. He poked his head in the door. 'Just to let you know Joe Johnson won the snooker.' It was his effort to make everything seem normal, he was way off target. I have a strong recollection of him saying to me, 'One day you'll understand,' the inference being it was something to do with my mum, but I don't know whether it was that night he said it. I didn't think I'd ever understand.

Fast forward a week and it's the FA Cup Final. The local hype was off the scale. Liverpool and Everton, first and second in the league, the best two teams in the country from a city that had in many ways been written off by the government of the day. This was a city sticking two fingers up to that government, a mass exodus of Scousers travelling down to Wembley for the final. All travelling together, all coming together as one.

I had a ticket. It was £6 standing up behind the goal. Uncle Arthur got one, too, but Grandad didn't qualify. It used to be the last digit of the serial number on your season ticket that dictated whether you got a ticket or not. For all these games that number rotated and Grandad had missed out.

And in an act of unbelievable kindness, Arthur let him have his ticket. He said that this was the first Merseyside final and probably the last in Grandad's lifetime, so he should have the ticket. That was Arthur all over, one of life's good people, a lovely, kind human being. He even took us to the coach at Hunts Cross and I can picture him now, stood on top one of the bridges over the M62 in his 'lucky blue gansey', waving us off.

I had been sworn to secrecy about the situation at home, wasn't to let anyone know, particularly my Grandad. I think my mum was ashamed of what had happened, even though it wasn't of her doing. I don't know whether she thought she could resolve things and he would come home before anyone found out, so I wasn't to say a word

My cousin Alan looked after me on my first trip to Wembley. Our Alan was a tearaway and had spent his late teen years bunking on trains all across Europe to follow the reds through the late '70s and '80s. Our Alan knew every trick in the book.

When we got there, he took me all around the ground. If you've ever seen that footage of the lads swinging from the towers, trying to get through the window, I was stood underneath watching it live. A few minutes later, everyone started humming. I didn't know what was going on until Alan told me it was to mask the noise of one of the gates being kicked in.

We had tickets in different sections, but he worked it so we were standing together, told me where to stand relative to the bar, so I didn't get crushed, and generally kept his eye on me.

I'd never been in anything like it. The constant movement and swaying, the singing, the smell of the stale beer and sweat. He said it was just like standing in the middle of the Kop.

I don't even have to look up the team for the day—it's imprinted in my mind: Grobbelaar, Nicol, Lawrenson Hansen, Beglin, Molby, Whelan, Johnston, Macdonald, Dalglish and Rush. Steve McMahon was on the bench. Gary Lineker scored to put them 1-0 up at half time. Rush scored in the second half and a woman next to me told me, 'When Rush scores, we never lose.' From that point it was nailed on. Johnston got the next and then Rush finished it off, smashing all the cameras behind the goal.

After the game we were back on the coach when Grandad, who had cut quite a glum figure since Nan died, came skipping through the car park. The look on his face was a picture. It was a boss day all round—the best.

My dad moved out and into a flat in Cheshire somewhere. From that day, I pretty much cut him out of my life, for a few years at least, and the damage done on that night has affected our relationship to this day. He destroyed my mum and undermined every relationship in the house, which disintegrated over the next few years. My sisters went out with him every weekend, bowling or the park or McDonald's. I never did. Never wanted to. He gave me the responsibility of looking after my mum, not explicitly, but that's what happened. I made up my mind very quickly that I hated him and would do without him.

He'd met someone else who worked on his ship, had been at it with her on his two-week rotations. Fifteen years younger, classic midlife crisis I thought, until I found out later that he had been at it with a string of other women, including the bloody neighbours! He sold the family car straight away, got himself the Manta, got us an old Chevette (which mum kicked off about and traded up to an old Astra). His new life without us was already all planned out.

But he was gone, and at almost the same time I had found a new level of football experience and I kind of transferred my allegiance from one to the other. I didn't need him anyway, I had the football.

FEBRUARY

Friday 1st February 2019

Friday afternoon and thoughts turn to football. Thoughts haven't actually turned away from football since the end of the game of Wednesday, but I have to live a functioning life elsewhere with work and family commitments, so thoughts turn to writing down my thoughts is probably a more accurate description.

My thoughts are we have been spoiled by the incredible football and run of results we have had so far this season and to be peevish about two dropped points against another Premier League side who are mid table, organised with some good players, is probably a bit arrogant and unfair.

Liverpool didn't play badly the other night; they just didn't quite click and didn't get the run of the ball. Even into injury time I was thinking to myself, *Well, we got one against Everton,* but in reality that is unrealistic. We did get lucky against Everton, wonderfully lucky, but the law of averages says we only do that so many times.

We currently have 61 points from 24 games. That's over 2.5 points per game. Before Wednesday, we hadn't dropped a point to anyone outside the top five teams (that includes United!). Not a single point dropped. That is not just good, it's bloody freakish and we can't do it forever. We'd like to think we can, but no team can continue at that rate. Even the Arsenal Invincible side

217

drew about 12 of their games (I say this because the feeling and reaction since was that we had got beat—we didn't, we got a draw in poor conditions).

I think we have got used to winning as the norm and, if anything, dropping a couple of points at home could be a good wake-up call against complacency. I'm going to stop looking at social media I think. Gobshites on there with enormous overreactions about players and not being able to cope until the end of the season—it's a game at the end of the day, and, as much as we all love that game, I think we need to get perspective. (This is me writing two days after the game about perspective it should be noted!)

The negative talk is about Sturridge and Lallana. And while I agree they didn't improve things the other night, the reaction to be them being played is so OTT. At the beginning of the season, Sturridge was like a new player—a player reborn who was going to be our secret weapon, challenging the existing front three, bringing a new dimension to our attack. Everyone bought into that. Everyone wanted him to stay. And if anyone wants to think back to the wonder goal that saved us a point at Chelsea in the early days of the season, we were all very much on the Sturridge bandwagon.

Since then he has hardly had a run. The front three, supported by Shaqiri, are very much in place and there isn't the opportunity for Sturridge to get a game. My concern is the front three have been overplayed and we will suffer for it at the end of the season and Sturridge should have been given more of a run. To throw him on last 15 and continually expect him to do something is actually unfair on the lad (I think Sturridge is great!).

Lallana is a different story. Three years ago, he was pivotal in that team, he was that player that was leading the press and the embodiment of the Klopp tactics—intelligent, skilful and committed. But he has been so unlucky with injuries and in the time he has suffered, the team has evolved and moved forward. If he had remained fit, there is a good chance that he would have remained firmly part of the picture – in the same way that Milner has – and as new players came in he would have retained his place, or at least been part of the rotation pattern.

But with injuries, he has been unreliable and has never been able to get back to the level he needs to be, and because of that he can't get in the team. I was going to say it's Catch 22, but I have just finished reading (listening to the audiobook of) *Catch 22* and I don't think that's actually a good example of the definition; let's say Chicken and Egg.

People are asking why we haven't sold him. I would say as part of Klopp's ongoing evolution, he has gradually upgraded players rather than wholesale change and Lallana is pretty much at the front of the queue to be upgraded in the summer. But, in the meantime, he is an option as substitute, understands the Klopp way of working and is probably a good addition to the squad, probably more for his experience than his playing ability at the moment.

The person who has been moved on in the transfer window is the forgotten man, Lazar Markovic. You always just forget he is still there—I was amazed in the summer when he popped up again and even more amazed when he wasn't sold again. He was going to be the next Ronaldo, so they said. Flashes of a good player but somehow never cut it under Rodgers and clearly didn't impress Klopp or any of the half dozen clubs he played for on loan in the meantime. Good luck to the lad at Fulham—looks like he's on a hiding to nothing there!!

Monday 4th February 2019

Liverpool playing the Monday night game this week. Everyone else has played and, like last week, I feel a little bit like the pressure is on to keep ahead of the pack. City beat Arsenal yesterday. Chelsea, Spurs and United all won. We are two points clear of City with tonight's game in hand.

There is a narrative being built that we are nervy. It comes following the draw to Leicester last week so it's hardly the end of the world, but the media are building the story and the fan base is getting worried. Thirty years of not winning does that to you.

Team announced and both Henderson and Wijnaldum are out, not even on the bench, so I am assuming they are injured. With Milner back into the team at right back, Fabinho and Keita are in the midfield alongside Lallana.

At the beginning of the season, Fabinho and Keita would have been seen as the golden ticket but at the moment they are very much unproven. As for Lallana, this could be a chance to impress and get some confidence back in a midfield three. Time to dig in, I think.

***

Half time and it's 1-1. Despite a lot of possession, I think it's fair to say we have ridden our luck there. We have gone back to 433 with Lallana in midfield. Mané scored first after great work by Lallana on the right wing. He released Milner who was clearly offside. Massive mistake by the linesman, but he cut the ball back to Mané who finished well.

Liverpool seemed to settle down after the goal and I thought another would come but there has been some shocking defending from their free kicks. They scored off the first one and could have had another two in quick succession. For some reason we have been pushing the defensive line so high and, on each occasion, West Ham have broken the line. The last one, just before half time, was awful defending and the lad really should have scored.

I am willing Keita to play well, but he just doesn't seem to want to. He seems so timid and lackadaisical. Fabinho is dominant and doing his best to boss the midfield but isn't getting the support he needs. Lallana is flitting about as he does and he's had some good moments, but the power and drive you want to see from Keita just isn't coming. Henderson and Wijnaldum both injured. We are missing them.

***

Bloody hell. One-one. Another two points dropped. City just two points behind now. West Ham organised just like Leicester like week. I can't really remember us having a chance to score. Couldn't break them down. Didn't really deserve any more out of the game. Origi has a chance to score with the last kick of the game. I guess there are only so many times you can do that.

Keita looked a little better towards the end of the game but still not doing enough. Firmino not impressing and was brought off. Salah barely made an impression. Again, it was Mané who looked our best option but just couldn't find the space in an organised defence.

TV pundits starting to talk about the bubble bursting. I'm going to have to switch it off.

Wednesday 6th February 2019

Just 13 games to go. It's not far off at all. I was disappointed after the game on Monday that we had dropped to just three points ahead at the top of the league. 'Just' three points. Spoilt and unrealistic, that's what I am becoming.

If you would have asked me at the beginning of the season whether I would be happy with a three-point lead going into the last third of the season, with 62 points from 25 games, you can imagine what my answer would have been. Of course I would. Wouldn't anyone?

But now we have dropped points to the 'other' clubs the perception has changed. From having the chance to be seven points clear this time last week, we have now dropped to three.

I think all of our expectations have become unrealistic. The run we have been on has been freakish. The law of averages dictates it couldn't go on, but the expectation is such that anything less than a win is not good enough.

The next game is key to us. Home to Bournemouth at the weekend. They play a more expansive and attractive game and that might be an advantage. I don't think they have the desire or the capability to play the organised defensive structure we have seen from Leicester and West Ham in the last few days. More tellingly, I don't think Eddie Howe has the same ability to be as tight as Puel and Pelligrino.

The narrative has changed. In the game the other night, the commentators talked about the incessant push from City, seemingly forgetting they got beat by relegation threatened Newcastle less than a week before.

Memories are short in football and the story that fits at the moment is Liverpool are tottering and City are in pursuit. I prefer to think it's a blip, a couple of games where we have struggled as we prepare for the Champions League and the title run-in. Better to come now than in ten games' time.

Tonight, City play Everton. It's rearranged in advance due to City playing in the League Cup final in a couple of weeks. If they win, they go top on goal difference. I'm sure they will; Everton are shite! They have been interviewing bluenoses in Liverpool today and most them want their own team to get beat. Bitter bastards.

Thursday 7th February 2019

Sure enough, Everton got beat by City last night. Photos going around of their fans cheering when City scored. How bad can it be when you are doing that?

The latest one going around tonight is if you type 'define woe' into Google, the following comes up. It's priceless.

woe

/wəʊ/Submit

nounLITERARY

great sorrow or distress (often used hyperbolically).

'the Everton tale of woe continued'

The result of last night's game is City go to the top of the league on goal difference. It's certainly a topsy turvy league. Only a week ago, we were going to watch Liverpool with the chance of going seven points clear.

The game in hand will be played in a couple of weeks against United. After being in all sorts of trouble under Mourinho, they are currently 10 games unbeaten under Solskjaer and are the form side in the league, so it will be a high stakes game to regain top spot.

Before that there is Bournemouth and a chance to regain our winning ways and try to relieve the pressure that is slowly but surely building.

Saturday 9th February 2019

I think it must be paranoia. That must be what I'm suffering from. Everyone is against the reds; everyone else wants them to fail.

The media narrative is such that you would think the club has imploded and we hadn't won a game all season. TV montages with a cracked glass filter. Slow motion footage of players and fans with head in hands. Crisis in big red letters. Sky Sports really do just pander to the lowest common denominator. Everything sensationalised. Everything is a story.

Twenty-five games into the season. One defeat and just five draws, three of which are against direct rivals ... away from home. The current 'crisis' stems from two draws in the last week against mid table teams who have the best record against the top six. It's not a crisis.

Bournemouth today and while on the one hand I'm saying it's not a crisis, on the other hand we really do need to win today to regain the confidence and momentum. It looks like Henderson and Wijnaldum are both fit and bringing them back will add a bit of steel and dynamism to the team. The forward thrust and aggression that I think we were missing against West Ham in the last game. I wouldn't mind seeing Lallana in the midfield with them two. A bit of imagination and creativity to add to the power. See if that can better unlock the front three.

Lallana has had a lot of stick recently, but I don't think he has had enough time on the field to get into a rhythm. He's been so unlucky with injury, but when you go back to the last time he got a run in the side, he was almost the missing ingredient in midfield. Leading the press, unlocking tight situations. With defences sitting deep at the moment and starving Salah and Firmino of the ball it may be Lallana who can create the space ... as long as he has the energy and power of Hendo and Gini to support him.

**

Back to winning ways. Back to what has become normality.

We beat Bournemouth 3-0 and I have to say we were excellent. Never looked in doubt. The flow had returned to the team, the so-called nervousness not on show at all.

The front three were excellent. They had returned to a front three in a 433 rather than the 4231 we have seen in recent weeks and looked far more in tune with each other. The defence were rock solid. Milner at right back for most of the game and then replaced by Trent to see out the game. He looked strong when he came on and could have scored.

The big difference was in the midfield and for me it was the return of Wijnaldum that made the difference. He turns the game over so quickly and effectively that he makes the rest of the midfield look better and in turn brings the front three back into play. He was excellent, even scoring a beautiful lobbed goal that left their keeper looking completely lost in no-man's-land. Pushing up to support the front three he had other chances too, but his ability to recycle the ball and move it on quickly sets up opportunities for others to finish.

Fabinho was solid at the base of the three but the big difference was Keita who is now benefitting from a run of games and beginning to show what he is made of. It's beginning to look like it has clicked. It's taken longer but those shoots are there. The timidity is slowly disappearing and we're starting to see the first glimpses of what he could become. Not yet the domineering force, but beginning to influence and create.

Mané scored the first followed by Gini's lob. The third was a work of art. The type of goal that you see in videos on how football should be played. A defence splitting ball from Keita to set Firmino free, he looked like he was going to lash it in but instead went for this reverse pass that allowed Salah in running from the inside right. It was a foregone conclusion that he would score. What a goal.

I feel relieved. I feel like we have breathing space for a few days, like the spotlight on the crisis can be lifted. For the past ten days we have only been as good as our last game and while that hasn't necessarily been bad, it hasn't quite been good enough. We were too much for them today, they couldn't compete. So we are as good as our last game and that puts us top of the league, at least until City play tomorrow.

United won again at lunchtime, that's something like ten games unbeaten. They are our next game in the league and that will be the game in hand we have over City. Stakes are high, I have my ticket for Old Trafford, bring it on.

Tuesday 12th February 2019

Champions League starts again today, which means we are in the final stretch. Twelve league games and potentially seven knockout games to focus the mind. We have got ourselves into position on the final bend and we now have to accelerate into the final straight.

We don't start until next week with our home game against Bayern Munich, but the hype has started today with United taking on PSG. When the draw was made, you wouldn't have given United a hope, but things have changed quickly. Solskjaer has turned around a very talented team to the point they are arguably the form team in the league. Combine that with both Neymar and Cavani being out and PSG having a talented but very small squad and all of a sudden they must be going into that game with some confidence.

Liverpool have a week off, courtesy of being knocked out the FA Cup, so they have travelled to Marbella for a bit of training in the sun. They went to Dubai a few weeks back and the results since haven't been the best, so let's hope Spain is a better place for a relaxing holiday.

City beat Chelsea 6-0 in the end and looked like they could pretty much score at will. It puts them top of the league as in recent weeks they have managed to build a 10-goal advantage, which may prove critical as we move towards the end of the season. They had been that far ahead on goals in November, but our great scoring form through December had eradicated that lead and we actually went ahead of them at one point, but their free scoring form in recent weeks has restored the advantage.

Although they are top, we have that all-important game in hand. City are playing in the League (or whatever the hell it is called) Cup final next weekend and at the same time we play our game in hand – against United at Old Trafford – and I have a ticket!!!

United at Old Trafford is such a nerve-wracking game. I have been there when we have won—we beat them in April 2004 when Murphy scored and there I was on TV going absolutely mental in the stands. I've also been there when we have been beat and it's a cold, depressing place. I was right behind the goal for an FA Cup game in 1999. Owen scored really early on in the game and we then held them out until the very end when they popped up and stole the game away from us in injury time. That was Solskjaer with the winner, the pixie-faced fuck.

So from Christmas, when they couldn't get a win anywhere, they are now in blistering form and stand in the way of us going clear at the top. That said, if we play anywhere near the way we did on Saturday, it will be a cracking game.

I can't get over what a difference Gini made to the side, despite the fact he had been up all night with the shits. For me he has been one of the players of the season so far. Unheralded, widely perceived to be the player who would make way for Fabinho and Keita, he has made the difference all season. Not always clear what he is doing and what he is bringing to the game, he is continually running, pushing, pressurising, facilitating. While the focus is on VVD, Alisson and Salah, Gini has quietly plugged away but has really made himself indispensable. The two games he missed last week only served to emphasise his value to the team.

His contribution, combined with the improving form of Keita, and the pictures of Oxlade Chamberlain in training today have given me the tingling feeling that it is all coming together at the right time

Monday 18th February 2019

A few days with nothing to add. Liverpool have been away in Spain, Social media is awash with nice images of the team having fun, riding bikes etc. but an absence of real news. There appears to be a desire to focus on Keita and I am taking this to mean he will get more game time in the coming weeks and we will begin to see the player that we have been waiting for.

The positive I have taken is the inclusion in the photos of Oxlade Chamberlain, who appears to be training with the team. How far away he is from being absolutely match fit remains to be seen, but it is certainly encouraging to have him on the fringes of the squad and competing for a place. He could certainly make a hell of a difference to the squad and provide another option on the bench. He will be like a new signing next season, all being well.

Ahead of tomorrow night's Champions League match against Bayern Munich, Klopp has had his press conference. The big news is that Firmino has missed training today with some kind of virus so is clearly a doubt for the match tomorrow night. How realistic this is I don't know. These guys are superfit, like finely tuned machines, so a cold or a bout of the shits shouldn't present a massive problem assuming it passes in time. I should point out at this stage that I am not a qualified doctor and really my opinion in this matter is completely uninformed!

If he is out, that would be a blow, but that is why we have a squad. We have Sturridge or Origi who is able to step up if they need a central striker in a 433, or if they want to move to a 4231, then Shaqiri could be brought in so there is no lack of options. I suppose the real blow is that they will have been preparing for the game with Bobby in the team so that time will be thrown out of the window if he isn't well. I don't think it's the end of the world!

The news that we did know about is VVD is suspended for the game and now Lovren has been confirmed as injured, leaving us with Matip as the only recognised centre back in the team. It looks like Fabinho will be able to step in at centre back—he did well there over the Christmas period when he was called upon and Matip appears to have played himself into a bit of form so we should be OK, but it is something of a baptism of fire to go into the game with what would be our fourth and fifth choice centre back. VVD has become the lynchpin of the side since he joined, and it will be a challenge for the rest of the team to step up in his absence. It will also be interesting to see how Alisson performs and whether he can organise the defence in VVD's absence.

Tuesday 19th February 2019

I always seem to be in trouble. Doesn't matter what I do. Wrong.

I was already in the bad books for going to the game tonight. If I'd have left at 7.15 and driven like a madman to get there, it still would have been wrong. So I've gone out at five, bought a few beers for the train, 90 minutes' heavy drinking in town and then on to the game. If I'm going to be in trouble anyway I might as well enjoy myself.

Tonight is the Champions League last 16 and if you can't enjoy yourself when you are at home under the lights to Bayern Munich, then when can you? Nothing beats a European night at Anfield. Nothing at all. From the minute you walk in and see the lush green pitch under the lights then you know it's going to be a proper night.

Bayern Munich tonight. European royalty and they will be terrified. Terrified of the team and terrified of the atmosphere in the ground. There will be an air of respect in the atmosphere. It won't be feral, like a United or Everton game. It will be a majestic atmosphere that shows due respect for the opponents. It will be loud and imposing. Alcohol fuelled. It's a five-pint game. It will be the only place to be. I can't wait.

I haven't heard any further updates on Bobby. My guess is he'll play in a front three. Midfield is difficult to call. Fabinho will be in defence, which counts him out. It's three from Hendo,

Gini, Milner and Keita.

I think the first two are nailed on. At the moment I would put Gini down as almost first name on the team sheet. And then Henderson is there to be solid and creative. The big choice is between Milner and Keita. He likes Milner for these games. His commitment and experience shines through. He was central to the Champions League run last year. Just when you thought he was passed it and not getting a look in, he was drafted in for the big games. You always know what you're going to get with him. Blood and sweat. With the defence weakened he may look for that extra solidity in midfield.

And then there's Keita. Improving with every game and ultimately the future of the Liverpool midfield. Klopp needs to show some confidence in the lad. That's what he needs to progress ... the confidence of the manager. At some point he is going raise his level and show why we paid all that money. I am desperate to be at the game when he steps up.

My call now is Milner. Solidity. Protecting the defence. Not conceding an away goal. God, I feel so boring sometimes.

***

A game of chess. Ninety minutes and two good footballing sides just nullify each other. I can't remember a clear chance for either side. The game was snuffed out in midfield and never gave enough space to create even the sniff of a chance.

I started the game thinking this would be free flowing and attacking, but it felt like we both just wanted to settle. Our weakened defence wasn't threatened, which is a relief. It just puts all the pressure on the return leg. I am struggling to name a man of the match just as much as I can't name anyone who had a poor game.

When all is said and done, we were playing European royalty and, as much as they might be in transition, from a tactical point of view they were head and shoulders above anything we have seen in the Premier League.

The return leg has to be more attacking. We have to get an early goal and hold it from there. Another game of chess.

Thursday 21st February 2019

On reflection, I think I'm OK with the result the other night. I think I had underestimated Munich. Heard all the stories about them being on the wane and kind of written them off. The fact I had money on us winning 3-0 tells me that.

When you look at the team they had, it was dripping with quality. Martinez in the middle, alongside Thiago and James Rodriguez. And Lewandowski up front (although I'm not sure he actually touched the ball). It was a great team.

I think perhaps we showed them a little too much respect, we maybe could have gone at them a bit more, but I understand we also had to protect what was potentially a suspect defensive partnership. I think at the end of the day, both teams were happy to hold each other at arm's length.

I thought Henderson was outstanding. For all the quality on display he was the pick of the midfielders. But it was work to shore up and be safe rather than create. He didn't stop. Keita too had a good game. He's getting better every week, showing greater consistency, being more involved and then showing the occasional flash of brilliance, of what is to come.

Going to Munich in a few weeks, I'm confident we can get a result. With VVD back in the side, we have strength from the back, from the base of the team. He will make all the difference as the team's strength stems from him. He will release Robertson and Trent, allow the midfield to be further forward supporting the attacking three. We only need a goal and then they need two.

This time I am not underestimating Bayern, they are a great

side, I just think we have enough throughout the team to get the result we need. But that's a long way away.

Before that we have United at the weekend. And what a different game that is going to be from the game at Anfield just eight weeks ago. United were a disgrace that day, absolutely awful, doomed under the horrendous atmosphere created by Mourinho.

A couple of months on and United are flying. Unbeaten in the league under Solkskjaer, Pogba is like a new player, creating and scoring. Rashford is the same, on a hot streak of form, and Sanchez is like a ticking time bomb, waiting to explode onto the scene. At the same time, Mr Big Hair has already been shipped out and Lukaku has become peripheral. They are a real tricky proposition and it should be a great game.

It's our game in hand over City, we need to win to get our noses back in front and put the pressure back on. There's still ten games to go, so there is time to make that back, but even more important is the momentum and the confidence that comes from a win. Even more important than that ... it's Fucking United.

Sunday 24th February 2019

Sunday morning of the United game. It's a while since I've been to Old Trafford and I'm so excited about the game. Can't help think it's a must-win game. All of our games have been elevated to this state recently. Must win. If they don't win then they've bottled it. It's a media thing. All or nothing. Hype and I've been sucked in.

The game doesn't need any more hype. Artificial hype. End of the world hype. It's United against Liverpool, which for as long as I can remember has been the biggest game of the year anyway.

United are riding the crest of a wave since the return of

Solskjaer. It's surprised me actually how long the run has gone on. There have been eleven wins and a draw in the league since he came in. There is no doubt he had the quality of players to be able to go on a run like this, but how he seems to have simply flicked a switch and created automatic momentum is almost eerie.

I can understand a couple of games, new manager bounce and all that, but to turn it into a run that has gone on this long, beating Spurs, Arsenal and Chelsea on the way, is quite a feat. By all accounts he has changed the culture of the team and of the club almost overnight and lifted the toxicity that existed under Mourinho.

When he was brought in, it was almost a joke. After a poor run at Cardiff a couple of years ago, he was worse than unproven. He was disproven, coming over from Norway. At the time it was a joke. Two months on it looks inspired. At the time, it was all about Pochettino coming at the end of the season. As the wins rack up, it looks more and more like he'll be retained permanéntly. Even Klopp said so this week. Whether that's just a bit of toffee remains to be seen.

It was the dream scenario for us in December, he goes on a run and gets the job permanéntly, at which point they get embroiled in another cycle of rebuilding. The popular choice, which stops them making the difficult decisions that clearly need to be made. There is a lack of experience behind the scenes there, no one in real control and, until that changes, they are going to be on this merry-go-round.

But enough about them, bollocks to them. We have enough to go at their dodgy defence and if we can nullify their chief threats, which appear to be Pogba and Rashford at the moment, then we have a good chance.

It's not must-win, there are another 11 games after this, that's 33 points to play for, so we need to play our best game, and if we can bring that, then I think we have a better than even chance of winning what is effectively our most difficult remaining game of the season. After today, we have Chelsea and Spurs at home and then teams from the bottom 14. Old Trafford represents our biggest challenge on the run-in.

VVD will be back, marshalling the defence and quietly controlling the pace of the game from the back. After his performance the other night, there is a shout to put Fabinho next to him, but more likely it will be Matip in the continued absence of Gomez and Lovren.

Midfield could be any three of five and I wouldn't be disappointed at any combination. Would be good to see us take the midfield to them, and I would say we should continue with Keita as he seems to be improving with each game. I'd have Hendo and Gini in there with him, but any combination involving Milner and Fabinho would be fine too. At the very least we have substitute options.

Tingling with anticipation it's fair to say.

***

Finished 0-0. We battered them into a goalless draw with all the possession and barely a chance.

First time in Old Trafford since we beat them in 2004. A long time ago. Rather than pretend to be a writer I will revert back to corporate style bullet points to try to cover some of the key points from the afternoon and the game.

1. We are top of the league. This is the first and most important point and shouldn't be forgotten in the general disappointment of not beating them. Even if it's only a point, it's a point clear at the top with just 11 games to go.

2. It's not nice to be called a murderer when you're just having a day out. It was feral going into the ground. We'd had a couple of pints before the game in Manchester so came in from that side and the atmosphere was really quite intimidating. No

colours obviously, but even walking in you were conscious of catching someone's eye and then asking why you weren't singing about Ole Bloody Solskjaer. As we got to the ground itself and walking through the turnstile there is a thousand-people screaming murderer at you. Really?

3. Our midfield. Point three was just going to be about Fabinho and what an incredible footballer he is and will yet prove to be. He was imperious today, control and vision but with a bite. But to just focus on him would be unfair as I thought Gini and Hendo were great also.

Gini in the first half, winning the ball, linking things up, pressing and scurrying. Hendo in the second running the game from the right side of midfield, linking up and bringing Milner into the game who had been picked ahead of Trent at right back. It amazed me when he was taken off as he seemed to have the game in the palm of his hand. All three were head and shoulders above the United midfield, which is why it's such a shame that we haven't been able to convert that dominance into a win.

4. VVD only runs when he wants to. He is the definition of nonchalance. He obviously thinks the game is running at his speed. Even going for corners, his swagger dictates the play. He walks everywhere but seems to be everywhere all at the same time. I can't quite get my head around it.

5. The people in the South Stand are a different kettle of fish to those in the East Stand. On previous visits to Old Trafford I have always been closer to the East Stand behind the goal. The United fans behind the goal are animals, absolutely feral. As many of them looking across at the away fans as watching the game. Looking for trouble. Looking for a target. If it wasn't for the line of ineffectual students in Day-Glo jackets you'd be quite scared.

Today, I was at the other side, butting up to the United fans in the south side along the side of the pitch behind the dugout. These are clearly the tourists, people who have always wanted to go the game and have now been and will never go again, because the idea of going to Old Trafford is far better than actually going to Old Trafford.

A stand full of fish out of water, not quite knowing where to look and clearly intimidated by being ten feet away from three thousand baying Scousers. It was the fans that Ferguson had been referring to when he said they were shite. I can't believe there aren't people out there who are more deserving of a ticket to such a game and the clubs are happy to take the money from these people, most of whom didn't look like they really wanted to be there.

6. Ole can park the bus just as well as Jose can. For all the fantastic football that I have heard about since Solskjaer started, we certainly didn't see it today. They set out with a complete lack of ambition. They parked the bus. A line of five behind a line of four. No interest in trying to win the game other than trying to pick something off at the end.

If I'm being fair (which I suppose I'll have to be) they had three injuries in the first half and had used all their subs by half time, which means to an extent they had to adjust their game plan and sit back, but I think the disappointing thing is we were unable to break them down and create space. For all the dominance of the midfield, we failed to get the front three into the game. Shaw took Salah out of the game and Sturridge was anonymous when he replaced Firmino, who also came off in the first half. It's really going to be our undoing if we keep getting shut out by these teams.

Overall I'm disappointed. I think they were there for the taking today and we played badly and fell short. It might prove to be a good point in the long run, but we are good enough to have had three.

Still top of the league though. I'll just leave that in there!

Monday 25th February 2018

There are a few things you miss when you go the match. Don't get me wrong, I don't think there's anything better than going to the match and being part of that atmosphere, but you miss some of the detail in the emotion of the moment. You only get to realise how good it was in a replay of the incident. There were two things that I missed at the match on Saturday, one good and one bad.

The bad was the free kick that Liverpool completely mucked up in the first minute. Now, I didn't miss the free kick itself, although I did miss how it came about. It just sort of happened and from our end of the ground, I couldn't quite work out what had happened. It wasn't remarkable and I'm not going to dwell on it.

What I am going to dwell on was the remarkably bad indirect free kick. Having seen it a few times now, it amazes me that a group of professional footballers could get it so wrong. An indirect free kick. It means you can't go direct, there has to be more than one touch before the ball goes in the net. We get that. Two touches. How Liverpool conspired to take three touches I will never know. Intricate? It was beyond intricate ... it was just plain wasteful, tapping it round the penalty area like it was Tiki fucking Taka.

Twat it. That's what you do. You twat it directly at the goal, at the wall, at the goalkeeper, you just hit it as hard as you can, preferably with the end of your toe, in the hope it takes a touch or a deflection before the power and the momentum of the ball takes it into the net. It's not rocket science. Well, it's not science, but you do need to hit it like a rocket. For God's sake, lads. Rant over.

The second thing I missed was the Alisson save. Again, I didn't miss it; it was directly in front of me. A heart-stopping moment when they sprung through the defence and Lingard was one on one with the keeper, moving at pace, an almost certain goal. I didn't miss how quickly Alisson came out and took the ball away from him. I didn't miss the guttural roar from the Liverpool end as it happened. In real time, I didn't miss such an incredible save.

What I did miss was the intricacy, artistry and precision of the save and you can only really see and appreciate that when the action is slowed down so you can see each advancing frame. What a piece of football. That he could put his arms around the player's feet and push the ball away without getting anywhere near his feet was almost beyond belief. That he could do that at speed makes him superhuman.

Unbelievable game-saving save. That split second alone makes him man of the match in what was otherwise a rather disappointing display.

And now straight on to the next game. We have a run of four now against the weaker 'other' sides in the league, starting with Watford on Wednesday. This is where we need to pick our game up now, putting these teams to the sword. Continuing to pick up points and keeping the momentum, keeping the pressure on City at the same time.

We also need to start scoring goals. Our attacking payers need to step up. Our outstanding defence have put us in this position, with untold clean sheets and just 15 goals conceded all season. Our attacking players now need to pick up the responsibility for putting this to bed. Not only winning but winning by margins that will reduce the City goal difference advantage, which is back up to 11. They are clearly not going to stop scoring, so we need to score more. Show them we are not for breaking.

Wednesday 27th February 2018

I said we had to score more, didn't I? We outclassed Watford tonight 5-0. One-way traffic from start to finish, Watford never got a look-in. Any sign of the nervousness that is apparently plaguing Liverpool wasn't on show at all. We were magnificent in every department.

Firmino injured and Origi replaced him, although out on the left with Mané playing through the middle of a front three. What a game he had with two goals in the first half, both provided by balls fizzed in from Trent, the first goal a header, the second a cheeky back heel, when it looked like he might not be able to turn round quick enough.

With two goals in the bag, Liverpool were cruising for the rest of the game. Apart from a couple of rare attacks from Watford, we never looked like conceding a goal, it was more a question of how many Liverpool could score.

The midfield three of Fabinho, Gini and Milner were dominant, Divvy scored a goal from the edge of the area, but it was Mané playing central and coming deep that really caught the eye, providing all of the link-up play we normally see from Bobby - with an incredible burst of pace when needed.

Salah too had a great game, constantly stretching them down the right wing and playing against (and beating) three men for most of the game. His threat created the concern in the Watford defence, which in turn created all the space for Mané.

Lallana came on for the last twenty and won the free kick that led to the fourth, another precision ball in from Trent and met by the mighty VVD. Five minutes later, with the Kop singing his name, he popped up again and got the fifth. He was majestic at the back, controlling everything on the pitch without breaking a sweat—and then pops up with two goals.

Jesus, we were good tonight, right through the team. Stepping up after the weekend and showing why we are top of the league.

In a full programme of games, City got a 1-0 win against West Ham through a very soft penalty, so not only do we retain our rightful place at the top, we have also reduced the goal difference deficit to six, which will help no end.

Everton at the weekend. Come on.

Interlude 8 - My Team

When I look back at the mid-1980s, I always see a watershed. A point where the team transformed and suddenly became the team for which I had ownership. It was the beginning of the 1987/88 season.

It wasn't a complete overhaul of the team, the majority had been part of that trophy-winning evolution but there were a few meaningful additions (and departures) where I felt we had gone from the team that I had inherited from those that had watched Liverpool before me to the team that was 'mine'.

After winning the double in 1986, the title went back to Everton the following year. They won it by a fair margin too. There was a bit of a transition in place in the team. Ian Rush was sold to Juventus, leaving at the end of the season, and Dalglish had come pretty much to the end of the road during the season. He only played 18 games. The front two that had been there for the past six seasons had come to the end of the road. Paul Walsh played a few, but it was clear there needed to be someone to replace Rush.

They got a record fee for him, over three million, which was a fortune at the time, and they also had time to work out how to spend it. Dalglish took his time. They didn't replace him with one player; Kenny overhauled the whole attacking side of the team. Aldridge arrived in the middle of the season, followed by the magical combination of Barnes and Beardsley in the summer and then finally Ray Houghton a couple of months into the

87/88 team. Other additions had been made such as McMahon, Spackman and Venison ... before you knew it, you had what looked like a new team. My team.

The 87/88 was also my first year in the Kop. Grandad had renewed my ticket after the cup final and I had another year in the main stand. But after that he said I had to pay for it myself. The decision was between a £95 ticket in the main stand and £45 in the Kop. It was a no-brainer and for economic reasons I became a Kopite!! Of course, it wasn't just economic. I was ready for it; it was a rite of passage, my next step in the journey.

My first game in there was Rush's last game at the end of the 86/87 season. A dress rehearsal to check I was up to it. Our Alan looked after me again and I got a spec near his, low down behind the post on the Kemlyn side. It was a very different way to watch the game. From the helicopter view of the stand to standing almost at pitch level. The perspective was different, but the excitement was amplified. I got so close to the players. Almost like you could reach out and touch them.

There I was. New team. New spec. A watershed. And what a team it was. They were magnificent that first season. Unbeatable. We had the league virtually won in the first two months. Unstoppable.

With a change of personnel, there was also a change in system. In England in the 1980s, nothing strayed very far from 4-4-2, but here was a team to stretch that idea. You could call it a 4-2-3-1. Aldridge up front on his own, Barnes, Beardsley and Houghton behind him, Beardsley in what would now be called a number ten role. Behind that were two sitting midfielders, usually McMahon and Whelan, though you would hardly call them sitting in the modern way. They were more the old-fashioned box-to-box midfielder, McMahon in particular.

It was a formation that was in its way revolutionary. The rest of the league certainly didn't know what to do with it. The focus always on Barnes and Beardsley but Nicol played so well too, on the overlap with Barnes down the left side. He transformed the full back position into an attacking outlet, in the way we are used to it now. He scored six in the first six games before anyone even thought about how to stop him.

There was a problem with the Kop that year and we missed the first couple of games at home. They were hastily rescheduled as midweek games, which seemed to add to the excitement. Banned from Europe, these were the only floodlit games we would see for a few years. The game I remember is the one everyone remembers. The mauling of Forest. We battered them 5-0. It was the game Tom Finney said was the finest example of football he had ever seen. He was right.

That was a midweek game too. We'd beaten Forest in the FA Cup semi-final at Hillsborough the previous weekend and this was the second game in four days. The team was Grobbelaar, Gillespie, Ablett, Nicol and Hansen in defence. Spackman and McMahon in the centre of midfield and then the four of Houghton, Barnes, Beardsley and Aldridge up front. Molby and Johnston on the bench.

Liverpool were a class apart. To be fair, they were far more experienced. Forest had a very young side with an average age of just 22. Since the glory days of Forest in the late '70s and early '80s, Clough had managed to keep them there or thereabouts but they had never been able to scale the same heights again. This was a young team in the midst of another transition whereas Liverpool were damn near the finished article.

Two goals from Aldridge, and one each for Beardsley, Houghton and Gillespie. As well as Tom Finney on TV that night, I managed to get on too. Clearly visible in the Kop, right behind the goal in my black Puma tracksuit getting thrown about and absolutely in my element.

We won the league easily that year and reached the FA Cup final, where we were (in)famously beaten by Wimbledon. It was a foregone conclusion that we would win that game and with it the second double in three years and it came as an enormous shock when we didn't. The Aldridge penalty miss was the biggest shock. My Uncle Arthur had said that season he was the finest penalty taker he had ever seen with his no-nonsense approach, and I had that in my head as I saw him line up to take it. He missed. It was unfathomable.

After the game, we were waiting in the coach park and there was a double decker bus full of Wimbledon fans. They looked miserable as hell; they must have been shell shocked. And then this old guy walks across the car park holding the FA Cup. It was Bobby Gould, the Wimbledon manager. Even then they didn't seem to liven up; they must have thought it was a practical joke!

While I think I took things in my stride at home, things were becoming more difficult. Mum struggled on her own with three growing kids. She developed a level of bitterness about my dad leaving and I was party to much of the ill will that went between them. She started drinking a little bit too. It was probably more than a kid of 15 should have to deal with. Money was shorter than before, so I got myself some part-time jobs. I was determined not to have to ask anyone for money or assistance. I would be responsible and sort things out for myself.

At the weekends I would stay over at my Auntie Pat's more often. Go back there after the match for my tea – always the same home-made burgers – but then sleep over and go out with them on the Sunday, almost like a surrogate family. I was avoiding being at home, I now realise.

Things came to a head in January 1989. An argument between my mum and sister Katy and she was taken across to my dad's. A falling out with a teenager that we all thought would be resolved in a few days and my mum fully expected her back. She never came back. Not permanéntly anyway. Dad enrolled her in a local school and before anyone realised we had been split up. That did it for my mum. She couldn't cope after that. The drinking got worse. The pressure on my other sister increased. We all took some emotional damage.

Except for me, I think by that time I was getting used to taking things in my stride. Nan passing away, Dad leaving. These were just things that happened. No big deal. Sister being taken away, that was just another thing to get on with. I just wrapped it up in a little box and packed it away, not a problem. Looking back, it was horrendous. As a teenager it was just normal life and something that can be packed away amongst the everyday schedule of school and part-time jobs. There was another match around the corner too.

MARCH

Friday 1st March 2019

There was lots to talk about today. I was going to write about the Derby at the weekend or about VAR after a really good podcast I listened to yesterday on the Anfield Wrap. I am still hoping to write about the outlook for the season with just ten games to go, but work is busy at the moment and sitting down to type even a short piece is difficult.

Looking forward to the Derby at the weekend. We really need to beat them. It goes beyond local rivalry at the moment, we need to beat all the teams we come up against and to be honest it doesn't really matter that it's Everton—it's just another one of 'the rest' that we need to get past. Of course, I've only said that to try to provoke the fume – could have said 'one of the smaller teams' in the league – although it's unlikely that any of the bitter ones will actually be reading this.

We need to beat them because they're Everton. It's always good to beat them. The last couple of games have been brilliant. The Origi goal before Christmas was one of the most surreal football moments I can remember. Twenty seconds of 'What on earth happened there?' And then Mané's late goal at Goodison last year. Is there anything better than beating them with a late goal, just at the point the supporters are cracking open the champagne to celebrate a goalless draw?

The level of bitterness is quite sad really, I don't know how it has built up to the point it has. They are beginning to become defined by this bitterness, by their negative view of Liverpool rather than their positive view of their own team. I get the feeling they would rather see us lose than Everton win. Their need for us not to win the league is becoming almost obsessive; a quick trip around Everton feeds on Twitter is quite illuminating. As far as I know, this isn't one of these rivalries that descends into violence (not on any major scale anyway) as it can in some places, but the atmosphere has really changed.

It's a while since I've been to Goodison, not since I've been back from Australia. In fact, the last one I went to was the night before I emigrated to Sydney in late December 2005. We battered them that night, Crouch, Gerrard and Cisse all scored. It was a great way to head off.

The first games I went to there were in the late '80s. Barnes and Beardsley time. One in particular we went to was a midweek game, it may have been the first game after Hillsborough. As a parent now, it boggles my mind that we would have been allowed to go to that game unaccompanied. Not that there was any danger as such, but just with the emotion being so raw at the time.

Me and my mate Stuart went together. We were still at school and we decided to go without a ticket. We had been before, but it had always been with a grown-up and a ticket. We were a bit more grown up now and didn't think we needed either. So we walked around the ground looking for a ticket, asking around, two spotty school kids trying to look like we knew what we were doing.

In the end we met this lad who had a couple of tickets. 'Wait here,' he said, 'my mate's got them.' We'd scored! So we stood there and waited for him and sure enough he was back five minutes later with two tickets for the Liverpool end. I don't know what we paid him but it was certainly higher than face value. But we didn't care, we'd got tickets, and we carried on walking down the road, feeling smug. That was until we went about 100 yards and came to the Everton ticket office, which was open and selling tickets for the game—at face value. It wasn't even sold out. We'd been done.

God, we felt stupid, another minute's walk and we'd have got them for ourselves. Of course, by the time we got back into school the next day, the story of our night had been distilled to forget that part of the story. I still see that lad at the match now, he must be fifty now, but I still recognise him.

In the '90s, I got invited to a couple of games in their corporate boxes, which was an odd experience. They didn't invite me to the derby; it was to games against other teams. Nice enough day out, nice people, nice meal, a few drinks. But it was horrendous sitting in that box waiting for a goal. If Everton had scored, everyone around me would have gone mad, and I just couldn't. If the opposition had scored, I don't think I would have been able to stop myself. And because I was young and trying to be on my best behaviour at a work-related thing, the whole day was quite uncomfortable. I went twice and they were both goalless draws—small mercies I suppose.

So much for being too busy at work, where did all that come from?

Saturday 2nd March 2019

So here we are. The final straight. Ten games to go and we are top of the league with 69 points. There are only nine teams who have had this many points at this stage of the season and the other eight have all gone on to win. That's a good omen but it only means we could be the first not to. I know, it's negative. Stop it. Be a believer.

The other eight haven't had Manchester City breathing down their necks, just a point behind. There is no margin for error at all. Our maximum possible haul is 99 points and we are going to have to get bloody close to that to beat them.

The result against Watford the other night gets us back in the groove and then we have Everton tomorrow. Momentum and belief get us there. We have ten games left, two against the top six, eight against the rest. Both of the top games are at home. Beyond that, our most difficult game is the derby. Five at home, five away.

Spurs seem to have dropped away from the top two and if they're not careful could be drawn into a four-way battle for third and fourth. It leaves us and City. They also have just two games against the top teams. One of them is United at Old Trafford which, due to fixture congestion and the FA Cup, has already been moved back to late April, which ramps up the pressure on an already massive game. I'm sure they'd have rather got that out the way now.

It's a battle of wits. Of psychology. Of spin. Not until the last game of the season do the two teams play at the same time, so one team is always putting pressure on the other. Most times it's City playing first and I fear that gives them an advantage.

They play Bournemouth away today, which I expect them to win, but after a nervy 1-0 win midweek you never know if they are getting the yips themselves.

***

They did beat Bournemouth, but again just 1-0. Some people would say grinding out wins is the sign of champions and that is two 1-0s in a row. Others would say they are bottling it and struggling to put teams to the sword. I'll agree with the others.

The big thing about the 1-0 is it gives us an opportunity to pull back more goals. They are seven ahead of us at the moment and that could be the crucial point at the end of the season. We caught up by four on Wednesday; it would be great if we could do that against Everton tomorrow. Smacking half a dozen past them would be magic.

That said, I'd settle for another 1-0 win in the 96th minute as that was possibly the best thing ever!!!

Sunday 3rd March 2019

The day is here. We need to beat them. Feel better about our chances after the Watford win the other night. Hopefully got ourselves back into a groove and if we have done that we should roll over these. We need to hope that we have managed to shake off the stutter of the draws in the last few weeks. Need to be brave, play our game, don't get dragged into theirs.

Firmino out, which is disappointing. I was hoping he would be back by now. I suppose they can't just bring him back too quickly or he will never recover and burn out. He's on the bench so he can't be properly injured. Maybe it's more of a tactical thing, to use him in the later stages of the game if we need to make an impact.

Origi holds his place and I thought he was good on the wing the other night. Must be difficult for these players on the fringe when there is a well-established first team. They can play well when they get their chance but know that as soon as the first team player is back, they will be back on the bench. Origi has scored some vital goals, not least the one against Everton a few months back, but is never going to be a first team regular. Must be difficult for Klopp to manage some of the expectations.

In midfield, Fabinho is holding again alongside Gini and Henderson who returns to replace Milner. I always look at the starters, but I don't know how big that is for the players themselves. Milner is on the bench and my guess is he will come on and play the last half hour or so if everything goes to plan. We seem to have reached this situation where we play four very similar and interchangeable midfielders across the ninety minutes, if nothing else to keep the energy levels up, because it's that midfield energy and dynamism that is driving this team. They are the difference, in my view anyway.

Come on Liverpool, let's do these.

***

Nil-nil. Bastards. That has pissed me off so much. They brought us down to their level; we just couldn't get out on top of them. That was the danger, that they were going to make it a game played on their terms and we didn't have the gumption today to control and win as we have done for most of the season. It's becoming a bit of a recurring thing. That's the fourth draw. We should have won all of them, but we haven't had that extra yard of pace or final pass—or maybe just that bit of luck that's needed.

We had chances; Salah should have won the game or at least got the first goal that would have led to more. We weren't really troubled at the back. Firmino came on with Milner after an hour or so but didn't really have the impact. It was one of those games that you could see petering out to a draw rather than one where you thought you might pick up a late goal. I suppose they're all like that until you get the late goal, aren't they?

The danger is that the whole season is petering out. That's eight points dropped now in about a month. Still not got beat, but a draw is two points dropped and we've had too many in a short space of time. Between this game and the United one, we'd have been better being a bit braver, winning one and losing one, and we'd still have three points rather than the two we have now. The way it's going that point could be all important. We've dropped into second behind City after that result. There's still a long way to go, but there is a point where we need to stop dropping points.

So while I'm all down about it, no doubt the Evertonians will be out all night celebrating their famous goalless draw. They'll be saying its them who won it for City. Sad, isn't it?

Tuesday 5th March 2019

Had to switch off everything. Everything is doing my head in. Media, social media. Feel like I'm surrounded by it so have taken refuge in one of my audiobooks. At least in there no one is going to say that Liverpool have bottled it, that this is the end of their season and the experience of Manchester City is shining through and will take them unbeaten to the end of the season. How many rent-a-voices can they get on to say the same thing? They are talking about Klopp making too many excuses, that he hasn't got the ruthlessness.

They are touching a raw nerve with it. I think I'm only re-acting in this way because something deep down knows it's true. Not the Klopp stuff—he is beyond criticism in my eyes. And not that we've bottled it necessarily but that lack of title-winning experience. City are not blowing teams away by any means but they are doing enough to win each game at this cru-cial stage of the season. People seem to forget they have lost four games already this season, so they are not infallible by any means, but just now, when they need the points they are getting them.

And just when we need them we are falling a little short. We have changed in style this season from the cavalier attack-ing, flowing football that took us to Kiev to a more controlled style, designed to choke opponents. Don't get me wrong, we can attack and score for fun when we want to – just witness last week against Watford – but in the last couple of draws we have not been able to resurrect that attacking spirit to sneak the win-ning goal.

Look, I know we can't do it every time. I know that really,

honestly I do. And I am sure we have had more than our fair share of late goals this season, but that builds an expectation that we can do it every time. Hence the disappointment when we don't. Even as the most blinkered of fans, I realise that. I just don't like other people telling me.

Wednesday 6th March 2019

Having a difficult time at work. They are going to close the factory and make people redundant. They are going to do in Stoke, which is widely known as Brexit Town because of the 70% leave vote. They are going to do it the week before Brexit Day. And they don't think they are going to be inundated with press and bad feeling. The naivety is staggering—either that or they don't care. I have had to start apologising for being so negative in meetings. Not negative I tell them but practical. Some of the people who work for me are going to be affected. I feel sick about it.

I have had to cancel my trip to Munich next week. I'm really disappointed but it clashes with announcements about potential job losses. I have to be responsible and be there. There are some days when you can make yourself scarce, but this isn't one of them. My team will be looking to me and it's important I'm there. I'm gutted but I know deep down I am doing the right thing.

I'm also missing the game on Sunday. We're supposed to be going to Sheffield to watch Embrace. It was a Christmas present for me and my wife, I had it all booked and was really looking forward to it. Something else has come up so I've had to cancel but had already got rid of my match ticket.

Life conspires to frustrate me—this is all just about to get good and I feel like I'm missing vital games. Take a deep breath. It's only football (bugger!).

Sunday 9th March 2019

Burnley at home today. I've known I was missing this since November. Supposed to be over in Sheffield last night watching Embrace and I had promised my ticket to my mate who is going to take his lad. I've had to cancel at short notice and it's too late to take the ticket back.

Enough about my woes. City beat Watford last night, which puts them four points clear at the top this morning. We really need to win today.

The dropping of points over the last few weeks has been disappointing, but we have stayed in the race for the title. If we don't win today, then we effectively lose touch with City and it will become very different to begin to reel them back in. On paper it looks like we have an easier run-in than them, but they are so far superior to just about every other team in the league they are likely to roll over most of them and it's not beyond the realms of possibility that they go the rest of the season unbeaten.

We need to win to stay on their tails in case they slip up. If we can stay in touch, the chunk of light sits right at the end of the season. Both City and United have progressed in the cup and the game they were due to play in the league has been rearranged towards the end of the season. They play each other just two or three games before the end. That could be the crunch game, I would say their most difficult game, and we need to be right on their shoulders.

The word is that Liverpool have bottled it. They have struggled to score and have had goalless draws three out of the last four games. The positive to that is we are keeping clean sheets. VVD is imperious and controls each game from the back; we never look like conceding a goal. The problem is further forward where the front six do not seem able to connect.

The talk is of the front three, but I think it's wider than that.

The front three need the ball from the midfield and while they are winning the ball and controlling the game there is a gap between them and the front three and the ball is not finding itself in the correct space.

Firmino not fully fit so unable to play that pivotal role. Salah and Mané trying their best but not able to get space and time. Opposition defences seem to have worked us out and are able to hold us at arm's length. The anomaly amongst the goalless draws was a 5-0 demolition of Watford last week, which was as good a performance as we have seen all season, which makes it all the more frustrating that it's followed by a 0-0 and at Everton too.

I think we need something more creative to link the midfield and attacking three. It's all control and no breaking forward. Keita seemed to be coming into form but then hasn't featured, with Klopp preferring the stability of Fabinho, Henderson, Wijnaldum and Milner. Shaqiri doesn't seem to have had a look-in for a couple of months either and he could provide the creativity we need.

***

I've driven to my sister's where I am going to watch the game today. She's not in, so I'm sitting by the beach in Prestatyn contemplating life in general. I've been here before. It's amazing to watch the power of the wind on a bad day, watching the people get blasted by flying sand as they try to walk their dogs. As I type, the team for today beeps into my phone for the game, which kicks off in an hour.

He's playing Lallana in midfield, which surprises me. Alongside Fabinho and Gini. Henderson Keita and Shaq all on the bench. No sign of Milner. Maybe he is saving them for Munich on Wednesday. It's certainly a strong bench for the game.

***

Half time. Winning 2-1 and fully deserve to be in the lead after being cheated out of their opening goal. Burnley scored direct form a corner in the sixth minute with Alisson clearly being held down by their players. How the referee and linesman have missed it I'll never know. Alisson even gets a yellow card for his reaction.

It wasn't long before we were controlling the game and have got the goals the play deserves. A tap in from Bobby and then Mané sweeping one into the corner. Conditions look bleak—like they were on the beach earlier. Wind, rain, sleet and snow. We need another goal to put ourselves clear so we are not sucker punched by the conditions late on.

***

Liverpool win 4-2. Another goal from Bobby after Salah was brought down and we looked comfortable. Then we concede a goal in injury time and it's the proverbial squeaky bum time only for Mané to break away and score with the last kick of the game. A point behind. Eight games to go.

Terrible conditions to play a game of football, but I have to say the professionalism and approach of the team are beyond question. A dubious goal to go behind and then a bit of a scruffy one at the end to potentially put the wobblers under us, but we have faced off all challenges and come through with another fine win. Lallana was great today—it's such a shame for him that he has been hit by so many injuries in the last couple of seasons. He adds a level of skill and finesse that can really influence a game.

Tuesday 12th March 2019

Woke up early this morning with a text message. It was a re-minder from the airline about checking in for the flight to Mu-nich. The flight I decided not to take. What a way to start the day.

Munich game tomorrow. Gutted I didn't go, but looking forward to watching the game. City went through tonight win-ning 7-0 so all the other English clubs have gone through to the last eight. We don't want to miss out. We need a scoring draw or a win after the goalless first leg. We are currently alternating between scoring a bagful and not scoring at all so it's difficult to call.

Lallana played well at the weekend. Man of the match per-formance. Everyone was surprised and a bit gutted that he got into the side but was well justified in being picked, really push-ing the pace in midfield, being forceful and creative. When we have looked for that creative midfielder who will break the lines we have been looking to Keita and Shaqiri. To add an in-form Lallana to that list for the run in is a real bonus. I was hoping we could add Ox, too, but he had an injury problem in his first game back so realistically he is going to be next season's 'new signing'.

I don't think Lallana will get in the starting line-up tomor-row. He always seems to like Milner for these games and I think Gini is picking himself with his performances. It's a ques-tion of Fabinho or Henderson. I'd go for the latter.

Wednesday 13th March 2019

Wednesday night and I have raced back for the game. Busy day and haven't had time to think about the game all day but listen-ing to the build-up on the radio. Going to be a big game. Mu-nich coming back into form and it's 0-0. All to play for.

He has dropped Fabinho, which is a bit of a surprise, and gone back to his tried-and-trusted trio of Hendo, Gini and Milner in midfield. He must have a game plan to ensure we are tight and responsible and not leave ourselves chasing the game. Fabinho obviously hasn't broken fully into Klopp's circle of trust, although he has been the pick of the midfielders recently and the type of player we haven't had for a while. I think he will be the future pick, next season and beyond he will be the fulcrum of that side, but for the time being the other three are the safe pick.

Keita didn't travel because he is injured so he isn't an option, but with Lallana in a bit of form and Shaqiri we have good options if we need to break forward later in the game. Fabinho is also on the bench and is a good option at the base to release one of the other three forward.

Come on, Liverpool.

***

Half time and it's 1-1. That's enough to put us through on the away goals, but in my current state I don't think my heart would hold out at that score for the whole second half.

Hendo went off early so Fabinho is playing at the base of midfield as he has been doing so well in the last few weeks. Very cagey first 25 minutess. Hardly a chance. Both teams feeling each other out. Then Mané gets the ball on the edge of the box from an incredible long ball from VVD. Neuer comes out and misses it and Mané turns him and chips the defence. Beautiful goal. Even better that I had a tenner on him to do it.

The game livened up from there. Pace picked up noticeably but not opened by any means. Ten minutes left and Bayern score. Ball in from the right and Matip turns it in. He's an easy target and will no doubt get some stick for it, but if he hadn't the guy behind him would have scored anyway. I think Robertson is more at fault for losing his man.

Going to be a tense second half, I think.

***

Full time. Wasn't tense. Was never in doubt. Finished 1-3. We held them out and they never got close. Towering majestic header from VVD puts us ahead and then another goal from Mané closed it out. It was a joyous masterclass of football and it puts us in the last eight. All four English clubs have made it through and with a couple of the big clubs knocked out there is an opportunity to move forward.

Gutted I haven't gone to the game tonight. I was dying to go to Munich. That was the only place I wanted to go and when it came out of the draw, I knew I wanted to go. Ange even paid for me to go for my Christmas present. But with everything going on at work, it wasn't realistic.

I feel like I have missed a famous night now. I'm absolutely gutted. I should have been in that stadium with my mates, it looked awesome and I am so disappointed that I didn't go. It was my choice. No one said don't go, but I realise I made the right choice. I must be growing up.

I'll just have to hope we get matched with them again next year. Fortunately, as we are now in the last eight, there are other away days to look forward to. Happy to get anyone in the draw and fairly sure we would be top of the list of teams the others don't want to face.

Friday 15th March 2018

Champions quarter final draw. Live. You're lucky, dear reader; you're going to get ball by ball commentary!

Open draw apparently and they are going to draw all the way through the final. There is a load of guff being talked. No one cares, just pull the bloody balls out.

All four English clubs have gone through so there is bound to be an all English match. Hope ours isn't one of them.

First one out is Ajax. That would be a good draw. Looks like they are one of the easier teams although they battered Real Madrid. Next one out is Juventus. Ajax vs Juve.

Next one Liverpool. Come on, you red men. Get a good draw, lads. The tension. Hurry up! Porto. Boom. Great. Best draw goes to Liverpool.

Spurs next. They get City. That means United get Barcelona. Sherlock Holmes level deductions there.

Don't care. We got Porto. While there is no easy draw that must be the most favourable. We battered them last year.

Now they are going to draw the semis. Stop bloody talking and pull the balls out the bowl. Yes, yes, yes... We all know how it works... Spurs or City will play Ajax or Juve.

That means we play Barca or United if we can beat Porto. And we came out last so we will be at home in the second leg. This is like the BBC, isn't it!

Now, who will be the home team in the final? The other side of the draw so if we make it we are the away team. What that actually means I'm not sure, probably less tickets knowing our luck and UEFA's incompetence!

I'll take that draw. Porto follows by United or Barca. Brilliant.

Before that we've got Fulham this weekend to go back to the top of the league. Momentum. Come on, you red men.

***

Excited about the draw today. Feeling really upbeat about it. Porto is a good draw and gives us the best chance to progress. I can see us being in the semis with Barcelona, Juventus and City. I think it rightly puts us as one of the best four teams in

Europe at the moment.

Focus on the league though this weekend. City are playing in the cup so we play the extra game on Sunday against Fulham and if we can get a good win and score a few goals it will put us ahead of them for the next few weeks and increase the pressure on their game with United, which will then be the game in hand.

The squad seem to be coming into form too. Maybe, just maybe, the two warm weather trips that were so derided in the wake of the poor results may now be beginning to pay off. After this weekend there is an international break so the team can get a break and be ready for the last seven games, which realistically we need to win to be in with a shout.

Lallana was a revelation last week and did well when he came on in Munich. He's like a new player in the squad. They have announced that they expect Ox to be 100% fit after the break, which is another great option off the bench. Keita was injured and missed the trip to Munich and I feel like this is just not his season. He needs to get fit and ready for next season after a year of acclimatisation. It's a shame but we are now in the final stretch and we need players who are in form and performing rather than playing them into form.

Fulham have been letting goals in for fun this season and this is our opportunity to reduce that goal difference. That could be vital on the last day of the season.

See what tomorrow brings.

Sunday 17th March 2019

Away to Fulham today. This is the game where we have the opportunity to go back to the top of the league. Need to put these to bed.

Team is out. Lallana gets another run alongside Fabinho and Gini in midfield. Henderson injured after the other night. What a great player Lallana is to have available to bring in when the games are coming thick and fast. I think he must be one of Klopp's favourites and I believe he is a real influence in the camp, injured or not.

The rest of the team has reverted to type. Back five and front three as you would expect. I don't think there will be much rotation in these areas through to the end of the season. It will be the same eight players barring injury or suspension. The freshness in the team will come from the middle.

Come on, Liverpool.

***

Half-time. One nil. Mané scores. Again. There's not a lot to say. Safe at the back. Dominant in midfield. Salah continuing to work hard. In the end we get the goal we deserved. Mané scored through a very crowded box after a run and a good interchange with Robertson. All been coming down the left today.

Need to pick up the pace in the second half. Try to reduce this goal deficit. This is a chance to improve our position in the league. Don't want to get to the last day and find we need additional goals. We need to get them now.

***

Finished 2-1. Klopp of the League according to Sky. I'll take that.

We won in the end. One-way traffic but then conceded a goal after a sloppy slice at the ball from Milner and an uncharacteristic back pass mistake from VVD. Ryan Babel stepped on to score and equalise with fifteen minutes to go.

To be fair Babel looked gutted. I remember ten years ago, when he joined Liverpool, he was going to be the next big thing. The player you willed to be amazing but had too many other things going on in his head to succeed. When it looked like he was going to make a career as a DJ, he has managed to keep his football going, is back in the Dutch squad and has fetched up at Fulham after nearly ten years playing in the Turkish league.

So fifteen minutes to go and we needed to win. To be fair to the lads, they stepped up the pressure and got the reward. Pressure told on them in the end and we got the penalty. Milner converted and from then it wasn't in doubt.

We are top. Two points clear but played a game extra. There is nothing in it.

Friday 22nd March 2019

A short note. It's international week. Why they have to have international week is beyond me. We are six weeks out from the end of the season. Everyone focussed on the run-in. Champions League quarter finals coming up and they think that anyone would be the slightest bit interested in watching an international match. I don't even know if they are friendlies or competitive. Who cares?

I am over in Chamonix skiing. Getting away from life and having fun for a few short days. A week till we play Spurs and the run-in really starts.

Off to the snow...

Saturday 30th March 2019

So this is it. The final push starts this weekend. Teams have been away on international but now they are back. There has been no news to speak of, nothing to write about, the world has been dominated by the failure of the Brexit process for the past fortnight. International games went under the radar as they tend to do nowadays and football has effectively been missing.

The football is back and there is now an intense six-week

uninterrupted sequence of games that will take us hopefully to that point of fulfilling our destiny. Klopp was back in a press conference yesterday and his key word was resilience. That is what will be required to win this league.

We have seven games left to do that, plus a minimum of two in the Champions League, with a quarter final clash against Porto coming up in the next few weeks. Beyond that, potentially either Barcelona or United in the semis but we don't need to count our chickens at this stage... Let's just look at the league.

Seven games. The most difficult is tomorrow. Home to Spurs. Beyond that another tough home game against Chelsea, three games against relegation threatened Southampton, Cardiff and Huddersfield and finishing up with games against mid table Newcastle and finally Wolves at home on the last day. There are no easy games in the Premier League as the old cliché goes, but that run-in I see as favourable. We have a real chance.

We are top of the league, two points clear but have played an extra game. City have eight to play. They also have a six-goal advantage at this stage, which could be crucial. Their game in hand is a midweek game against United in late April. I can't remember ever saying this, but that is a game I want United to win.

They have appointed Solskjaer as their permanént manager now and that will be their biggest game of the season as they try to secure some local pride but more importantly a place in the top four, which is currently being hotly contested by United, Arsenal, Spurs and Chelsea. Just four points between them, only two of the four can qualify for the Champions League. All to play for.

The media narrative is that we are bottling it ... or bottled it over the last section of games at least, whereas City have the stronger mentality and are more experienced in this push for the title. They are odds on to win the league with bookies and commentators are all behind them. We are the slight outsider in a two-horse race. City play Fulham today at lunchtime. You would think it's a nailed-on win, but the important thing is how many they score. They could run up a cricket score against a poor team and that could put the goal difference out of reach.

***

Nine p.m. End of a busy day. City won as predicted but only 2-0, which is good as it keeps the goal difference within reach.

I've been preparing all day for our holiday tomorrow. We are off to Australia for three weeks in the morning. It's been booked for over a year and I'm really excited to be going back to a place I consider one of my homes. We lived there for seven years, had the best time in Sydney, lived and worked, had our little boy, became Aussie citizens. This is the first time we have been back since we returned to the UK in 2012.

I know what you're thinking. *He's missing the game tomorrow, what sort of fan is this?* I know. I've been thinking the same. When you book these things a year out, you don't factor in the fixtures; you'll assume you'll miss a game, maybe two. What you don't realise is it will be Spurs, Chelsea and a quarter final of the Champions League!

I'm disappointed to be missing them. Not more than that. I could go further and say I'm distraught, gutted, but that would be a lie. I'm so much looking forward to going away with family and catching up with old friends in Sydney.

That said, I'm absolutely furious that the Spurs game was moved to a Sunday afternoon rather than a Saturday teatime because I will be on a plane and will miss the entire game. These Sky people really are inconsiderate bastards. I'm going to be on pins for the whole flight to Singapore wondering how we got on. I have enquired to see whether they can live stream the game onto the plane, but apparently that is not an option. Sodding Sky, someone has to be blamed and it's them.

The other two games I'm not too concerned about. I had seven years in Sydney and barely missed a game. Of course, it's not like being in the ground, but at least watching it on TV at stupid o'clock in the morning gives you a connection. Coverage of the Premier League is very good in Australia, at least it used to be, and the Champions League used to be on terrestrial TV, so I won't be missing anything.

The Porto game will be an early start on a Wednesday morning, probably in the house where we are staying, and if I can rouse enough support Chelsea could be a big night in the city, although I won't be broadcasting that too loud at home!!

I'll be back for the last two home games, so I can only hope we are still in the running by then. Can only hope. For God's sake, how negative is that? I don't know if you can do a written Freudian slip, but that is bloody close. The lion-hearted fan inside me is obviously having a quiet day and the cracks of doubt are showing. Match day tomorrow, I'll be a different person.

The only thing I haven't talked about is the team itself. From what I can see, we are in good

shape after the break. It looks like the only person still on the injury list is Ox, and we'd virtually written him off for the season anyway. Gomez is back, which is a great boost. I doubt he'll be straight back into the team, but if he can play himself into match fitness in the coming weeks he should be back in the first team. At the start of the season, at times he looked like the senior partner alongside VVD, which really is saying something.

Looks like Henderson and Keita are maybe carrying knocks into the game, but with the strength in depth in midfield we can carry those setbacks in our stride. Fabinho has made himself indispensable; Wijnaldum has been our best midfielder all season and plays with such intensity in these top-of-the-table clashes. Milner never lets anyone down in these games; these are the type of clashes he was made for.

That's before we start talking about a resurgent Lallana, Origi on a diet of raw meat and Shaqiri desperate to prove himself after a quiet few months.

I should have started on this before I got into the 'can only hope' territory. Just writing about the team for a couple of paragraphs and I am almost instantly bounding with confidence.

Sunday 31st March 2019

Sunday morning and flying in a few short hours through to Singapore for a stop-off before continuing to Sydney later in the week. Liverpool playing Spurs at home today. I'll be mid-air and won't be able to see it, likely won't even know the score. That is not what I need at this stage of the season!

Spurs are the best of the rest. Up till about six weeks ago, they were part of the race for the title but are too inconsistent and have dropped back into the pack of four fighting it out for the Champions League spots. They have everything to play for because two of the top six are going to lose out and they don't want to be one of those, especially not with this new stadium to pay off.

They can be great on their day, I don't really see what Kane does, but he seems to keep scoring anyway. But we can be better. Salah not scoring too many recently, but his work rate never fails and that creates problems for the opposition. They are watching him constantly and that is letting Mané step in. Between the pair of them, fed by Bobby, they need to have the best six weeks of their lives. Ripping defences apart, scoring goals, creating terror and excitement at the same time.

It is a must-win game. At this stage they all are and even if we win them all, we may still come up short. We are a point behind and I could see City winning all of their remaining games, they are that good. But they also have a very busy fixture list, and something may have to give. At the most they are going to lose one and if they do that gives us a sniff. But even then, we would need 20 points to overhaul them and the only way to amass that many points is seven wins out of seven. It's a must-win game, they all are from here on in.

Come on Liverpool, I can only imagine what you'll be doing, but I'm positive you will be doing it well.

Interlude 9 - Hillsborough

My match-going routine changed that year. It was the year my best friend Stuart got his season ticket and I started going with him, standing right in the middle of the Kop.

I haven't mentioned Stuart, but he has been almost ever present in my life. Born in the same hospital a few days before, our mums had met and become friends at prenatal classes. He lived around the corner as a kid and has always been there. Forty odd years on he is my oldest and most trusted friend and we still sit together on the Kop. Since 1988, my football life has always had him in it.

At the start of this season, we started going to the away games. We both did a milk round in the morning and that helped to pay for our away trips. It was the cup games we went to rather than the league games, they were the exciting adventures of the time in the absence of European football.

That season, we had been away to Arsenal in the League Cup and then replay at neutral Villa Park. We'd also been to all of the FA Cup games that season so far. Coach up to Carlisle in the third round and then down to Millwall for a more unpleasant experience in the fourth. I don't think I'd go to Millwall again! We struggled to get tickets for Hull but went to the screening at Prenton Park that we counted as an away and then home to Brentford in the sixth round.

It was cool going to away games. I thought so anyway. Still at school and studying for GCSEs, I used to think going to these games was a real adventure. We came back full of stories. Running the gauntlet through London after Millwall, being there when a load of lads emptied an off licence and then getting drunk on the way home. Standing next to the guy who cracked the roof of the bus at Villa, being raided at The Rocket on the way home from Norwich. We were good kids really but were on the fringes of the regular away game travellers and we revelled in it. I for one thought I was really grown up. So, of course, we were going to go the semi-final. That's what we did. It wasn't in question.

My memory of Hillsborough is a series of moments, crystal clear moments. I don't remember every detail, but the moments are enough for me to piece together the day.

We went with another mate, Ian, driven by his dad Jimmy. That was how we went to all the home games then. Jimmy was a real character. From the middle of Liverpool, he had spent years at sea before settling in Warrington. He'd been going to the game since the '50s and had untold stories about his life at sea and going to the game. Jimmy had one flaw. He was a terrible driver.

That day, the four of us went in his car, but his driving was particularly bad. As we drove through Glossop on our way to the Snake Pass he struggled with the pre-match traffic jam, constantly over-revving the engine and it was almost inevitable that the car was going to break down. It had overheated and as he took the radiator cap off he dropped it somewhere under the bonnet and couldn't find it. It was comical really. He took us all for a pint in a local working men's club while we waited for the AA man.

But the man didn't come, and all the match traffic had gone by then. We were going to miss the kick-off and that couldn't happen, so we flagged down a coach bringing people back to Sheffield from Manchester Airport and jumped on, leaving Jimmy back there on his own to get the car sorted. Three 16-

year-olds on our way to the game.

We got to Sheffield just after three o'clock. The driver took a detour and dropped us off only a hundred yards or so from the ground and we ran down, eager not to miss anything. Turnstiles were empty. As we were going through we could hear a voice over the tannoy telling people to get off the pitch. I turned to Stuart, something was going on; we had to be quick. And we ran straight down the tunnel.

It was the same infamous tunnel the fans had gone down when the gates were opened shortly before. But the gates were closed now. We didn't know what had gone on. Everything looked normal. Outside, the place was empty as everyone was in the ground. We were late and wanted to get in.

We got onto the terracing just as the players were leaving. It was busy in there. Packed. I tried to get into a better position, but there was no movement. People were on the pitch but there was no trouble, no fighting at least. We didn't really know what was going on at all. I don't know how long we were in there. It couldn't have been long.

We were at the back of the section, probably about fifteen or twenty yards from the front and had no idea the extent of the problems down there that were causing people to spill onto the pitch. At the back around us, there was a sense of unease and panic. We had only just arrived but were amongst people who had been there in the building crush. People couldn't move, and I felt like we were just adding to the problem.

We still thought the game would be going on, that the players would be back out soon and we didn't want to miss that, but at the same time, the sense of something being wrong was evident Lads were being pulled out of the terrace up into the stand above. That wasn't right. We pulled back and went up the tunnel we had just come down. Back to the area behind the stand.

There was a person on the floor who was struggling. I could see he was struggling. He was surrounded by others trying to help. They were shouting for help. There was a policeman there, not really doing much to help, and the others were shouting at him. Pleading for him to do something. They were angry. It wasn't that the policeman didn't want to help; he just didn't know what to do. We knew something wasn't right although clearly not the extent. We knew we had to stick together, and we took the stairs up to the stand above so we could see what was going on. I don't know what happened to that person on the ground.

By the time we got up there, there were many more people on the pitch. People being pulled out of the terrace and being laid on the floor. There was a shout from the Forest fans at the other end and an angry reaction from our fans. The Forest fans couldn't see what we could see. That something was really wrong. The police formed a line across the pitch, while fans started the rescue effort. They started tearing off the advertising hoardings, running people off to the far corner. Ambulances began to appear and come on the pitch. We watched. We didn't know.

Again, I don't know how long we were there. I think we were still up there when someone said that someone had died. It was just a rumour, maybe a report on the radio, but that put everything we could see in a different context. It was difficult to comprehend—someone had died. We'd been in crushes at the match before, but nobody had died. It didn't register as even a possibility.

At that point, we were still thinking about our own problem. Stranded in the City, how were we going to get home? We didn't know, but by then, Jimmy had fixed the car and had driven across, probably more aware of the extent of the problems than we were through radio reports. He stood on a wall outside the ground in his white factory overalls so we could see him. We didn't see him.

We walked out, not quite sure where to go. There were

people queuing up at phone boxes. People queuing up at houses to use the phone. Local residents helping. People walking back to their cars. We ended up at a row of minibuses parked on an embankment just off the main road. We needed a lift. I can't remember how many of the minibuses we approached, but eventually we found a group of lads who would help. They said we'd have to sit on the floor of the van, but that was alright as long as they could get us home.

One of the lads in the van was from Sheffield. Jasper his name was. We drove to a place not far from the ground. I think it was his mum's. A flat over a hairdressers and we all trooped in, maybe a dozen of us, guys we'd only met ten minutes before.

It was only then that I phoned home. It was my first chance. By then it was confirmed people had died. My mum sounded frantic. She burst into tears and so did I. Up to that point I had been quite calm, but I started crying.

We didn't know these lads, certainly didn't know their family, but we were offered cups of tea and bacon butties. The lads were at pains to ensure the whole group paid for the hospitality and I remember a pile of five and ten-pound notes next to the telephone.

You could see the ground from the flat. A big window in the living room next to the TV. The floodlights were on, casting a kind of halo glow around the stadium, and I was listening to the Des Lynam reporting as the news came through on the TV. The death count was rising.

I couldn't say how long we stayed there. I think it was dark by the time we left and headed home. We stopped at a pub on the way back. Probably as a toilet stop more than anything, but we had a pint in there. It seems horrendous to say that now, but we did. We knew what had happened by this point. But I really couldn't say how we were feeling.

And then we drove home. We chatted to the lads all the way, although I can't remember what we chatted about. We knew all their names by the time we got home, but it's only Jasper that I remember. I decided to look them up afterwards to thank them for looking after us. But I never did.

They dropped us off at Burtonwood services. We hugged each one of them. My mum and Auntie Pat and Jimmy were all there. I guess Stuart's parents too, but I don't remember them. I just remember my mum. She gave me the biggest hug. A desperate hug. She'd lost so much in the years before. I can feel that hug now and understand it better as a parent than I ever did as a child.

And then we went home.

APRIL

Monday 1ˢᵗ April 2019

Singapore. A 13-hour flight not knowing the score. As we came in to land the phone went on, picked up a signal and I knew the score before we touched down. Relief.

A close one. A last-minute mistake by the keeper at the Kop end. It's Jordan Pickford all over again. We have certainly had our share of good fortune this season. I have done the obligatory search on YouTube and found the Russian highlights. Great goal from Bobby from an incredibly fast-paced ball in from Robbo on the left. A great goal and it looks like we had more good chances in the first half especially.

Having conceded a goal with twenty minutes to go and almost another with minutes to go, but for amazing defending by VVD, we had nearly thrown it away. No room for error. We made the error but got a reprieve. How much is that going to count at the end of the season?

I haven't got that much more to say. I wasn't there; it's all regurgitated, nothing original. Suffice to say we got the win, that's all that matters at this stage. On holiday now.

Tuesday 2nd April 2019

Two a.m. Curse of the jet lag. Hiding in the bathroom, wide awake, trying not to wake the kids up so they can get back into a normal routine. Working my way through newspapers and social media to get a feel for the atmosphere and the reaction to the game on Sunday.

I was dismissive of it yesterday. Just a win. It was nothing of the sort. It was a massive season-changing win. Because I wasn't there, it's impossible to get a sense of the reaction, the relief, the wild reaction to getting that goal in the final minute. It must have been mental in there.

I think back three months to that reaction to that goal against Everton in the derby. The place went berserk, absolutely crazy. It must have been the same. Now, this isn't Everton, there won't have been that primal response in the same way. Going from absolute frustration that we haven't put this shite team away to a madcap moment of hilarity that we have pinched the game through the worst of all mistakes, via the side road of confusion as to what actually happened there and surely someone is going to disallow it.

It can't have been like that surely. But it would have base instinct coming to the fore. Six games out. Our biggest and hardest remaining game of the season, the disappointment of being pulled back, the relief of not conceding a breakaway and the madness of how a World Cup winning keeper can make such a calamitous error at such a crucial moment. It would have been crazy, almost too much to comprehend. And I bloody missed it.

That's the experience of the match goer. The difference between the person who watches on TV and reads the newspaper reports and the person who stands and cheers and shouts. I want to be the match goer.

Thursday 3rd April 2019

Other side of the world. Woke up this morning to find City won again last night. Cat and mouse. They beat Cardiff, which you would expect – Cardiff are more than likely going to get relegated – but they only beat them 2-0, which I am looking at as a positive. It puts them a single point ahead with a nine-goal advantage. Same games played.

It turns out that was their game in hand. We play Southampton tomorrow night and they are playing in the FA Cup, so they get that game in hand back. That will be the United game in a couple of weeks.

Liverpool need to win and keep winning, that's the only thing for it. Keep winning. We need 18 points from 18 and to finish on 97 points and anything less than that and I'm afraid we're done for. City can't finish on 97 points. They can finish on 98 or they can finish on 96 or below. Ninety-seven is ours and that's what we need to get to.

I was thinking we needed to be ahead on goal difference. I can't see either side dropping points in more than one game. They lose one and we draw one, puts us both on 95. So the goal difference does matter. It really matters. This is where we need to throw caution to the wind and not just win but win well, racking up the goals.

It's a while since Salah has scored, he's played well but hasn't scored; he needs to get back on it. We need fours and fives. It's in our grasp but we need goals. At the weekend, Klopp played a blinder. Spurs equalised, and we needed to win. He brought on Fabinho and took the game to them. He trusted the defence to keep them out and he put his fist round their throat, pushed up everyone except VVD. We needed the win; he got it. Now we need goals, he needs a plan for them.

Second would be heart-breaking. It would be a phenomenal achievement in terms of points, but it would be gut wrenching and soul destroying at the same time. After 32 games, we are up there with the record breakers, the best teams ever (or at least in the Premier League era). City's total last year is the top. They finished the league on 100 points. Then it's Chelsea. Mourinho's team from 04/05, who choked all before them, only conceding 15 goals. Then it's City and ourselves. Fourth best ever. Of all United's successful assaults on the title, they have never amassed this many points at this stage (just thought I'd get that in there ... the bastards).

Any other time a team has got this many points, it's been pretty much a one-horse race, so to have us still in contention is unprecedented and outstanding. Somehow, I don't think second is going to be seen that way.

Friday 5th April 2019

Back in Australia. Back in Neutral Bay where we spent so many happy years living the Aussie Dream.

Arrived back last night and off to the Airbnb apartment we have taken for a couple of weeks. Internet working and amidst exploring the area with the kids, I have been looking for solutions for watching the Southampton game.

They have all the Premier League over here. They used to show it on FOXTEL, their equivalent of Sky. Every game. But this has since been bought out by the phone operator Optus. I've decided I don't like Optus. They have exclusive rights to both Premier League and Champions League but have decided that they don't want visitors from the UK watching it.

It's a TV subscription service much like Sky at home. In addition, they have up an all-singing all-dancing app, which streams every game directly onto your iPad. It should be a piece of piss.

But only if you're Australian. I don't know how much of it is the Premier League protecting their asset when assigning rights, but they have made it very difficult for anyone from outside the country to watch it. You can't download the app with an English Apple account. And you can't change your English Apple account to Australian without an Australian credit card.

Tried everything. Live chat with Optus. Email to Optus. No chance.

They must know that loads of English visitors would gladly pay a premium to subscribe for the short time they are here, but they haven't set it up, so I can only imagine it's part of the Premier League rights package. They hate us clearly. It's a 6 a.m. kick-off so the pub isn't really an option either. Although you never know.

***

A solution. It's a good thing to have mates around the world. Caught up with my best mate from when I was over here. All different now with kids in tow but was great to catch up with him.

He's English but has been here a long time now and is fully entrenched in the Aussie ways. I have returned back to the flat armed with his Apple ID and his Optus log-in. And before you know it I am all set for the game. Alarm set for 5.55 a.m.

Come on, Liverpool. There's always a way...

Saturday 6th April 2019

Six forty-five a.m. Half time and it's 1-1 at Southampton. The iPad works and I'm watching the game live. Magic!

The football isn't magic. Liverpool struggling a little against an impressive Southampton who have also adopted a pressing game under their new manager. From certainties to go down at Christmas, I reckon they will be safe from the drop if they continue to play like that.

They score early on through Shane Long who found loads of space in the box from a cross. Liverpool tried to push forward but were held back by their pressing game. Midfield trio of Fabinho, Gini and Keita haven't quite clicked and have been unable to get the ball through to the front three.

There have been a lot of calls for Fabinho to finish the rest of the season as first choice holding midfielder, which I tend to agree with, but he hasn't had the best of games there so far. For me they are missing Henderson, but I guess he is being held back for the Champions League in midweek.

Keita was quiet also until he pops up for his first goal for Liverpool. Great cross from Trent to pick him out and he did well to get up for the header... He's only little!

Need to push on in the second half now.

Throw the dice.

***

Get in there. Fucking get in there. What a release that was at the end. Thirty-five minutes at 1-1. Getting closer but not playing particularly well and not really looking like making the break-through. Playing better than the first half but not well enough to get the goal they need. It wasn't a pleasurable experience.

And then Salah gets the ball inside his own half and runs and runs right down the middle. Bobby draws off to the left for the pass, but Mo somehow dink's it into the space between the defender, the keeper and the right-hand post. What an incredible goal. What a time to score. Eight games and 55 days without a goal and he picks this perfect moment to put us ahead. His 50th goal for Liverpool in record-breaking time.

Top off after the goal. Look at me he says. Just look at me. I can imagine every red in the world went mad. I'm sitting on the toilet with headphones in at 7.30 a.m. If I'd have gone mad and woke the kids up it would have been World War Three.

I didn't feel like going mad anyway. It was a sigh of relief and a release of tension through my whole body that had built up through the half. Legs were numb from sitting in the loo too long. It was just complete relief.

The nearer we get to ninety minutes the more my mind starts doing gymnastics with the points combinations. What ifs. The goal lets go of all of that. We're going to win. Then Hendo steps up with a great surging run from midfield to make it 3-1. Game over. Another goal taken off City. Only seven now.

Hendo and Milner came on at sixty minutes. Trent and Gini both not making an impact. We needed impact and experience. And the pair of them delivered it. Some people don't like Henderson. He changed that game today. The look on his face as he scored said it all. Winner.

We are back at the top. Two points clear. City don't play this weekend. They are in the FA Cup instead, so we stay top for at least a week. They play just before us next Sunday so we could be top again.

I keep on wanting to say we are going to win the league. We keep putting in these resilient performances. Coming back. Winning late. The type of things that champions do. But it's not in our hands. 82 points with five games to go and it's not even in our hands. For Christ's sake. Good win today. Got to keep going.

Tuesday 9th April 2019

Next part of the run-in. Porto at home in the quarter final. Switch from the constant mental calculations of the Premier League to a much simpler proposition. Hopefully that is beating Porto, putting ourselves a couple of goals clear ready for the second leg in a week or so's time.

I am a day ahead of it all in Sydney so will be watching it at 5 a.m., headphones in, wishing I was standing there amidst the noise in the ground. We played them last year in the last 16 and absolutely battered them 5-0 before a goalless draw at Anfield in the second leg. I always think it's better to play the second leg at home, but that's the luck of the draw, so we need to get our noses clearly in front.

Robertson is suspended so I guess Milner will be drafted in to cover at left back. Moreno is a forgotten man. Milner is an intelligent player and really bolsters the midfield when playing as a full back. With VVD in the central defensive slot and so much energy in midfield to cover the full back positions and the inner channels, we don't need necessarily a traditional defensive left back.

Other than that selection, the only question is the middle three. In these types of games Klopp has gone to his tried-and-trusted triumvirate of Hendo, Milner and Gini, but with Milner at left back my guess it will be Fabinho coming in and allowing the other two to rove forward.

Gini has been our most consistent midfield player all year but has looked a little tired of late, so I could see Keita getting a run in his place possible, particularly after his goal at the weekend.

It's a sign of how far we have come that this weekend we qualified for next year's Champions League. The last two seasons it has been a last game of the season thing, which added some unwanted drama to the day. Last year, with our run to the Champions League final, our league run really suffered and we went from cruising for the CL spot to leaving it late to qualify after a run of draws.

The situation is very different this year. We have qualified with five games to go, letting the others fight it out for third and fourth. We can't afford any dropped points as we go for a much bigger prize. The likelihood is we will crack 90 points for the season, which is incredible progress for a team.

A great first 11 plus a bench full of options. A far cry from the bare bones we had reached by the end of the season last year when we were literally down to the last man and the only option we had on the bench was a half-fit Adam Lallana. This is a testament to our squad building over a two to three-year period and our squad and player management throughout the season. It's not just the on-field play where we have improved, we are a more improved unit all round.

Wednesday 10th April 2019

Five a.m. start for the Porto game this morning. Half time and I would say a fairly comfortable 2-0 lead. Liverpool have had most of the ball, but Porto have had the odd attack and have looked dangerous on the break without really having an outstanding game.

Keita got the nod ahead of Gini in the end and popped up with a goal after about five minutes. Slightly deflected but we'll give him the benefit of the doubt that it would have gone in anyway. Ten minutes or so later and Bobby has a tap in from six yards, but the praise needs to go to Henderson in midfield for splitting their defence and letting Trent loose to put the cross in. A brilliant passage of play.

Bobby should have had another later on after another great pass from Henderson. I like Henderson although I know many don't. I think he's great at the base of midfield, but with the form of Fabinho you can't really argue that he's getting the position. I think the positive from that is Henderson playing further forward with proving runs and intelligent passing.

It's a bit like the Henderson of the 13/14 season. Breaking forward from midfield, third man running but also able to spot and deliver a telling pass. I still think the downfall of that season was losing him for the critical couple of games at the end of the season after the late red card against City. (Rather than the Gerrard slip espoused by lazy gobshites everywhere.)

Lovren back in the side, which was a surprise. I don't know whether Matip is being dropped or rotated. I thought he had been fairly solid of late. He has played every game, though, in the absence of Lovren and Gomez so maybe just getting a rest.

Can't complain at Lovren, been solid enough at the back but then again anyone would be next to VVD.

***

Full time and a 2-0 win. If I was being picky, I would have pre-ferred a third goal to make the tie absolutely safe, but it didn't come. We contained Porto and they never really got a sniff at a goal, but to be able to relax completely next week we needed a greater margin.

Nothing much to say about the half really. We were in charge, a couple of chances; Mané had a goal disallowed for offside. I'm not over the moon about VAR. I'm not in favour of it anyway, but the way the game is constantly under review off the field is a bit unnerving. United beat PSG last month on the back of a very innocuous handball and you can see the potential for conceding penalties through very debatable ball-to-hand situations, with the game being stopped and called back on the whim of some guy in an editing room somewhere.

Our goal was called offside tonight but there were no com-plaints and really the linesman should have seen that anyway. I'm not going to complain until something serious goes against us – and to be fair won't complain at all if it goes our way – but I don't like this addition to the game and where it is leading.

An interesting subplot in the other game. Spurs beat City 1-0. I would still fully expect City to go through next week, but it is an added thing that Pep has to think about over the weekend, does he have to rotate and weaken his team for the league game to ensure he has his first eleven ready? It's all small margins but it definitely gives us a following wind.

Saturday 13th April 2019

Still over in Sydney. Sad news came through today that Tommy Smith passed away yesterday. He was just before my time so never actually saw him play, but he has always been referred to by family as I was growing up. When a player was too soft, it was Tommy Smith he was compared against.

He was also a link to that great Shankly tradition, one of the players who came through the academy under Shankly and knew the Liverpool way, which gave him the freedom in the eyes of many to be outspoken about some of the modern players and practices that would have been frowned upon in his day.

It was a little anachronistic, but ultimately he was a guy who deserved the respect of the entire city for his commitment to the club over nearly 20 years. Scored the goal in the first European Cup win, too, which is not to be sniffed at. There when the breakthrough was needed.

RIP Tommy. It's sad you never saw this great team come to a triumphant conclusion. I am sure there will be a great tribute to him at the match tomorrow.

Sunday 14th April 2019

Chelsea tonight. One thirty a.m. kick-off over here. The next big test.

It's difficult to assess where Chelsea are even up to. Started the season well, looked like Sarri was a genius. There was that late goal from Sturridge at their place that rescued a point. At the time that seemed like a great point against a resurgent team.

Since then, it's difficult to say what they are going to do from week to week. And that's the worst thing about this game. Don't feel we know what we're facing. After losing touch with us and City, they looked for a while like they were going to miss the top four, but good results in recent weeks and they look to be on form. Hazard is on form and that's the danger.

As for us, well, this is the final countdown now. We have rotated where we can all year, but these players need to be hunkered down for these games. Six, possibly eight games in the next four weeks. Don't talk to me about being tired. If they're tired now, they can go home!!

Front three pick themselves. Alisson, VVD and Robertson are also nailed on. The other centre back is a big question. I thought Matip played well recently, Lovren is fit and came straight in for the Porto game the other night. Gomez was on the bench so he must be fit too and out of the three of them, he is the pick. He's definitely the one with the long-term future, whether he needs to play himself in for a couple of weeks is the question I guess. There's also a doubt over Trent too. Gomez could cover there maybe or even Milner if he needs that experience on the pitch.

This is the time of the season when Milner is going to be in the frame for every game. He was the experienced head in the run to the final last season and that is going to be invaluable in the coming weeks as a starter or a sub or generally just a wise head in the camp.

As for the midfield you can pick any three from six and I'd be happy. Fabinho, Hendo and Gini would be my guess at the moment, although Keita also deserves a shout. Don't care who. Just beat these plastic bastards.

Monday 15th April 2019 (Part One)

Alarm set for 1.30 a.m. After a long and busy weekend, I don't want to fall asleep and miss this game, but my mind won't really let me switch off from it.

City have beaten Palace. Fucking Hodgson. So it leaves us needing to win. We needed to win anyway. There is no room for error. Side as expected. Matip gets his place back, which is fair based on his recent form. Keita gets the nod in midfield ahead of Gini.

The closer I get to this game, the more I'm shitting it. Looking ahead in the fixture list I have been thinking it wouldn't be too bad as their form is poor, but I know how tight it can be against these in recent years.

Come on, you mighty red men!

***

Half time. I was right. Very tight indeed. Goalless but all about a battle in midfield, which is so congested. Chelsea making it that way. Looks like they are playing with half their team in the middle just trying to stop our flow. We look a bit overrun at times with Henderson and Keita struggling to keep up. Fabinho is solid and good job too.

Need to get control in there to make things happen. This is where the experience of Milner could be crucial. Not many chances. Mané had one at the end there that he would have scored when he was in form a month ago. At the back they haven't really had a chance, but Hazard always looks menacing.

***

Full time. What a half. What a win. Two nil. What a fucking win.

A great half of football between two great teams. So different to the cagey first half. It really opened up. We started in another gear. Went for them and two goals in two minutes early on in the half. After being quiet in the first half, Henderson stepped it up from midfield. Put in a great cross for Mané to finish.

The release. The relief. Crowd went berserk. That's what we needed. I'm lying here in bed with earphones in next to my sleeping wife. It was all I could do to restrain myself from jumping up. Could feel myself shaking.

Two minutes later and Salah hits a monster of a shot from 25 yards. It went so fast, so straight, but somehow looked like it was going in slow motion. It was like time slowed down for a second as it went in. Christ knows what the keeper was thinking. To be fair, he had the presence of mind to at least dive for it but was nowhere near. What a peach of a goal. The place just went berserk again. That was it. That was what we needed. We had just blown them away. Another gear. Another level. Unbelievable performance.

To be fair to Chelsea they can back. A quick sub after the goal seemed to release Hazard and give him space. He could have scored two in the five minutes after our goal. Fine margins. Hit the post and then Alisson got his foot to the next.

We calmed down, regained control. Held on. We win. And back to the top of league. Two points clear. Four games left and we are top of the league. I'm off to sleep. Or I'm going to try if I can calm down.

Monday 15th April 2019 (Part Two)

Waking up this morning after the Chelsea game. All the coverage of the game, the goals, the reaction. All the plaudits for Salah, the Klopp press conference. All good. But waking up this morning it is the 15th April. It's the Hillsborough anniversary. The date etched indelibly into the mind. Hillsborough.

There was a beautiful well-respected silence at the game. Always observed so well by all supporters, even the Chelsea fans who are not known for any type of decorum or tolerance. Hillsborough crosses the boundary of football.

It's about people respecting people. It's about people understanding what happened to innocent people on a day out and how the memory and the rights of those people were trampled on by authority. It's about how the families of those people were treated when all they wanted was to understand what happened to their loved ones. It crosses every boundary.

Thirty years on. It's frightening to think it was thirty years ago. A lifetime. So much can happen in that time. I visited Anfield last year during the week and had time and space to stand in front of the memorial. All those people were so young. It hit me like a hammer. I never properly realised how many of them were so young until I saw it etched into the memorial. So many teenagers, so many in their 20s. People with lives ahead of them. I was 16 that day. I had my life ahead of me too. But I came home.

Where I sit in the Kop now, I am surrounded by guys of my age, plus or minus five years or so. When we got thrown together during the seating of the Kop we were in our 20s. Twenty-five years on, we are all in our 40s and 50s. We've had lives ... careers, families, successes, failures, good times and bad times.

That was taken from those 96. Taken through incompetence, disdain, a lack of duty of care. Then the truth was then taken, through callousness, corruption, self-interest, and contempt. It's an outrage.

For a long time, I felt guilty about Hillsborough. Guilty that I came home. That through a twist of fate I wasn't standing in that pen or behind that gate that was opened. I should have been. I would have been if all had gone to plan.

Thinking about it now, it was guilt. I ignored it for a while, looked the other way. It should have been me. I don't feel like that now. I feel sad for the lives that those people missed out on. I feel empathy and admiration for their families and the campaigners who have worked tirelessly. I feel anger at the injustice and the people who created that injustice and continue to hide behind it.

The tribute yesterday is just a minute of contemplation and

thought. But it brings people together. The recognition that we are just people following an interest and a passion and no one should suffer or die for that passion. Hillsborough is a unifying force in that sense. And when we get carried away about the day-to-day pantomime that is the modern game, we should remember that really, it's all just about people.

Tuesday 16th April 2019

Just four weeks to go now to the end of the season. Four league games, all of them very winnable.

For a couple of months now I've been waiting for the moment when I can say, 'We're going to win the league.' That moment when I was convinced. When we had put in a performance that was league winning and I knew in my heart of hearts that we were going to kick in and win.

The performances have been there. Spurs a couple of weeks ago with a last-minute winner. The win against Chelsea at the weekend when we turned up the gears, did what we needed to and then held a very good Chelsea side at arm's length. They were league winning performances.

But I still can't say it. I can't say it because it's not in our hands and as much as we continue to rack up points, City are racking them up at the same rate and have that all-important one-point advantage. We need to face up to the fact that we could amass 97 points this season and still not win the league. Finish the season with a single defeat and not be crowned champions.

Only one side has scored this many points at this stage of the season - and that was City last year. They are a hell of a team, possibly the best the Premier League has ever seen (although I don't believe that myself), and they could go in and follow up their 100-point season last year and win it again with 98.

I don't know whether I'm ready to think about that possibility yet. Scoring 97 and not winning the league. Would that be a failure? No doubt it is progress. No doubt it is a phenomenal achievement. But it's not winning is it? And that is what we set out to do.

The next week is crucial in how that shakes out. We play Cardiff at the weekend. City play Spurs. I know which is the most winnable of those two. Before we play our next game, at home to Huddersfield, City have to play the all-important game in hand, away to United. I think it's safe to say it will be the first time I have ever wanted United to win. The moment I walk across to the dark side. But, unfortunately, I think that will be our last chance.

Before that the return against Porto on Wednesday night.

Wednesday 17th April 2019

Last full day in Australia. I'm lying here on Shelley Beach in the sand, Manly looking beautiful across the water. Body surfing at Freshwater this morning. It's been a fabulous holiday. Sydney is a special place that means so much to me and my wife and we feel happy and blessed to be here again, showing the kids our old life and meeting up with loads of good people who have been friends for a long time. Still thinking occasionally about the football though!!

Champions League last night. Barcelona outclassed United and saw them off. The shock of the night was Ajax beating Juventus in the away leg, just like they did with Real Madrid in the previous round. They have become the dark horses in the competition and will be a tough opponent for whoever goes through between City and Spurs. At the moment, they look like a lucky miss.

Of course, we won't be playing anyone if we don't see off Porto tonight. A 2-0 lead from last week might seem safe, but I won't feel relaxed until we get an away goal. The concern is it's 'only Porto' and the greater focus is on the league game against Cardiff at the weekend.

After a good game last week, Lovren is unwell, so isn't in the squad. Matip deserves to keep his place I think. He is injury prone but has had a good run and it would be a shame for the lad if he loses his place. That said, there is no room for sentiment and Gomez is the best of the three in my opinion ... assuming he's fit of course.

Other than that little dilemma, the squad appears to be fit and firing at just the right time. Their front man looked a real threat last week but wasn't good in front of goal. It only needs him to get one and it's a very nervous remainder of the game. An early goal to the good will settle nerves.

***

Half time at Porto. Somehow, we go in a goal ahead. It's one of the most one-sided halves of football I have seen this season. Porto have been on the front foot from the start with some good chances and domination of play throughout. We had a single chance that fell to Mané. It looked like he was offside, but after a couple of minutes' review, the referee gave it.

I don't like VAR at all, but I'll take that. No one could see the goal until the review had actually happened and I didn't think for a single minute it would be given. But it was spot on. Mané was onside when the pass was made but moving so quickly he looked way off by the time he tapped it in.

That has changed the tie. Porto now need four and, as hesitant in defence and careless in midfield as we have been, I can't see them getting four goals at all. If anything they may have just punched themselves out, which will leave us better opportunities in the second half.

***

Full time. We won 4-1 and in a really smug way I am going to say I was right. Porto had nothing much to offer in the second half. They had punched themselves out and left themselves open too often. The key goal was Salah running through into a beautiful pass from Trent and, at 2-0, the tie was over. They pulled back a consolation goal but had nothing left and Firmino scored, followed by a header from VVD.

We are through. Professional and assured Liverpool seeing off a potentially difficult second leg. We are boss. The experience and the composure throughout the team is so reassuring to watch and then combine that with their ability to destroy sides. It's a joy. Something we have waited so long for. We now have one of the best teams in world football.

Barcelona awaits in the semi and I am excited already. The idea of Messi and co. coming to Anfield is something dreams are made of. But they'll be having nightmares watching this Liverpool team in action. We have now beaten both Bayern Munich and Porto in the away legs. It's a far cry from our supposed poor away form just a few months ago.

While our game was a procession, the other game was anything but. A right ding dong and Spurs have knocked City out. City won 4-3 on the night with the first five goals coming in the first 20 minutes.

City had a winner at the death that was ruled out by VAR. Made all the better by Spurs' final goal being allowed by the same system when it looked like handball. So that is their quadruple out the window. Let's hope there is some kind of psychological hangover that affects their ability to get the treble. With a game as emotional as that, losing it in the way they did, you couldn't blame them if their hearts were just a little bit broken.

As for Spurs, they'll be on cloud nine, but at the moment it's so tight for that third and fourth spot they can't afford to be letting any opportunity to gain points slide. They will play Ajax in the other semi in a few weeks, but will need to win a couple of games before that.

Despite their game in hand, I feel like we have our foot on City's throat. They have shown themselves to be mortal. This is the time.

Friday 19th April 2019

Flying back from Australia. Christ, it's a long way. Modern communications make it seem like that's not the case. Live TV, newspapers, email, social media. It's all instant. It's only when you're sitting in a plane for seven hours to Singapore and then another 14 hours back to Manchester that you realise how far away it is. The other side of a planet. Literally.

It's a shame it's so far. We spent so long there and tried to make a life there. We loved it there, made so many great friends and memories. But then we decided to come back and have another life over here. The distance dictates that the two lives are separate. You can't just pop over to sample your old life. It's a commitment. You are either here or there. You can't do both.

We have had the best two weeks being over there. We have taken a wonderful journey down memory lane with friends. It will be a while before we go back. But not seven years.

Flying home, I am reading Ian Salmon's book on the 2015/16 season. *They Say Our Days Are Numbered - Liverpool's Season of Change.* It's excellent. A mini review of each match in the context of his life. His writing style is engaging, and I am thoroughly engaged with it. It has made me realise two things.

First of all, he is a far better writer than I could ever hope to be and my idea of writing a book that may be published has taken a severe knock when I look at what is 'the competition'.

Perversely, I think the 15/16 provides better content than the current season. That may sound strange as we pursue this record-breaking points haul, but it actually becomes difficult to continue writing when everything is going well. Ian has had the benefit of a season of change. The departure of Rodgers and the arrival of Klopp and the start of the journey.

Which brings me on to the second realisation. How far we have come in the last three seasons under Klopp, and how lucky we are to be in this situation we found ourselves in. At the start of the 15/16, we were a club in disarray. Many believing the manager should have gone at the end of the previous season. The majority believing he was a dead man walking. Disquiet amongst the fans. Another season of rebuilding just over a year after nearly winning the title. How it all went so wrong so quickly.

It's easy to forget the state of things just three short years ago. The core of a good side. Players with potential but not gelling as a unit. A divided fan base not enjoying the Liverpool match-going experience.

And then the arrival of Klopp and how he changed things in a slow but effective and all-encompassing revolution. I remember his original press conference and how he said we would win the league within three years. How he took a mixed bag of players and stood behind them, brought the best out of them. Not straight away. It was not a linear thing. But week-on-week the trajectory was in the right direction.

At the end of each season there has been evolution. Better players brought in year on year. Sticking with players and improving them when other managers would have sold them on. Being honest with players who weren't going to cut it. Being brutal when needed. Blooding new players.

Selling players for world record fees in order to finance this evolution. Reaching a point where every new player who comes in is genuinely world class. Mané, Salah, VVD, Alisson,

Fabinho. A supporting cast of quality players throughout the squad.

Three years in and we are top of the league with four games to play, in the semi-final of the Champions League. In the words of a previous manager, a few games from greatness.

I think with this steady progression it can be difficult to see how far we have come. These are special times and we should realise what we are watching because it doesn't come around very often. We are watching a world-class team coming into focus. And there is still improvement to come that we will see over the next couple of seasons. We have the capability to sweep away all before us.

One of the things that Ian identifies is that 2-2 draw against West Brom. That was a turning point. The point when it started to come together. When it started to click. There was a lot of piss taking in the media and across social media when he brought the team down to the Kop end after a draw. But the crowd were behind the team that day. They were part of that comeback. The release was immense when Origi got that equaliser. You had to be in the ground to realise it. We were together from that moment.

It's a magical thing to be a part of.

Saturday 20th April 2019

Just 22 days to go to the end of the season. Four games to go in the Premier League and a double header against Barcelona. It's crunch time. Six games in three weeks.

We already have 85 points on the board. By any stretch of the imagination it's already a successful season. Either ourselves or City are going to end the season as the highest point-scoring runner up, with a points total in the mid-90s. The highest runner up to this point is United with 89. In that season they hadn't progressed to the semis of the Champions League either.

Klopp is saying there is no high-intensity training. The intensity is coming in the games. The hard work has been done, the fitness is there, the fight is plain for all to see. In the league it's a case of who blinks first.

City play Spurs today. A repeat of the Champions League quarter final, which is being called a modern classic. Pep is adamant there is no plan B. They will continue to play the game they have for the last two years.

The defeat against Spurs – and the nature of the defeat – must have had an effect on them. To think you are through with a last-minute goal, only for it to be disallowed by VAR must have some kind of impact on the team. Pep's celebrations turning to disbelief on the touchline were hilarious. They were to me anyway. But that outlet of emotion must take its toll. If not on him then on the players themselves. The team-talk before the game today will have to be a masterclass.

I can see it going one of two ways. Spurs will be on a high and in a mood to take the game to City. If that happens, then it could be close, could be exciting. Alternatively, Spurs could experience the wrath of a team at the height of its powers and be absolutely spanked. I'm hoping for the former but expecting the latter. We only need a draw. Fingers crossed.

***

Fingers crossed my arse. City win 1-0. It was a close-run thing. City scored very early and held on. Tense game and as long as it was 1-0 there was always a chance. Next step. We need to beat Cardiff and then assuming we can do that we need to look to United to beat City midweek. You know, I've always like that Ole chap.

Sunday 21st April 2019

Cardiff away this afternoon. Another must-win. After City's win yesterday, we are back in second and a win today would take us back to the top.

I don't think it's particularly relevant, but we also have the opportunity to reduce the goal difference deficit. I don't think it will matter now, only an outside chance, but I would like to think we can reduce the deficit. Just in case.

There are a number of reasons I want to beat Cardiff. There is the obvious reason of course—to go back to the top. But then there is the Warnock factor. Beating him at any point is good. The self-serving slimy snake. Just to see what he whinges about after the game.

It's a must-win for them too. Currently third from bottom. Huddersfield and Fulham have already gone, and Cardiff are hanging on. They beat their closest rivals Brighton midweek, which gave them some hope, but they are still three points from safety with three games to go. This is not going to be an easy ride.

The positive that we have is the size and strength of the squad. Reading Ian Salmon's book about the 15/16 season it's amazing to see how badly the squad was affected by injuries. Really down to bare bones. I think that came from Klopp arriving midway through the season, realising the squad weren't fit enough and increasing the intensity of the training. That put him on his arse three months later with hamstrings seemingly popping for fun.

Alongside the improvement in the squad is the leap in terms of how they are managed. Klopp has learnt a lot over the past three years, the intensity of the Premier League and how players need to be cajoled through. We reach the critical part of the season with just about a full squad of players and all of them coming into form. It's not by accident you know, it's experience and planning. Professional long-term approach to building a world-class all-conquering football team. It'll continue to get better too.

But for now, let's just focus on Cardiff.

***

A win. Another win. On to 88 points. That's more than Liverpool have ever got before. And still three games to play.

I'm not going to say it was never in doubt. We owned the game but got to half time goalless. Missed three good chances and you wonder (worry) whether it's going to be your day.

Second half we were assured and in control, then Gini scores from a corner and you see what it means to them all. He went fucknuts. They all did. You could see how much it meant, how fired up they all were. It wasn't just scoring a goal. It was more than that.

Game was over then. We got a penalty. Some people were saying it wasn't a penalty. How it wasn't a penalty I will never know. Salah was wrestled and pulled repeatedly until eventually he went down. It wasn't football. Nailed on.

After the game Klopp talks about the conditions. They had let the grass grow long and hadn't watered it, to stop our passing game. To try to slow us down. Klopp knew this would happen so created the same conditions at Melwood to train in. Every detail. A winning approach.

In other news United got spanked 4-0 by Everton. Things must be bad. It doesn't bode well for Wednesday and United taking points off City, although they are desperate for the points now to get into the top four. Hopefully they'll put up more of a show.

Wednesday 24th April 2019

Well, this all feels a bit odd. Not right really. Manchester United, my own personal anti-Christ, are playing tonight and I am desperate for them to win. Want them to win more than anything. I've been racking my brains as to whether this situation has arisen before, and I really can't think of an example.

I've never wanted United to win. In my conscious football-supporting past, I have always wanted them to lose; no matter what the game, what the relative position of the two teams are, it has always been a good thing when they concede a goal, drop points, have an injury, a setback of any description. It's in my nature. Like I don't want to get stung by a wasp or eat beetroot, I don't want United to succeed.

It started in the '80s. Ron Atkinson, Bryan Robson, Norman Whiteside, Jesper Olsen. I was probably too young to understand that violent and toxic relationship of the time, was certainly too young to be involved in it, but I hated them, we all did.

I grew up in Warrington. (Bloody hell, I hear you cry, he's a bloody woolly back.) For those of you who don't know the recent history of Warrington, who have never even heard of Eileen Bilton, Warrington is a 'new town'. It has its own industrial history; it's a traditional Rugby League town really, alongside St Helens, Wigan and Widnes.

In the 1960s and 1970s, young couples having children were encouraged to move out of Liverpool and Manchester into the new housing estates being built in Warrington. I was one of those thousands of children and grew up with children from similar families. On our side of town, they were mostly from Liverpool, but there were many from Manchester. Aspiring working-class families, football-loving families, everyone had an allegiance.

In my school, it was almost a three-way split between Liverpool, Everton and United. In the mid '80s, they were the most successful teams in the country... Liverpool and Everton in terms of trophies, United in terms of media hype. It was constant at school. The Liverpool and Everton kids kind of stuck together, their families had common ground, similarities. It was United kids that were the common enemy. Alien.

And what was all this about United anyway? They won the cup... So what? We were winning the league and the European Cup. Why did they get all the hype? In a world where nothing really existed before 1980 in anyone's memory, why would United get all this coverage and hype?

As I got older and we would start going out on the piss, we would go into Warrington on a night out. You'd meet more people from the other side of town, the Manchester side. This animosity would meet in the middle. Fucking United ... we hated them.

It got really bad in the '80s. I remember one home game when the clubs tried to diffuse that tension by doing something 'nice'. It was when the Liverpool team used to run out before the game and kick signed plastic Crown Paints balls into the crowd. Everyone wanted one of those balls. Well, I did anyway. One year, they thought it would a good idea if the United team ran down to the Kop End and kicked the balls in while the Liverpool team went down to the away end. Who thinks of this shit?? Sure enough, every ball was burst and slung back onto the pitch. Fucking United.

So now it's 2019, I have 40 plus years of ingrained hatred towards this team, but tonight I desperately want them to win. It feels instinctively wrong, but I am forcing myself to look at the bigger picture. City needs to drop points and, with four games remaining, this is probably the best chance of them doing that. Local derby, at Old Trafford, United need the points to get the European place.

I was going to say local pride, but I am not seeing a lot of pride in the United side at the moment. They were spineless in a 4-0 defeat to Everton on Sunday. Normally, this is wonderful. To see what has happened to them since the departure of Ferguson (I didn't even start on Ferguson did I) is hilarious. To see them stagnate and disintegrate is something I have waited for since the early '90s. It's a comedy, where every episode is better than the last.

Moyes was a great start; to think he was the natural successor to Ferguson was a brilliant opening episode. The wonderful years of 'David Moyes is a Football Genius'. That Ferguson stood there in the middle of the pitch and announced it and told the crowd to get behind him just made it so much better. Then Van Gaal. The idea that this guy was going to turn it round and things just got worse.

The funniest part has to be Mourinho. That a club with such history and pride would stoop so low as to bring in this footballing whore was priceless. And the fans loved it. They got behind him. Sold themselves out. And sold themselves out for a busted flush. The dishonour that man brought to that club over that period. The Ferguson fume must have been immense.

And now Solskjaer. God, they love him. Or they did. The support for the guy at Old Trafford a couple of months ago, it was huge. He was the new messiah. And no wonder. A run of games, a run of wins, playing attacking attractive football, using the same players that had deserted Jose. Ole was the man to bring back the United of old, to bring back the traditions of Sir Alex. Ole understood the club, understood the fans, he was a man to trust to bring back the good times. Don't worry about his lack of experience at this level, his previous absolute failure at Cardiff; Ole will bring back the spirit of '99.

And they've given him a contract and that is the most priceless move of them all. Since they've signed it, he's dropped off a cliff. Out of the cup, out of Europe, dropping points in the league. After recovering to fourth and a Champions League place, they are back in sixth and looking unlikely to even get into the Europa League.

He looked lost on Sunday after the game. Managing a team of overpaid, underperforming superstars. The dead cat has bounced and there is no way he can see to resurrect it. He needs a clear-out of these players, he needs to identify players with heart and galvanise them into a team. I don't think he's got it in him. But tonight, I'll be right behind them. They might just be able to do it, stranger things have happened. Come on Ole, Come on the Red Devils—great bunch of lads. (Makes me feel a bit sick)

***

City won 2-0. Hate United, always have, always will.

Thursday 25th April 2019

Good news and some well-deserved recognition as the Players Player of the Year is announced and VVD gets it. The talk was it being between him and Sterling, but I think common sense has prevailed. Virgil is a worthy winner.

Since he arrived at the beginning of last year, he has been majestic and has moved the team to another level. I can't remember seeing a player who has allowed a team to step up in such a way. Teams can bring in forwards who score for fun, such as Salah last year, but VVD seems to have allowed the team to prosper.

As well as his own playing ability, positioning sense and reading of the game, he seems to exude a calm that flows through the rest of the team. He makes everyone around him more relaxed, which in turn has created a stronger and more cohesive unit.

They are so calm and assured at the back, since bringing

him in we have lost the tag of defensively suspect that had hounded us for years (again referring to Ian Salmon's book on 15/16 where it was a common failing through the season).

Going forward, he is the core that all our forward play seems to stem from. His ability to play a long ball to put a player through or open up space sits close to someone like Alonso. And he has scored some great headers at crucial times too.

It's not just him. He has been surrounded by other good players. Trent and Robbo to either side of him, Alisson behind him is immense and now Fabinho sitting in front means that we have the most cohesive defensive unit I can remember.

It's difficult to compare players between eras, but I have to say he is the most influential defender on the performance of a team that I have seen—he has been a game changer in both a micro and macro sense. Changing games, changing aspirations.

Within all this arse kissing, we have to tip our hat to Klopp in all of this. I well remember the fume of the previous season when we didn't get Virgil (and Keita) and Klopp didn't move to the next name on the list. In both cases, they were the only name on the list and he took so much criticism for it.

That is what long-term planning is about. It's about sacrificing in the short term in order to be able to fulfil the plan. He knew what was required, he knew what he needed and wasn't prepared to sell himself or the club short in order to realise the long-term ambition. That should give everyone heart. That is why we have Klopp and that is why we trust and support him.

As for the PFA Team of the Year, we are also well represented but at the same time it is harsh on some of our players not to be recognised (not that they care if we can go on and win the league). We have had Trent, Robbo, VVD and Mané all included in the team. Four from 11. Manchester City have the other six and then somehow there is a place in there for Pogba, which astounds me.

I think Alisson is unfortunate not to get in ahead of Edisson, but it's a close call. Aside from that, you can't really question any of the other City players. Despite my obvious bias, you have to recognise how good the City team and players are. Laporte, Fernandinho, Silva (Bernardo), Sterling and Aguero. I'm sure I could make an argument that any one of our players could get in ahead of these, but I would only be being peevish. I think the positive to recognise is that we are now sitting alongside the other great team in the land.

As for Pogba, well, that's a different story. No doubt a great player, he has been held up all year as an example of unprofessional, the unacceptable face of football. How his fellow professionals could vote him into the team is beyond me.

I think Wijnaldum should feel unlucky here. For me he has been the pick of the Liverpool midfield this season. Looking under pressure for a place at the start he has been the most consistent and influential midfielder throughout. When other players have taken time to settle or been out of form, Gini has performed at a consistently high level. He's one of those players that you can't necessarily see what he's doing, but he's in there, working away, making the team tick along. He's a player who you only really notice when he's not there.

He's not high profile, he flies a little below the radar in many senses, but he'd be the player I'd have in that team— Pogba, my arse.

Friday 26th April 2019

Shock horror. I'm actually going to the match. Out early(ish), a few pints, going to Anfield, shouting, singing. Supporting. That's me tonight. Come on. It seems like ages since I've been to Anfield. It was late February, but then there was the trip to Old Trafford to consider. It's good to be back.

It would be better if I could see out of both eyes properly. I don't know what is going on, but my eye is so sore. I know it's sore because of the amount of weeping water it is creating. I have a permanént tear stain down my face and shirt.

I soldiered on at work, but they just told me to go home. The doctor doesn't know. The optician is disinterested. My wife is concerned and I am in extreme discomfort. The other passengers on the train are appalled at the weeping mess sitting next to them. At least we know how everyone feels about it now.

I don't really feel like going. But I have missed so many games I am desperate to see the end of this amazing season. And I have a pass, which I'm not going to waste.

I'm thinking about the game. After the United no-show the other night we are back to simple maths. Three games to play, as it stands City have the advantage. They need to drop points. I am surprisingly relaxed about the situation. It's not in our hands, there's not a lot we can do except win the games we have. If we do that we get 97 points, which is so high it is freakish.

If City had dropped points the other night, I don't think I would have felt the same. The pressure would have been on. It would have been intolerable. We play before City for the next two weeks. If we win then the pressure sits on them to win each time. The pressure is all on them. They are the front runner; we are on their shoulder, ready to overtake at the first sign of weakness.

If they don't show any weakness, then we come second with 97 points. It's disappointing but we have the third highest ever points total and have been beaten by a team who has accumulated 198 over two seasons.

We are not at our peak, there is growth potential. We're going to get better and we will win in the future. We have the potential to be one of, if not the best team in Europe for the next three to five years and I'm looking forward to it.

We might not win the league and I'm OK with it. There,

I've said it.

Huddersfield tonight. They've only scored 14 points all season and are already relegated. We won't show mercy, but an eye will be on Wednesday and the game at Barcelona.

Salah has been in New York this week after being named as *Time Magazine*'s Top 100 most influential people. That in itself is beyond wonderful and we should all burst with pride at the thought of having that type of role model at our club. It might mean he gets a rest tonight. Or it might mean he scores a hit trick to celebrate.

Pulling into Lime Street. It's been too long. Come on, you mighty red men.

***

Five nil win. Never in doubt. Not really even a contest. Men and boys. Keita scores before anyone really realises we've kicked off and Salah and Mané get two each in their own private spat to win the Golden Boot.

As much as I am at peace with this whole situation, this puts us top of the league with 91 points and still games to play. What the win tonight means is the pressure is on City. Pressure to win.

Sunday 28th April 2019

Pressure back to City today. Playing Burnley and they need to win.

Stuff to do today, but I am wandering around with one of those little Apple AirPods hanging out of my ear. Tidying up the garden, playing with the kids, off for a game of tennis shortly. I can't stop and listen, don't want to listen but want to know what's going on.

John Murray and Pat Nevin in my ear. It's not the words

I'm listening to, it's the tone. Murray's tone. His Geordie dulcet tones playing away in my head. Complemented by Nevin's brogue. I'm listening for the raise in voice, the speed up in pace. Approaching half time and I've heard it a few times. It stops me in my tracks but yet to score. Three minutes to half time. Nil nil. Come on, Burnley!

***

Twenty-nine millimetres. That's all they won by. Jammy bastards. Couldn't watch it but listened. They sounded utterly unconvincing but got the goal midway through the second half. Had to go to goal line technology. Twenty-nine millimetres is about an inch. That's how close it was. Although not as close as the 11mm that ours didn't go in by against City in the only league we have lost so far this season.

I kept on listening. Or rather I kept the thing in my ear. I thought right up to the end they might concede a goal. We only needed one. But no, they have slithered over the line and got the three points. They are slithering. We are barnstorming. But they are the ones with their noses in front. Leicester next for them. Rodgers. You never know.

Monday 29th April 2019

Feel like we're running out of games. Only two left now. Only two more chances for City to drop points. At this stage I am supremely confident that we'll win both of our games, but my fear is that City will win both of theirs too.

While we are taking games in our stride and look imperious, they are looking nervous. It's experience and muscle memory that is getting them through games. They were anything but convincing against Burnley yesterday. Eventually got a goal that literally crept over the line and then resorted to the dark arts of time wasting to see out the game.

I think our only hope is that Leicester can get themselves in front next week. Then it will be interesting to see how City react. Can they pull a game back, have they got the quality (yes), have they got the heart?

It's funny that Rodgers is in charge. That he is our hope. He's got nothing to lose. He's a guy who'll take an opportunity when it's out in front of him. He needs to prove himself. He got some bad press walking out on Celtic before the end of the season and he needs a win. An opportunity to prove he can influence things. He's never coming back to Anfield and there are mixed feelings about him amongst the fans. Taking points off City will make him far more respected and appreciated than his three years as manager ever would.

Come on Brendan, pull your finger out, lad.

Tuesday 30th April 2019

Watching the Spurs Ajax first leg. I think Ajax are the definitive dark horses. In the wilderness for years, they have brought together a team of young players and this is probably their one year before the squad gets raped by the big teams across Europe and it is back to the drawing board.

They looked like the easy team in the draw but, having beaten Bayern to get out of the group stage and then knocking out Real Madrid and Juventus in the last two rounds, both with outstanding away wins, they have every chance of winning the competition.

They look a level above Spurs. First half especially, they could have been far further ahead than a single goal. Spurs are playing better in the second half but don't look like they have the quality to break through and score. They are without Kane and Son and you wonder where the goal is coming from.

Ajax have their away goal now and they will be happy to

take that into the second leg. I can see it finishing 0-1.

Looking back to the previous round, all of the first legs were tight; there was only Liverpool who had more than a single goal lead. All very cagey, no one wanting to commit. That seems to be at odds with how it has gone in previous years with Champions League games becoming goal fests.

There is obviously a greater focus on the defensive side of the game and this is where Klopp has been ahead of the game. In a defensively oriented era, he has broken the bank to get the best defender and goalkeeper in the world and it has clearly paid dividends. At a time when keeping a clean sheet is everything, our back five have kept 20 in the league already this season. A club record and up amongst the best in Premier League history.

Gets me thinking about the game tomorrow. How is that going to play out? I'm not sure Klopp knows how to play a cagey game. He goes all out to take the game to the opposition through his world beating front three and is safe in the knowledge our world beating back five will shut the opposition out at the back.

The only question is the thrust and mindset of the three midfielders. Are they set up to defend or attack? We are picking three from seven at the moment, so there are untold numbers of combinations to drive the game strategy.

When I talk about shutting out the opposition I suppose I should be putting an asterisk in there. We've never had to deal with Messi before. I felt like I had ticked something off my bucket list earlier this season when I went to watch him play. Twenty minutes he was on the pitch. Set one up, scored one himself and then broke his arm and went off.

This time I watch him, he'll be playing Liverpool. The excitement and anticipation is off the scale. I'm not going to the game tomorrow, will have to settle for watching it on TV. But I will be there at Anfield for the second leg next week and I can hardly wait.

I've seen good players at Anfield before, both domestic and European, but the idea of seeing Messi there is incredible really. What do you do? Marvel at him, shout at him, scare the shit out of him? I don't know ... it's Messi.

I watched them play in October and, as good as they were, I still think we are better. I still think we are stronger in just about every area of the field, largely driven by the intensity and pace of our play.

The Messi factor is a big one because I think it's difficult to legislate for him, to plan for him. But the man who has to manage him has just been voted the best player in the English league and is probably one of the best defenders in the world. So we have the best possible person to be looking after the little magician. Messi apart, I think we can take it to them. Can't wait.

Interlude 10 - After Hillsborough

I buried Hillsborough. From the very next morning, I buried the whole thing almost completely. Not consciously, I didn't decide to bury it, but looking back it is clear that is what my young self had decided to do. I think it was a mechanism to deal with things. The same mechanism that had apparently been so successful with the series of recent losses and changes in the family. If I buried it, I was immune to it.

Straight away I pushed it down and out of sight. When so many people across the city and beyond were converging on Anfield to express condolences and lay flowers, I didn't want to go. Refused to go in fact. I was straight back to school and with other pupils asking if I was OK, I nonchalantly but politely shrugged it off. I think the three of us had been the only ones in our school to go, and no one locally had been directly affected in terms of losing people, so the effects and the grief were not immediate. I could keep it at arm's length.

I watched the coverage in the media and the funerals of those who died but didn't get upset. I attended the matches after Hillsborough as if nothing happened. Travelled to the first game at Goodison without a ticket. The semi-final replay at Old Trafford. The run of league games up to the defeat at Anfield by Arsenal when we lost the league. I was disappointed but didn't attach any additional significance to the loss, certainly wasn't one of those who cried on the Kop. I celebrated the Cup Final at Wembley as I would celebrate any other.

At school, on our last day, the tradition was to sign everyone's shirt. My sign-off was 'Double Double winners', which was very much at the front of my mind (it was the day of the Arsenal game). After that, I sat my exams with no issues and came out with good grades across the board.

About three months later, something came to the surface. My cousin's husband took me to the local pub and got me a bit drunk. When we got back home, my mum and Auntie Pat and her family were sitting in the back garden on a summer's evening. I got really upset that night, worked myself up into hysterics, crying about the man I had seen on the floor behind the stand and why the policeman didn't do anything to help. My mum told me about this the next day. I took the opportunity to bury it even deeper so there wasn't a repeat. It worked for a long time.

A couple of years later, I went to university in Sheffield (studied politics and in particular the growth of the Labour movement, my dissertation was on the Miners' Strike, which had made such an impression years before). I never made a connection between my time there and Hillsborough. Saw the plaque in the Broomhill Tavern to the supporters who had been there the night before the disaster but didn't feel an attachment. I did think fleetingly about going to find that hairdressers but never actually did it. I followed the progress of the Hillsborough case through the inquests and inquiry and the TV documentary but was always quite detached from it. Tried not to make the connection between the events of the day and my own experience.

I never talked about it with anyone. Never told anyone I had been there. If it came up in conversation with new people or colleagues as an extension of me being a Liverpool fan, I would let them quietly but firmly know that I had been there in a way that made it clear it was not a topic for further discussion. I politely just shut them down.

Never spoke to family or friends about it. And to this day, I don't remember having a conversation with Stuart, a friend who has been there ever since. It's just something we have never discussed.

To my eternal shame, I lost patience with the Hillsborough families. I couldn't understand why they kept on pushing, looking for information or some hidden truth about what had happened. Why couldn't they just leave it, move on? We all understood they had lost loved ones, but why couldn't they just get on with their lives? This pursuit of supposed justice was pointless. I was never outspoken about this, never discussed this view, but they were the thoughts that bubbled inside. Looking back, that was the worst thing that I did. To deny those families that support and respect and understanding. It was callous and mean. I feel tremendously guilty now about that denial.

And these buried feelings stayed that way for a long time. Until 2012, and the publishing of the Hillsborough Independent Panel report. It was just a few days before my 40th birthday, I had only been back from Australia a couple of months and that day I had an interview in Manchester. I remember them announcing the findings on the radio, primarily that it wasn't the fault of the fans on the day, and it caught my breath. That feeling when you think you are going to cry and you take a deep breath to suppress it.

I suppressed it all the way into Manchester and was stood in the lobby of an office building watching the BBC news. David Cameron was speaking in the Commons and he apologised—he said sorry. That was the moment it broke. I don't know why but in that moment I burst into tears in this lobby and just cried. People watching me. A grown man in a suit crying his eyes out.

The Prime Minister of the day apologising for what had happened to those poor people all those years before and for the lies their families and the people of Liverpool had been exposed to since. And it just released all of this emotion and guilt that I had carried inside me. Released it in a way that it just broke through my meticulously well-trained control of my emotions. Just in that moment.

That wasn't the end of it. I wasn't 'cured'. But it was the start of me accepting it more. Trying to understand it and why I had buried it so deep. I think I know the root of it. Guilt. I felt guilty about what happened and that was what I was hiding.

The fundamental guilt is that I survived. That I wasn't one of those poor people who died in such horrendous circumstances. All things being equal, I would have been in that pen. (Pen. The word makes my blood boil.) But for a stroke of fate, I would have been right behind that goal for that game because that's where we stood for every game at that point. And I have known that since I stood in that stand above the terrace and watched it all happen in front of my own eyes.

My mum used to say, 'There but for the grace of God go I.' She said it a lot when we were kids, when we saw people less fortunate than ourselves. It 'could' so easily have been me, but I think from a very early stage I have replaced that 'could' with 'should', and that is how it had been buried for all those years. I felt horribly guilty about not being in the middle of that disaster when all those other people suffered.

That is supported by guilt about all the details of the day. Having a pint while we waited for the car to be fixed, arriving late, worried that by running down that tunnel we had in some way exacerbated the problem, not stopping long enough to check that person behind the stand was alright, watching things happen from the stand and not helping, stopping to have a drink on the way home. I have come to realise the images I retain from the day are the parts of the day I feel worst about. All these things live with me, but they only float around the edges of that central guilt of surviving.

As I said earlier, the other guilt and shame is the betrayal of the families, which continued and grew over the years. I think I *probably knew all along why they pursued that justice but wasn't willing or able to support them. That was unforgivable. I don't know exactly what was driving these thoughts, the only thing I can surmise is the guilt around coming home that day when others died and every time I saw or heard them it reminded me of the fact. I just wanted them to stop talking about it. I can only apologise to those people who I recognise as some of the bravest and noblest people in our society. Their perseverance in obtaining the truth is a lesson to us all.*

I've tried to self-diagnose. I came across something called Survivor's Guilt. It's a recognised condition, a form of PTSD. And then I think I shouldn't be so self-indulgent to think I have this, something that is normally associated with holocaust survivors and returning war veterans. I wasn't in that crush that day; I didn't feel any pain; I didn't experience people dying around me. This isn't pain from a physical experience; it's a self-inflicted mental state. I have since spoken to people who have tried to understand and help, who haven't diagnosed anything but have at least considered it a possibility. I should talk to them more.

I feel slightly more at ease with it now because I am able, and allow myself, to think about it. I am not open about it (this is the first time I have ever talked about it openly), but I don't suppress it in the same way. There has been a weight removed in the knowledge that this wasn't the fault of the fans. My actions didn't contribute towards the outcome that day.

Hillsborough is still the thing that catches me out. When I hear people talk about it, I find myself catching my breath. When I mention it, I have to be careful that my voice doesn't crack. I suppose in a way that is progress. Something is still lurking there but it's not as far below the surface as it used to be.

MAY

Wednesday 1st May 2019

Here it is. The big game. Barcelona in the Nou Camp. Just watching the build-up as the team walks out and it looks incredible in there. Just done the mosaic around the whole circumference of the ground. What a stadium.

There's the lads. Up against the best in Europe. But we are going against them toe to toe. Surprising line-up. Firmino was declared fit but is only on the bench, alongside Henderson, which is a surprise. Gomez in ahead of Trent. His first start since December.

The midfield is a bit unexpected. Fabinho, Milner, Keita and Gini. According to the commentators they're playing in a diamond with Gini at the top. We'll see. Milner shaking hands with Messi. He looks like he belongs there with the look on his face. Serious.

***

Half time. It's a quality game of football. Hasn't quite come fully alive as yet, but the quality of the two sides is just outstanding. It's a pleasure to watch.

At home I have a projector with a big screen on the wall. Surround sound speakers. I don't get to sit here very often to watch the football but I am tonight and it's the perfect place to watch football. And this is a perfect game to watch. Sometimes going the pub to watch the game is the best option, but I feel I am just absorbing the football here. No distractions. Just watching the two teams go at each other.

It's 1-0 to Barcelona. A pass and a run that are the only two things that sets these teams apart. It was Suarez with the run and the touch to wrong foot Alisson. I love Suarez. I absolutely love him. He is the best, most exciting, most exhilarating player I have ever seen at Anfield. I love the way he plays football. His whole win-at-all-costs approach. He is a player that makes you stand up every time he gets the ball. Or he was. So for him to pop up and put us behind is difficult.

We have had chances. Mané should have had a penalty and both he and Salah have been getting space and time to run. I think they are missing Firmino. Bringing it together at the front. Gini isn't as effective in a similar position.

Just coming out for the second half. We need to try to get that away goal without letting the game get away from us. We need more of the same as the first half and hopefully we can get that moment of quality to level it up. I love football sometimes.

***

And then sometimes I hate it. Full time and I think the technical term for it is being Messi'd.

We have finished up getting beat 3-0 after playing so well for most of the game. We were all over them for the first part of the second half but couldn't get that final pass. With 15 minutes to go we are 1-0 down and then Messi pops up and makes it three.

First one pretty lucky, a combination of unfortunate errors and a tap in. The second a moment of pure brilliance. A free kick from over 30 yards. How on earth can he put it in past one of the best keepers in the world like that? Alisson wasn't even close.

So disappointing. Salah hits the post just moments after the third goal and you just know it's not going to be our night. Firmino came on too late, we had lost our dominance by that point and he never got into the game.

Three goals behind. It's doable, but it's a stretch. If we do it, it will be the best night at Anfield ever. Chin up. See you next Tuesday (as my wife tends to call me).

Thursday 2nd May 2019

Disappointed this morning after the game last night. Liverpool played well overall, but at the end of the day we weren't ruthless enough. Had enough chances and didn't take them. Barcelona took theirs, they had a competitive edge through the game, they knew when they had to absorb pressure and they knew when they needed to strike. For all our equality in terms of possession and passing, their experience and game play gave them that edge.

I think ruthlessness is an interesting concept in teams of where this club is at the moment. I think the team is ruthless enough, I think Klopp, for all his charm, is both loyal and ruthless. That game was planned to the last detail and we had every chance to win. The statistical balance suggests we should have scored at least one, but on this occasion we didn't. The same balance suggests they didn't really deserve three goals, but the scoreline shows us they got them. In a certain light, you could see it as an anomaly—but that doesn't really help us now.

In terms of balance, you never know, the same two teams could go at it in the same way next Tuesday and that statistical anomaly could fall in our favour. That's why we go to the game I guess.

I do think we need to be a bit nastier. I think we need to

take something from Suarez who was an aggressive, needly little shit the whole game. You could see him, always looking to wind someone up, push it a little bit too far. I used to love him for it at Liverpool. The type of behaviour you can really get behind as a fan but hate when you see it in the opposition. We don't have that in the team (possibly Mané and I was hoping to see it in Keita this year) and I think we need just a bit of it. We have model professionals and that's great to a point—I just wish sometimes there was a bit more gnarl to them.

The ruthlessness question is more about the fan base. The reaction to the game last night is so interesting through all the different channels that are available to vent your opinion. There are, of course, those who go straight to the criticism of the team.

Questioning every decision of the manager, every move the players make—calling the players for lack of application or effort or making mistakes, not giving the credit they deserve when they are playing a game at a level we couldn't have dreamed about five years ago. I don't think these people are ruthless, I think they're just stupid. Thankfully, you don't get as many of them at the game as you used to. The quality of football is overwhelmingly good and I don't think right minded supporters who are watching the game and understand it (the key point) will criticise in that way.

The stupid people are generally the preserve of the internet, social media and phone-ins. They are the sewers of the football fan world and luckily, they can be tuned out.

At the other end, though, there are the apologists, who excuse and justify everything that goes wrong, as if it is out of their hands—the people who lack the ruthlessness. When I was younger and we were winning the league every year, we didn't have this. When life was a bit tougher and people were a bit hardier, they had more of that ruthless edge. When we stopped winning things, we lost that edge. Ferguson picked it up in the

'90s and it filtered through the United fan base. A ruthless expectation of success.

I think I'm as guilty as anyone of it, but when I hear it sometimes – the apologies and excuses for why we haven't won – it makes me wince a bit. I've heard it on the podcast I was listening to this morning and it has made me think about it. There are so many outlets for football chat and analysis now that people become over absorbed in the football.

It's a long way from just going the match, talking about it with mates after the game, praising or slating as appropriate, going to school or work for the week and then going the game again the following week.

That was when people used to talk about what they thought about the game. That has now morphed into what people 'feel' about the game and I think a lot of the commentary is overindulgent. Maybe it's my British stiff upper lip, maybe it's my age; I'm just not comfortable with it.

There is talk following the game that we are playing at the highest level as if we don't really think we belong there, like this is fantasy land and we are lucky to be breathing the same rarefied air as Messi and co. I'm criticising here, but I am conscious I am doing the same.

I guess it's part of the club's journey and the need to build the fan base's ruthless streak. The fan base need to think we deserve to be here, that it is our right to be playing in these games based on the team we have, rather than thinking we are here based on someone else's grace and that gives us the excuse not to play well. Klopp has already made that transition – even if he talks it down – I think the fan base need to make that jump too. We need to stop being apologists. Get the swagger back.

Saturday 4th May 2019

It's coming to an end. Second last game of the season. It's May and we are still in the two big competitions. If I was being really positive I would say it's all on a knife edge. I want it to be on a knife edge and it still could be, but at the moment the probability is the knife is going to fall a very specific way – the wrong way.

I'm not having that right now though. We have to beat Newcastle tonight. Away from home, their last home game of the season, highly charged and alcohol fuelled (for the crowd at least) and Benitez in charge. It's not easy.

But having said that I am confident we will take the game to them and beat them. If we don't our league challenge is effectively over and after the journey this season, I'm not ready for it to be over yet. Barcelona was a dreadfully disappointing result after a strong performance. The team and the fans need to pick themselves up from that. Tuesday night will be a big night. But this Saturday is the biggest game in front of us.

If City had have dropped points last weekend, then the pressure would be on us tonight. But they didn't, so it's just up to us to throw that challenge back to them.

Firmino was a miss at Barcelona and he is not in the squad at all tonight. He obviously needs to be ready for Tuesday, so in that sense it is about using the squad. Not just the game in front of us. Sturridge in his place and we can only hope he puts in a better show than last week when he was poor.

Another shuffle in midfield and defence, Lovren and Trent playing in place of Matip and Gomez. With the strength of the squad right through I don't feel like these changes weaken us. We have an outstanding squad of 20+ players who are interchangeable based on the minutiae of any given game. Come on, lads.

***

Half time and it's 2-1. At times it looks easy and we should be out of sight, but Newcastle have made a good fist of it. A goal to make it safe. That's what we need. 'Race for the Title' they're calling it on Sky. Star Wars day and were still in a race for the title.

***

Jesus Christ. I've aged there. I feel like I've been through the mill. We won 3-2. We won 3-2. We just sat and watched it happen.

I'm not sure we deserved the win. No, bollocks to that. We did deserve the win because we wanted to win, but we didn't really look like we were going to win. We needed a goal. But they got the goal, pulled it back to 2-2. And we just didn't look like we were going to get the breakthrough. Then Salah goes down. Salah is down for an eternity, stretchered off in the end. No shape, no momentum. This was the night we lost it.

But no, this is the night we scraped it. The night we proved we can still do this, even in the scrappiest way. We didn't bottle it. We did it. Again.

I've sat at home tonight and watched this on TV. I wanted to watch it properly. Not go the pub and kind of watch it. I don't think I could have coped in the pub. All the blurts who start calling every bad pass. I had to be at home.

I've got my phone next to me and with the vagaries of the internet and live TV and streaming and delays and all the other shit I don't understand, my phone notifications are about three seconds ahead of what I'm watching. I know someone is going to score before I see it. And what started off as a real pain in the arse, spoiling my enjoyment, in the end became my saviour.

As I'm watching the game, I'm looking at my phone and

willing it to beep. I felt like Uri Geller, using the power of my mind to make it beep. Nothing to do with Liverpool on the pitch. It was all about my phone.

We score late. A free kick from the right. And as Shaqiri lines up to take it, my phone beeps a second before he kicks the ball. I know everything is going to be alright. It's relief. Relief that my phone has saved us. I am still letting that relief out when I watch the ball go in the goal. There was no screaming, not tonight. There was just relief that my phone had let me know it was all going to be OK.

It was a similar story with the final whistle. My phone knows ahead of time. My phone knows we've got another three points and the pressure has transferred back to City on Monday.

Another late winner. Surely our name is on this title. Surely all these things that have happened are not going to be in vain. This is fate. It must mean something.

My mind goes back to half time in Istanbul in 2005 and a confused conversation I had with my Grandad (who had been dead for 14 years at that point). Surely, we can't have all come all this way and been through all this drama to lose at the final hurdle. Look at us here, sixty odd thousand people in a stadium in the middle of a moonscape. Surely, we can't all be about to lose. Surely not, Grandad.

And look how that turned out. Probability, statistics, book-makers are saying one thing. I don't quite believe it. Not having it. Not yet.

Monday 6th May 2019

We've done all we can. A fabulous late winner on Saturday night. That's our contribution. Over to City tonight. From see-ing United as the last opportunity to drop points a couple of weeks back, I then transferred all hope to Burnley. And now those hopes rest with Leicester tonight.

I'm thinking they can do it. I've decided they can. I've decided they can hold out City tonight, score a goal and put the absolute shits up them. This is all about Rodgers. There must be a reason he left Celtic with two months to go before the end of the season. A reason he played such a shits trick.

I've decided the reason is tonight. He's got his chance tonight. To show himself as a real manager. Something he never quite achieved at Liverpool. He has the chance to do it tonight.

I can't listen to it. Just can't do it again. I hear they are without Fernandinho. That's a big miss. Another reason.

***

This is ridiculous. Sitting on the toilet. One ear pod in. Listening to *Five Live*. Forty minutes in and it's still 0-0. They can't commentate on the game but have the Monday Night Club with Kelly Cates instead. They're playing the noise of the City crowd in the background. That's what I'm listening to. I tune out Chris Sutton at the best of times, but tonight his voice is like white noise. Just listening to the crowd. Every time the volume raises they go over to the commentator. It's going to be a long hour if it goes on like this.

***

They won. By a single goal again. Limping in. Seventy minutes before they scored. Kompany. Relying on Kompany to drag them over the line. He can't be far off retirement, can he?

To the last day then. Barcelona tomorrow. Salah and Firmino both out I've just found out. Uphill struggle. Or it could be the best game ever.

Tuesday 7th March 2019

Barcelona at Anfield tonight. What a night it's going to be. Struggling to think of anything else. The challenge of the enterprise and how good it's going to be if we achieve it. Imagine if we do it. Bloody hell.

We are where we are. We'd like to be in a better position but we're not so there's no use crying about it. We need three goals and not to concede. If we concede then I think we've blown it. We are also without Salah and Firmino. Two of the best attacking players in Europe. Again, no use crying about it. They are the cards we have been dealt.

The perverse thing is the more I talk about the obstacles, the more excited I get about the whole thing and the more I think it's on. It's fucking on, isn't it! The bookies don't think so. Eighteen to one for us to qualify tonight. They have it wrong and I have a sneaky fiver to prove it.

If we go at them tonight and get an early goal, the place is going to go mental. Absolutely batshit like something we've never seen before. Get that goal and hold them out and anything is possible. Up to the very last minute anything is possible. I don't know how he's going to do it. I suppose that's why he's on the big bucks. He must have a plan. Take them by surprise.

I'm hearing Brewster is lined up to start. That must be the ultimate surprise. None of us have any idea about him, how on earth can Barcelona? I expect him to do something unexpected. I wouldn't be surprised if he has all of his most trusted lieutenants on the field to start. It wouldn't surprise me to get Fabinho, Henderson, Milner starting. To provide pace and power alongside solidity.

It's important to get a goal. But even more important not to concede one. We need to be still in this game at 70 minutes and that's why we need that solidity. From seventy, God knows...

Unleash hell I guess!! Whatever happens he's got to throw everything at it. Be brave. Scare the shit out of them.

Some big players at Anfield tonight. Some of the biggest ever. The difference tonight is how we treat them. We get under their skin tonight. Every kick the crowd will be on it. None of this deference. We don't need that tonight. Yes, it's Messi. He was good last week. We have to do everything we can to stop him being good again. Both the players and the crowd. Give them a night they won't forget. I'm winding myself up too much here. If I carry on like this I won't get to the ground!

***

Right. I've calmed down a bit now. Walked to the car. Chatting to people. I don't quite know where to start. Lost for words.

In the second half there, something made me think about my mum. On occasion, mostly when she was pissed, she would say, 'And I was there.' I never knew what she was on about. It was some Welsh comedian called Max Boyce in the '70s talking about the rugby in this lilting Welsh accent. At the end he would say, 'And I was there.' That was his line.

By the way. We won tonight. We beat Barcelona 4-0 and I was there. It was the best ever performance on the best ever night. And I was there.

I'm sitting in the car now. I'm exhausted. I've never seen anything like it at Anfield. This is better than 87/88, better than John Barnes. Better than anything I can remember in that ground. From the first whistle.

I can tell you when I knew we were invincible. In the 38th second, when Lionel Messi was tackled on the edge of the box and 50,000 people just ripped his head off. He was rattled. We had them rattled in the first minute.

Liverpool were rabid. Fabinho was rabid. What a performance. Yellow card early and he bossed the game throughout. He gets the first mention. Before any of the goals. Fabinho was the boss.

One nil up at half time. Origi with another goal. He'll be a legend soon that lad. They never laid a glove on us first half. Second half. Two more goals in the first ten minutes. Gini on at half time and two goals. Looked at the clock at 3-0. Sixty minutes. Thought we'd blown it too early.

But no. We came again. Missed the last goal. Too busy looking at what sub was coming on. It was a goal. What? Origi again.

We were great. There, that's all I've got right now I'm afraid. Four nil against the mighty Barcelona. Overcoming a 3-0 deficit. We were more than great. Invincible. Immaculate. I'm going to stop now.

Best night ever. And I was there.

Wednesday 8th May 2019

It's been the day after the night before. Just read back what I wrote last night when I got back to the car. It's a little bit all over the place. And that's me sober.

I've spent last night when I got home and then much of the day today trying to piece together what happened. Getting an understanding of how good it actually was. Social media, podcasts, radio, TV, it's been everywhere. There is no shortage of opinions and the general theme has been it was an incredible, almost impossible feat.

We were unlucky last week. Didn't get the rub of the green. We didn't deserve to go in three behind. But last night, I don't think there was any luck involved. Last night the team worked their bollocks off for that win. Motivated and focussed. Luck didn't come into it. They made their own luck.

To a man, they were immense. Alisson made phenomenal saves but that wasn't the story of the game. He didn't keep us in it in that sense.

Defensively impeccable. VVD marshalling the players around him. Solidity allowing them to push forward. Trent and Robertson shouldn't really be counted in the defence. They're attackers who happen to defend and they both did both parts excellently. Robertson was unlucky to go off at half time but Milner, having been great in midfield in the first half, continued to be great at left back.

I've already talked about Fabinho. He was a standout in a standout team. Henderson too, proves his value as captain. There was a wonderful moment in the first half. Matip has let something go, Henderson absolutely lays into him, then turns to VVD, pointing. 'You, fucking sort him out!' he shouts, pointing at Matip. Perfect illustration of the chain of command!

Up front, Divvy and Mané worked away, never stopping. Shaqiri on the other side, dipping in and out a bit more but continuing with the incessant high press. These guys must be so fit; they never stop. Gini, apparently angry with Klopp for not letting him start, comes on and scores twice. Take that Jurgen!!

The fourth goal. I wasn't the only one to miss it. I think half the ground did. Quick thinking from Trent. How do you catch the La Liga champions out like that? They should be docked a week's wages.

And the crowd. Oh, the crowd. The noise. I haven't been able to speak all day. Shouting, screaming, singing, cheering, booing. Constant noise. Trying to affect the game by my noise. Multiplied by fifty thousand. It was insane. Last night, I'm thinking it was one of the best. It couldn't be the best, surely?

It was the best. And don't call me Shirley.

It was the best game I have ever been to at Anfield. Thirty-five years with a season ticket and it was the best. It's a big statement. I had to think about what was better. In my mind last night, it was better than 87/88 team. I think that's fair. I think we are watching the best Liverpool team ever assembled. The best team to a man. It's a privilege to watch it, it really is.

It was different to Chelsea in '05. Different to Istanbul. On those games we were punching above our weight. Tactical thinking and taking our chance. That was a miracle. I don't think that was a miracle last night. That was Liverpool proving themselves to be among the world's elite. It was us showing them how it is done, standing on an equal footing, one of the world's top teams playing another of the world's top teams. And this is only the start.

Spurs won tonight. They made a big comeback too. Three-nil down at half time. They scored three goals in the second half, the winner in the sixth minute of injury time. They made it too. I'm a bit disappointed to be honest. It's the European Champions League, I wanted a European team. Seems a long way to go to play bloody Spurs. It'll be a close game though.

Tickets booked today. The whinge about the ticket allocation is for another day. Today was reflecting on Liverpool's brilliance and then booking the plane for the final. I'm going. After the disappointment of missing out last year, I'm there this time. Counting the days.

Saturday 11th March 2019

The remainder of the week had been focussed on the European football. After our miraculous win on Tuesday, Spurs achieved something on a similar scale. At half time in the away leg at Ajax, they were 2-0 down, 3-0 on aggregate. The tie was effectively over. I saw the half time score and started getting excited a about the idea of Ajax in the final, not even bothering to watch the second half. But they pulled it back. Lucas Moura got a hat trick in the second half, the last goal in the 96th minute to take them through.

This was followed up by wins for Arsenal and Chelsea on Thursday night in the Europa Cup and, for the first time ever, all four finalists for the two major competitions come from the same league. It's quite a coup for the Premier League and shows the quality of the teams. Well, the top five teams at least, there is a huge disparity between them and the rest.

Only the Manchester club's letting the side down. City destroying everything in their path but couldn't progress in the one competition their owners really want them to, and United seemingly disintegrating before our eyes. Their draw against hapless Huddersfield last week was the first time a relegated team has taken a point off the top six teams this season. As you will have noticed, I am taking great delight in reducing the top six to the top five as I see another summer of woe and further decline for our friends at Old Trafford. Great bunch of lads.

But the amazing football, the good side of the wider game, has been put in sharp contrast with the shadowy side of football organisation and administration. The details and arrangements for both finals are a disgrace and show UEFA's contempt for the fans generally.

The Champions League final is being staged in the Wanda stadium in Madrid, the new home of Atletico. The stadium holds nearly 68,000 people but both teams have been allocated less than seventeen thousand each. That's less than half the stadium. The rest of the tickets have gone to corporate sponsors and the UEFA ballot. And while a great deal of these tickets will find their way to Liverpool and Spurs fans, they'll do so at vastly inflated prices with all manner of people making money out of honest fans who just want to watch the game.

The corporate stuff pisses me off. Lots of them not interested in the game. Just interested in the day out. The free hospitality. I remember back to the FA Cup final in 1992. My dad (!) got hold of a corporate ticket for me. I already had a ticket but gave it to a mate and went on this ticket. Right on the halfway line. Had to wear a suit to the game. Surrounded by people who had no idea. As the teams came out, the woman behind me asked the guy next to her, 'Which team is in red?' Fuming. Then she asked, 'Which one's John Barnes.' I had loads of mates sitting at home and she is interested in is getting a blimp at John Barnes. It still annoys me now.

Loads of them not even interested in the game or who is playing, but they have taken all the flights at reasonable rates and all the best hotel rooms just for their free piss up.

And then there's the UEFA ballot. Now, I shouldn't complain too much about the ballot because that is the source of my ticket so far and while the idea in principle is a good one, the way they manage it is so poor, the market is flooded with thousands of tickets at vastly increased prices. With Spurs fans also in the mix now, the demand will drive the prices through the roof.

I'm quite fortunate in that I have a relatively well-paid job and can afford to pay these prices but the principle of it and the number of people who are making money out of a sporting event makes me sick.

The situation in Madrid is one thing, but the Europa final is even worse. In their infinite wisdom they have elected to stage the final in Baku in Azerbaijan. They are talking about extending the football family and the opportunity for smaller nations to take part. It's bullshit, it's all about their palms being greased.

Arsenal and Chelsea have only been given 8,000 tickets each and need to make their way 2,500 miles. You can't even get a direct flight! When they would get a better crowd and atmosphere at Wembley. Rant over. Last game of the season tomorrow!!

Sunday 12th May 2019

So here we are. Last game of the season. And we're not just going to clap the team around the ground. We're going to see if they can win the league. Thirty-eight games on and we have a punchers chance of doing this.

Same lucky T-shirt as the other night. Haven't even washed the luck out of it. Trying to explain to the family as I'm getting ready how important this is, why I'm so excited. Showing them the combinations of results that we need ... and those that we don't. They were oblivious. Nodding their heads. All they know is after today, Daddy doesn't have to disappear for the day every other weekend until after the school holidays.

Whereas I am so excited I feel like a school kid again. I was still at school last time this happened. It was 1990 and I was still in sixth form. Spent my entire school years watching Liverpool win the league most years and assuming that it would just go on forever, never having experienced anything different. How wrong could I be. Twenty-nine years on and it means so much more having waited my entire adult life for it to happen again.

It's out of our hands today. We just have to win our game and hope that City don't win theirs. The realist in me says it won't happen. City are playing Brighton who have only just escaped relegation and have hardly won a thing all season.

The romantic in me has an entirely different plan. The romantic says we score early, the news filters down to Brighton. City gets flustered and concedes a goal. The news feeds back to Anfield. The ground comes alive and we get another. City have bottled it. They can't get the two goals they need. Brighton are resolute. They're not going to be seen as the last day patsy in someone else's story. All their fans aren't going to the game to watch their team get beat. We win comfortably but spend the match watching Twitter feeds. They don't win and the Kop goes wild.

I always wanted to be romantic but generally the execution is poor!!! I don't even want to think about the situation where they don't win and we don't capitalise on it. Wolves are the best of the mid-table sides and have a good record this season against the top sides. At the moment, I have the ultimate belief that we'll beat them today. But an early goal for Brighton and all of a sudden that pressure shifts to Anfield. Pressure on the team and on the fans. There'll be heads going everywhere.

It's a big hope today. It's not our task to win, it's more a hope that someone else won't. The odds are against it. We are 6/1 to do it today. City are 1/8 on. They were 1/10 the other day so someone somewhere thinks are chances are reducing. Maybe it was after the game the other night. Maybe they think the momentum is with us. That fate is with us. Who knows?

According to the odds, today is more likely to happen than the other night. For us to qualify against Barcelona was 18/1. Statistically that means that us winning the league is three times more likely than us getting to the final. All these things are pointing one way.

I said to my wife this morning that it was unlikely. She said to stop thinking like that. Be positive. She is the most positive person I've ever met. She said to be positive and with the positive energy of fifty thousand people in that ground today, anything is possible.

Team news doesn't come into it at the moment. I believe we have a fully fit squad. It could be our strongest team with Salah and Firmino back. It could feature some of the other squad players. Big Divvy might come in; he certainly hasn't let us down this season with big, big goals at crucial times. To be fair, the squad have all stepped up when required.

Here we are. Lime Street and this is how I'm feeling. Come on, Liverpool. One last push!

***

We won and we didn't win. All at the same time. I'm a little bit heartbroken but I'm also seeing some perspective.

We went ahead early. Brighton also scored and for a few

moments there was a bit of madness. But very quickly City were back on top and it became obvious we were not going to have some sort of nail-biting finish. We've had enough of that already. We won the game. It was never really in doubt. Two goals from Mané. Run of the mill. I don't really know what happened elsewhere. It finished 4-1 to City, so I guess it was one-way traffic.

At the end of the game, Alisson got an award for most clean sheets. Mané and Salah shared the top scorer prize. It was all lovely. Lovely, lovely, lovely. But we didn't win the league. Everything is a consolation. We didn't win it. Now's not the time to be talking about 97 points. We didn't win it.

When I stopped writing earlier at the train station, I walked to the pub and I put 'You'll Never Walk Alone' on my head-phones. I was so pumped by the time I got there. Nothing was going to stop us. After the game. After we hadn't won the league I was quite relaxed, and then they played it again in the ground. That got me. That really got me.

End of the season was supposed to be today. We have an extension. Three more weeks and there is so much excitement to come. But today was the end of the season and we didn't win it. Right now, I can't put a brave face on it. Can't spin it. We were wonderful, but we didn't do it.

Smile as if everything is OK. Chin up. Well done, lads. What a performance!

Tuesday 14th May 2019

So I think it's fair to say I've been sulking a bit. Didn't want to write this. Been avoiding it. Had a read of the last entry, written when I was really down after the match—that's what this is all about, ups and downs. That was a down and I'm still a bit down.

I know, I know. We did brilliantly, we got 97 points; we should be so proud, any other year, freak situation yada, yada,

yada. I've heard them all. But we didn't win the league. We didn't win it and that's the one we all want to win, and I'm a bit down about it. Sorry. I know we're not supposed to be down about it but I am.

It's my own fault. I had kind of made peace with it after the City Burnley game and then again after the Leicester game and it was firmly put to bed after the Barcelona win. I had reconciled it all in my mind, put it in its own little compartment and then firmly closed the door on it. There may have been some brave talk writing in here, but that's all it was, brave talk.

But then it's still there, whispering away in my ear ... there's a chance, don't give up hope, anything's possible ... and before you know it, I was well up for it and it had become a nigh on certainty. And now, here I am with my hopes well and truly dashed.

Two days on and I'm still the same. I'm not outwardly whingeing about it, I have it bottled up, but it's definitely there. Disappointment. What can I say?

We look forward to the Champions League final; it looks like tickets are sorted pretty much but still waiting on the ballot. That is something to really look forward to, but the disappointment lingers.

I've switched off from social media. Can't be bothered with the increasingly classless City fans (and now the team too) and bitter Evertonians who have probably taken greater delight in Liverpool not winning the league than anything their own team has done all season.

Switched off from our own fans looking for reasons. Where did we let ourselves down? What could we have done differently? Where do we need to invest to strengthen?

In that sense I think I am still quite defiant. We had a great season. We only got beat once and that was by the team that ultimately won it. We didn't drop a single point to teams in the bottom half of the league; we were the flat track bullies that we needed to be. Two of our players were joint top scorers, our goalkeeper won the golden gloves, and another was the Player of the Year.

In historical terms (Premier League historical!), we got the third highest points tally ever, eighth best goals tally ever, third best defensive record ever, third best number of wins ever, second fewest losses (second only to Arsenal's Invincibles). In these terms, we pissed over anything United managed in their twenty years of Premier League domination. (Always fucking United!)

Compared to last year (the year when we swept away all before us with our attacking football and Salah was majestic), we scored an additional 22 points (29% improvement), scored an extra five goals and conceded 16 fewer goals (42% improvement).

We have at different times been immense, professional, controlled, dogmatic, focused, joyous, ferocious, breath-taking and lucky. Don't dismiss the lucky either; everyone needs a bit of luck now and then. We've been unlucky, too, but I think we've enjoyed the rub of the green on more than one occasion.

The unlucky is that we have done all this at the same time Manchester City have been imperious. Like a machine. While I feel like we have been caught in a wave of emotion and that has propelled us forward, at the same time City have efficiently swept aside anyone who came in their path. They have used their experience and their wealth of talent to pursue the league like a group automaton. They finished the season with 14 straight wins, for Christ's sake.

And despite all that hyperbole and justification, I'm still disappointed!

Wednesday 21st May 2019

The season has been extended due to the Champions League

final, but right now all is quiet.

Players seem to have had a week off and now they are back in a training camp in Marbella by the look of it. There is nothing official, no news coverage, but pictures begin to filter through Instagram of the training camp. The countdown begins.

Tickets are all sorted. Seven of us going and we have seven tickets. Not sure which one I'm having yet. Not sure how much it's costing me. All I know is all things going to plan I will be in that ground next Saturday night. The lads are doing the two-day trip, staying over for a couple of nights. I'm just doing the day return but can laugh off the obligatory abuse, safe in the knowledge I am going to the game.

Ongoing fume about the venues and ticket allocations for both of the finals. How something should be done about it. How someone should say something to UEFA. They say it every year and then the teams and the fans go to the game and then promptly forget about doing anything about the disgraceful political machinations as there's only an outside chance they will get to the final again and it will be someone else's problem. This is Liverpool's second final in a row with an improving team and next year's final is back in Istanbul!! Someone somewhere needs to start lobbying!

The appalling administration is brought into further focus this week when Mkhitaryan announces he won't be travelling to the final with Arsenal amidst fears for his own safety. How on earth can UEFA allow one of its showcase games to be scheduled in a country where they can't even guarantee the safety of the participants? It's beyond belief.

Have received my email from Liverpool today to vote for Player and Goal of the Season. It was an easy choice made tougher by my need not to conform. I ticked Wijnaldum. I think he's been great all year. The uncelebrated workhorse who puts it all in for the team and doesn't get the recognition. The player who looked like he was on his way out but has been reliable all season, stepping up when needed. As I write those lines it strikes me there is some sort of psychological trauma driving that decision. It's nearly a cry for help. I won't go there, but you know what I mean!!

In the end, I went for VVD (sorry Gini, I've deserted you too, we're all bastards). VVD is the Player of the Year. The whole league have decided he's the Player of the Year, and that's according to the players who play in it, so how can I say otherwise for just the one team? He's been imperious throughout. Head and shoulders above, both literally and metaphorically. Transformed the team. Beyond doubt.

There are other contenders. Alisson, Robertson, Mané, Salah. Fabinho started slowly but based on this calendar year would be right up there. Gomez for the early part of the season, Matip for filling the gap he left. It's hard to leave anyone out. The team has been bigger than any individual.

As for the goal. Well, that was a tough choice between two of them scored against Chelsea. Sturridge in the last minute at Stamford Bridge or Salah for that arrow at Anfield. I went for Sturridge. I went for that purely for the reaction it brought. To bring me up and out of my seat when I thought all was lost. To have me screaming and shouting in disbelief, bouncing around the room. It was a beautiful goal, brilliantly conceived and expertly executed. Phenomenal.

They didn't have the Origi goal against Everton in the shortlist. In terms of ongoing joy at the very thought, that deserves a mention, surely. Ten days and counting.

Friday 31st May 2019

One day to go. Excited doesn't begin to cover it. Thought of little else all week. Not even clear on what part I'm so excited about. Just the whole all-encompassing idea of going to the biggest game in world football ... again.

Media has been stepping up the coverage. Interviews, features, statistics. You can't get away from it and it's all fabulous. The Scouse contingent in Madrid is growing day on day. Building up to fever pitch. My mates are flying out today. They're like a bunch of kids. Pictures of them on WhatsApp on the plane. You'd think they'd never flown before.

I'm joining them tomorrow, flying out first thing. Been getting my stuff together this morning like a kid going on a school trip. It's going to be awesome. Christ, I hope we win.

Interlude 11 - The Last League

If you told me in May 1990 that I would be knocking on 50 and Liverpool hadn't won the league again I'd have said you were crackers. I was approaching 18 years of age and all I had ever known was a successful Liverpool, capped in the last three seasons by a wonder team graced by one of best players in the world, John Barnes.

In May, we had won the league comfortably. Barnes was the Player of the Year again, arguably better in a more central and advanced role than he had been in his first season. A joy to watch; played nearly every game and scored 22 goals. He was out of this world and took Liverpool to their 18th league title. They won it comfortably too finishing on 79 points, nine ahead of Villa in second and 16 ahead of Spurs in third. (An interesting note on this season is that United finished 13th with just 48 points. It was only three years later they won the league and started their run of success under Ferguson).

By this time, I had graduated to the middle of the Kop—right in the middle. I'm quite tall as were all my mates and we were those awful people who used to arrive at the game ten minutes before kick-off and push our way through from the side and then stand right in front of some unlucky person who'd been there since the gates opened. I know, bad, isn't it?

The trick was to pretend you could see your mate and hold your arm in the air as if you were catching his attention, 'Dave, Dave,' then turn around to the others, 'I can see Dave, he's there, come on.' There was never a Dave. I don't even know anyone called Dave.

The middle of the Kop was brilliant. It was where all the noise stemmed from. It was the catalyst. There were three lads (Peter, Dominic and Barry) who sat on the barrier and conducted things, but most games you would get to start a song. There is nothing like the thrill of shouting, 'There's only one Peter Beardsley,' and the rest of the crowd picking up on it and singing. And nothing worse when they don't. It was all about the timing, the mood and finding the right moment.

It was also when I started having a bet on the game, first goal scorer and correct score. Only a pound at the time but was great when you got it right! The Everton game that season, I had John Barnes and 2-1 and can well remember Beardsley bearing down on goal in the last minutes and willing him to miss. It worked too!

The team hadn't really moved on from the 87–88 season. Playing in that derby were Grobbelaar, Venison, Nicol, Hysen, Hansen, Whelan, Mcmahon, Burrows, Barnes, Beardsley, Rush. The only changes were Hysen coming into the defence (at the time I thought Hysen was great and a long-term replacement for Hansen ... how wrong was I!), and Rush for Aldridge, which was undoubtedly an upgrade, although I was never convinced Rush fit as well into the poacher's position in that system as Aldridge. Looking at it now, it probably looks more like a 4-3-3 with Barnes as a forward, which was unheard of at the time. Burrows was playing, but I guess that was covering for an injured Houghton.

The sad thing is that I don't actually remember them winning the league that season—I don't remember the game at home to Derby County when they were crowned champions, although I'm almost certain I was there. It was the norm, we were champions yet again. When I think about how much I crave that moment now, it seems almost criminal that the last time it happened, I must have taken it completely for granted.

That was the last league title. It was a watershed for every fan, although I clearly didn't realise it at the time. But the title win wasn't really the end of the chapter—and the end of this story. We have to move forward nearly twelve months for that and the two final chapters to my own little journey.

The first was the resignation of Dalglish in March the following year. That was a shock. Earth moving. Stuart and I had been to the game the night before at Goodison. A game of madness—an FA Cup replay that ended 4-4. An end-to-end game, it was like an out-of-control boxing match, we kept going ahead and they kept pulling us back. A last-minute Cottee goal taking it into extra time at 3-3 and then he scored again after Barnes had put us back ahead. Looking at the match reports, even Dalglish is reported as saying it was the best of games, no sign of what was to come.

It was the next day in school when it happened, coming out of a lesson to be told. We thought the other kids were winding us up and we went into the library where we could look at Teletext on the computers. It was true, he'd gone. It was beyond belief—we'd only been there watching them the night before and now he was gone. We were top of the league—how could there be any pressure?

He'd been the ever-present, the hero as a small child, the great player who I'd never quite got to see at his peak, the manager who had won the double, created the best team the country had ever seen—and he was gone.

There was great deal of conjecture at the time as to why, but none that really spoke of the effect of Hillsborough on the man. He bore the weight of the entire City and eventually it told. I don't think that was recognised at the time. There is a piece in the Echo on the day, reflecting on the reasons. Hillsborough (and Heysel) is a passing comment, certainly not central. Quotes from a range of players and managers and not one of them mentioned it, they all rather focused on the pressure of the football. I think it's only later when it becomes clear the effect of such a human tragedy on a good man.

And then my Grandad. He passed away on Father's Day, 16th June 1991. He was old by then, had been alone since the death of my Nan seven years earlier, and had been lonely, he missed her terribly. He'd had a couple of heart attacks in the early '70s and in that sense had done really well to last an extra 20 years. He died peacefully in Whiston Hospital.

In his final years, he used to stay over with us a couple of nights a week and was a calming influence in a home that was disintegrating. A well-placed word when I was overstepping the boundaries, a source of support for my poor mum. He continued to go to the match to the end. I passed my driving test and took him to the match a couple of times in that final season. I would drive him right up to the ground and, as he got out the car, he would put a pound in my hand and tell me what score to put it on. I wasn't allowed to tell anyone!

Of all the losses over that period, Grandad's was the easiest to take. It was his time to go and I had been lucky that I had got to spend so much time with him. I still think of him now when I'm at the match. He wanted so much to share his passion of the place with me and I have had it ever since. I have a lot to thank him for.

JUNE

Saturday 1st June 2019

Today's the day. Up at half past three for a half past five flight. A day on the piss, a football match and then arriving back at some point in the early hours tomorrow. Can't go back to sleep until I get on the plane so sitting here, bleary eyed, in the disgrace that is Manchester Airport.

Champions League final. Again. This is the fourth in my adult life. That's without the five when I was young. For a club to get through to the biggest game in world football (bigger than the World Cup now) so often is bordering on freakish. Trying to explain to the kids last night how important the game is, the magnitude of it. They nodded and smiled. *You say that every week, Dad,* I can see them thinking!!

This is my first since the magical trip to Istanbul. I've missed the other two, so really I have a 100% record. I'm the lucky charm. The trip to Istanbul was incredible. I'd left my job at the time and was about to start a year-long trip backpacking around the world with Ange that would ultimately see us living in Australia for seven years. We got back from the match, European Champions, after the most exciting, unbelievable game, picked up the backpacks and off we went.

I missed Athens, though not for the want of trying. I was living in Sydney by then, watching the match every week in the middle of the night and feeling very detached and far away

345

from the Rafalution.

Liverpool drew Barcelona in the last 16 that year and the odds on us even reaching the final were huge. So I put a biggish bet (biggish for me) on it right at the start and that paid for the trip. Tickets for the game were sorted. I was due to fly out on the Tuesday night, meet the lads in Athens on the Wednesday afternoon, fly back on the Thursday morning, to arrive back in Sydney on the Friday night a conquering hero. It was the ultimate trip. A defining trip.

Until I was playing tennis on the previous Saturday morning and I put my back out. Not just a twinge either. By the Sunday, I could barely stand up. I spent hours at the physio on the Tuesday. He worked and worked on me to the point I could stand up straight. But then I couldn't sit down again. I had to call the lads on the Tuesday and tell them I couldn't make it. Gutted doesn't even start to cover it.

Then last year in Kiev. I missed that too. We had a family holiday booked. A big one, going over to Las Vegas and Los Angeles. We had it booked nearly a year before to coincide with school holidays. I remember looking at the fixtures at the time and thinking, *That's the weekend of the final.* But the final at that stage was a long way away. Our first season back in the competition, making it to the final was the impossible dream surely.

We got through the group stage and then game by game we began to knock off the opposition. With every game Kiev got closer and closer and the realisation that I was due to be on holiday. And then we qualified and it was the big decision. Do I go or not? We took off for Las Vegas the morning after the final. Could I get back from the match in time to jump straight into the plane?

Kiev was a nightmare logistically and the route the lads took was like *Planes, Trains and Automobiles*, a five-day odyssey across Central Europe. I couldn't go but again I was gutted, it looked like the trip of a lifetime.

So that was it. I wasn't going to miss another. It was decided from that point on. The date was circled on the calendar for this year. Don't book a holiday to coincide with the final. I was adamant. This is before a ball had been kicked. Ange still booked a holiday, they are flying out of the same airport I'm sitting in now ... in about three hours ... I'm just not going with them!!

That's why I was working so hard to convince the kids what a big game it was and why Daddy's not coming to Tenerife!

It's a wonder we are here at all. An absolute wonder. Looking at the journey through the competition this year, it's easy to forget that we nearly didn't make it through the group stage. Never mind the miracle of Barcelona.

Starting off with a barnstorming win against Paris St Germain, it seemed like it was going to be walk in the park, but three poor performances away from home, particularly the one in Belgrade, and we really did defy the odds to even make it to the knockout stage. PSG with some of the biggest stars in the modern game and Napoli who at the time were the form team in Europe and we managed to squeeze through.

Thanks largely to a last-minute point blank save by the mighty Alisson against Napoli. Seen it so many times this week. The lad should have scored. He would have scored if he hadn't shit himself with this huge keeper running at him. What a save that was. A game changer. He paid his transfer fee off in that split second alone.

The rounds after that have been fairly straightforward. Bayern Munich looked like a tough draw and then not scoring in the home leg left us with a lot to do, but the return leg in Munich was a lesson in controlling a game. Porto was about as straightforward as a Champions League quarter final could be, although brilliantly managed to allow us to continue the crucial league form at the same time.

And then Barcelona. We were unlucky to be in that position after the first leg. We didn't deserve to be three goals down. That last Messi goal and then Salah hitting the post seconds later and we looked done for. Going into a return leg without two of our most potent players. It was impossible, wasn't it?

But that is why people go to the football. To be there on nights like that. When sporting miracles happen. I call it a miracle. It wasn't that. It was the perfect execution of a well-rehearsed game plan. An understanding of how to win and then showing some of the best players in the world what can happen when you get caught in the eye of a storm. I've seen so many people wearing this 'Never Give Up' T-shirt. It's more than football. It's a lesson in life.

And now the final. This time we go into the game as one of the elite teams in Europe. It's different to the previous three I've mentioned. In Istanbul it was freakish. Punching far above our weight. A team of inherited players peppered with upcoming stars. The idea that that team could get to the final, never mind win it, was entirely improbable. A fairy tale hyped by the drama of the final itself.

Then in Athens. A team in a rebuilding phase, working towards potential greatness. A club about to jump off a cliff into a financial abyss. But on the night, the luck ran out. Milan got their revenge. Revenge for a game they should have won two years earlier.

Both of these masterminded by the genius Benitez. Working with players while wanting other players. A seeming lack of emotion, a game boiled down to its working parts and how they fit together. Who knows what would have happened if he had still been there? A dynasty built a decade earlier maybe.

So different now. It feels like we got to Kiev on a wave of emotion last year. It just built and built. It was unexpected, but with the destruction of City and then Rome, it became inevitable. The luck ran out in the final. We were outmanoeuvred by a cannier team. And the goalkeeping was shit, obviously.

This year we are here on the back of an exceptional league run. That we didn't win the league is a statistical anomaly. Being in the right place but at the wrong time. We are the team that people fear, the team with the momentum. But now we have the team and we have the emotion running through the team and the club. Driven by Klopp. I'd like to think this is the start of things.

Taking off now. Going to try to bank some sleep.

***

As improbable as our appearance in the final seems after the games against Napoli and Barcelona, Spurs' seems even less likely. They were really poor in the group stage, only getting through with a draw at Barcelona in the last game, after Barca had already qualified.

Then they came up against City in the quarter final who were pretty much an unstoppable force at the time. They only went through in the end after a late City goal was ruled out for being fractional offside. In the semis it was Ajax. A goal down after the first leg at home and 2-0 down at half time in the return. The game was over. Only for them to pull back three goals in the second half, the last with virtually the last kick of the game. To say they have ridden their luck is an understatement.

I don't know how they are going to line up tonight. The question is all about their talisman Kane. I don't get Kane myself. Don't know what the fuss is about, but he continues to score goals. He's been out for the latter part of the season and the question is over his level of fitness. Will he be able to play? How much below full fitness does he have to be to get a game?

Then there's Moura and Son, their two other attacking players. I think Son is nailed on to play, but Moura got a hat trick at Ajax to put them through and he could miss out. Behind them two, it's Eriksen and Dele Alli. Two midfield playmakers both of whom can change a game on their day but strike me as inconsistent.

The talk is that Pochettino has to a choice between them and depending on which players get in the team, will dictate the shape they play. That you can't pick a formation and squeeze them all in together. Particularly if you want some midfield solidity behind them. He has Wanyama and Sissoko there and you would think he would want to play them too. Something has to give somewhere. He's only allowed eleven players; it says so in the rules.

But enough about them, they need to worry about Liverpool. I think there are three outstanding questions for the game tonight, one in each area.

The defence is sorted pretty much. The question is who plays alongside VVD? I'd go for Matip. I'd go on to say that is the fair choice, but I'm not sure how much that comes into it. There is an element of meritocracy in the way Klopp picks his team and, based on the way Matip has played since the turn of the year, he definitely deserves to be playing. He's been really strong and has become more assured with every game. I liked him when he first came to Liverpool but then he seemed injury prone and a bit flaky. He looks a bit gangly and awkward as he runs and that always seems to make mistakes or poor performances more memorable.

Gomez was outstanding in the first half of the season. In much the same way as Matip has done recently, he actually looked on occasion the stronger of the two centre backs when he was playing, even outplayed VVD on occasion (even if VVD was secretly controlling the entire game as it revolved around him).

So does he go back to Gomez now? The player with the strongest future, the player you potentially see occupying that spot for the next few years. Or does he remain loyal to Matip and reward his contribution to the path to the final? Of course, there is a world where Lovren gets in. Klopp likes him, he has the experience of these games and is generally very strong when VVD aids by pulling his strings.

Next question is attack. It should be a no-brainer. It should be Firmino, the lynchpin around which all the attacking movement revolves. The worker, the connector, the brain. But he's been injured. Missed the last few games. Missed much of the training camp with the team. I believe he only joined the rest of the squad on Tuesday this week. Doesn't seem like the ideal preparation. Klopp says he's fit and ready to play, but I think there is a doubt.

Does he start and get his fitness assessment while he's playing? What happens if he's not fit and we have to use a sub early, what happens to the game plan as no one else in the squad can quite do what he does? Even having him as sub raises a question. What if you bring him on to change the game and he's not up to it? Questions. The more I write about it now, the more I'm worrying myself!

Even if he doesn't play, then it has to be Origi. He's done enough. Deserves the chance. The season started with so much promise for Sturridge but, again, he hasn't lived up to it and while it appears he's avoided injury, he hasn't been able to influence games as you would expect when given his chance. Origi, on the other hand, has stepped up and done the business. God, I hope Bobby is fit!

And finally, the midfield question. The midfield is the big question as that's the dynamo that powers the whole Klopp machine. Strengthened at the back, potent at the front, the combination of the midfield provides both cover and ammunition. It's the freshness, power and pace of that three that will dictate this game.

I'm focussed on who is going to start the game, but that isn't how Klopp works with his midfield. Yes, it's about who starts, but it's more about how he rotates it in the middle of the game to retain that momentum. It's about four players, possibly five or six, and how they both start and finish the game.

I think it will be Fabinho at the base, alongside Henderson and Gini. The question then is how he will use Milner, because he undoubtedly will. Milner is like having a secret weapon. Milner can come on and chase a game, provide that impetus, or he can consolidate, protect and ensure we don't lose a winning position. We could go into extra time and Milner is a player with experience you want on the field to guide the others through it.

It's that four anyway, that's how I think they'll line up, but it could be Milner for Gini in a similar scenario. Add to that the options of Lallana, Oxlade Chamberlain and Shaqiri and there is no end of tactical options to change the game.

I'd like to think we'll have too much for them but don't want to underestimate what they can do. Kane, for as much as I think he is a bag of spanners, could pop up and score even if he only has one and a half legs!!

I think (and hope) the biggest difference between the teams is the experience of last year, of having been in the same game last year and the pressure and expectation associated with it. A massive game and so heart-crushingly disappointing to have lost it in such circumstances. The players know what to expect. The coverage, the atmosphere, the noise. It will set them apart. I'm hoping Spurs will be like rabbits in the headlights in such a frantic environment.

That's the hope anyway. Nine a.m. local time and just touched down. Twelve hours to kick off. Butterflies. Off into the city to find my mates, all of whom had a heavy night on the piss last night and are crammed into an Airbnb somewhere in the city centre. Then a day of sightseeing, or more likely seeing the inside of a string of bars on our way to the game.

Come on, you mighty Champions League final redmen!!

JUNE

***

Four hours to kick-off. It's building. There's a level of alcohol involved, which has now led me to delete the literary gold that I had composed while sitting on the toilet in the basement of the last bar we were in. One day, people will realise the depth of my writing. Maybe.

It's a balance now. Warning's going out that it takes longer to get to the ground than previously thought. While at the current moment we are ruling this local bar with our northern English charm.

The kick-off draws ever closer and we are frankly a bit too pissed to realise it. Supporter life. Right now we rule, we unknowingly accept we have no grasp on their language and arrogantly accept that they will speak ours. But we rule. Three hours to kick-off.

***

Half time. We are a goal up. I hate to say it, but it's a bit of a non-event. We got an early penalty, early as in the very first minute. Salah put it away.

But it's like it never happened. They've spent the rest of the game feeling each other out. No commitment, no attack, no thrust. It's like the goal never occurred and the two teams are playing a game of chess. Like they weren't expecting the goal and now don't know what to do. Yawn. We can only hope they are getting instructions now. Hopefully Spurs need to chase the game and we need to catch them on the break. Otherwise, quite frankly it's going to be shit. A complete non-event (except if we win). Sorry.

***

353

What do I say now? I think they call it winging it. This is the bit where you realise I'm not really an author and I don't really have anything worthwhile to say. This is the bit where you find out I'm overcome with emotion. That the minute we won tonight I burst into a flood of tears. Surrounded by my mates. They're jumping up and down, going mental, but as the ref blew the final whistle I was nigh on inconsolable. What the fuck happened there!? We won the European Cup, that's what.

Champions of Europe. We are now the best team in Europe and everyone in Europe has witnessed it. Champions.

I'm not going to talk about the game too much. It was a terrible game of football. No one really went for it. Like two teams feeling each other out. Spurs didn't seem to realise they were a goal down. No ambition to try to get back. No real chances either way. Divvy pops up at the end and puts it out of sight. We won, but it's difficult to find anything positive to say about the game. Dire. Crowd was quiet until the end. Tense in there I thought.

And then we get to ninety minutes and we are champions of Europe and an outpouring of noise and colour and emotion, overwhelming joy. With a couple of minutes to go we left our seats and went and stood with our mates. All together in a moment of triumph. How it should be. Big, meaningful hugs. The hugs of drunk people who have just realised their season's ambition but are knackered and don't know what to say.

Flying straight home now. The ultimate come down. I am exhausted. A day drinking combined with an emotional reverse enema.

Champions of Europe. I'll stop now.

Sunday 2nd June 2019

The morning after the night before. What a night but paying for it now.

I've come down from the emotions of the stadium after the game. I don't know what came over me. Floods of tears when the final whistle went, and the team started running onto the pitch. Whether it was emotion built up over the ninety minutes, over a season or over a whole lifetime of watching Liverpool, I'm not too sure. Whatever it was, I couldn't stop. Happy uncontrollable tears of joy.

And as I watched them lift the trophy, and a defiant roar went up around the ground, the tears were gone temporarily; I was screaming with the rest. We have been amazing all season and we have stuck it to them. Champions of Europe. The players on the pitch, the fans in the stadium, we all stuck it to them. I waited and waited in the ground to watch the celebrations, to join in and be heard.

Until I'd seen enough and off I strolled, back to the coach. I don't stroll very often. Normally I stride, at pace. But last night I just strolled without a care in the world. I called the family on holiday in Tenerife; they had stayed up to watch it. They were so excited we had won, excited for me and that I was there. And that's when the waterworks started again. Bloody hell! Whoever wrote that last entry in the early hours was a tired, drunk emotional wreck!

Thousands in the airport. A quiet buzz. Not the triumphalism that was happening elsewhere, more a mellow, self-satisfied glow right throughout the terminal. As is modern life, not so much talking about it. Everyone was too tired and drained to talk. Instead people reliving the game through their phones, social media and news reports, watching the goals, replaying the handball (it was definitely a penalty), absorbing the reaction, the scenes on the pitch and in the crowd. Filling up on every last moment. Champions of Europe—for the sixth time.

I got home at five. A really chipper taxi driver keeping me awake in the cab, talking about football, talking about how good Liverpool are, how much they deserve the win. He was right too.

A few hours' sleep and then up again to relive it, to look at the reaction. In Madrid and in Liverpool. Seen so many of those videos of large crowds and the reaction when the goal goes in, people going crazy, showers of beer in the air. Seen the video of Jordan Henderson hugging his dad—that got me.

I am so pleased for Henderson, so badly maligned by so much of the fan base, largely for not being Steven Gerrard. But you could see how much it meant to him last night, to be the next captain to lift the trophy, and he deserves all the accolades he gets. Maybe not the heartbeat of the team but definitely the heart. Good for you, lad.

I've read the reports. I was right about the game, a bit of a non-event, though why I had to be so negative about it at half time in the biggest game in world football I don't really know. Miserable bastard. I'll put it down to dehydration as I queued for a bottle of Coke! A poor game that never got flowing, it didn't reflect the attacking talent in the two sides.

Both Firmino and Kane played for their respective sides but neither made an impression, Kane was anonymous. I think both sides suffered from having a three-week break. It was too long and the momentum both teams had been carrying had come to a juddering halt. The newspaper reports say Spurs had the best of it. I'm not sure I agree; neither team looked threatening. The very early penalty kind of upset the flow of the game, not what anyone was expecting. Like starting the game with a head start and not having the tactics to address it.

So while last night's triumph didn't necessarily reflect the game, it has definitely reflected the season. A season where we racked up 97 points and still didn't win the bloody league, we needed something to show for the enormous efforts of the team—I think the European Cup counts as that.

It's been a marvellous season. A consistently high level of performance that for the most part has swept away everyone in their path. A wobble in the Champions League group stage, but a show of resolve to go through to the knockouts. A season really capped by the magnificent defeat of Barcelona at Anfield. They should have given us the trophy then really, not that we needed it on the night, just being in that ground was reward in itself.

I've had my own ups and downs. I am really quite proud of myself to be still writing this as we come into June, that I have stuck with it and as much as possible fulfilled the goal I had set for myself. Whether this sees the light of day is another matter. I am about to have a professional watershed, leaving my job at the end of the month, with the current plan to work for myself, possibly kicked off with publishing this book. My mum would be so proud; she always wanted to write a book.

I have picked the right year to do this. This is finest season of football I have seen. It's been a privilege, a pleasure and an honour to watch this side over the last nine months. I don't think it's a one-off either. I honestly believe this is the start of something; that next year we will be even better ... but then I say that every year!

Monday 3rd June 2019

Well, this is it. It really is the end of the season. And with it the end of my book. I thought yesterday was the end, the last entry. But that was before the homecoming parade. How could I finish the book without talking about the parade?

It was madness. It was the madness of Liverpool as a city, the madness of its people all coming together to express how mad they actually are and how the city is the best, maddest place on the planet. Three quarters of a million people out on the streets at six hours' notice to celebrate the homecoming of one of the finest teams the city has ever produced. Showing them how much it means, showing them how mad we all are together.

And at the moment, I think the maddest person there is Jurgen Klopp. He's mad, as mad as mad can be. He has curated a set of players and built them into a team with unshakeable belief. He has galvanised a set of supporters, made them dream and then delivered on that dream.

He has been inspiring and adventurous in his football. Last season was a feast of attacking, fluid, sumptuous football. He has been practical and controlling. This season we have seen a level of professionalism and control in games that has seen us turn into a machine. We are seeing something very special. And he has done it with a level of personal charm and focus that draws in everyone around him. He is the Shankly for a new generation.

Watching him since the game has been wonderful. One can only imagine the level of pressure that he has been under in the last few weeks, trying to bring this trophy home, trying to get this perceived, media driven, 'not-winning-a-final' monkey off his back. But now we see him relaxed, sitting on the back of the bus, beer in hand, giggling away to himself as watches the adoring masses swimming around him in a sea of red. He has brought so much happiness and fulfilment to so many. A mad adopted son of a mad city.

I've been struggling to think of a title for this book. A lot of it was going to be driven by whether we won a trophy or not I guess. Watching the interview with him after the game when he started singing. It was one of those 'embarrassing dad' moments. He started singing and he kept on singing. Normally, my stomach would have been in a knot, pleading with the person to stop—dying inside. Imagine David Brent doing it, you would want the ground to open up beneath you. But not Klopp, there are no sides to him, there is only him in the whole world who could have carried that off. A true one-off and a new hero.

I give you 'Let's Talk about Six.' (Baby!)